Writing for Museums

Writing for Museums

Margot Wallace

ROWMAN & LITTLEFIELD
Lanham • Boulder • New York • London

Published by Rowman & Littlefield
A wholly owned subsidiary of The Rowman & Littlefield Publishing Group, Inc.
4501 Forbes Boulevard, Suite 200, Lanham, Maryland 20706
www.rowman.com

Unit A, Whitacre Mews, 26–34 Stannery Street, London SE11 4AB, United Kingdom

British Library Cataloguing in Publication Information Available

Library of Congress Cataloging-in-Publication Data

Wallace, Margot A., 1941–
Writing for museums / Margot Wallace.
pages cm
Summary: "Whether written by administrators, staffers, freelancers, or interns, words are delivered by people in your museums with the knowledge, to be interpreted by strangers. Your story is told everywhere, and with each narration it reinforces your brand; hopefully every single word reflects your brand. If you ever wished for a good writer, right on staff, ready to take on project, major or routine, here's the help you're looking for. Writing for Museums will help all staff who write better—and result in clearer communication with and education for—all your visitors." —Provided by publisher.
Includes bibliographical references and index.
ISBN 978-1-4422-2763-7 (cloth : alkaline paper)—ISBN 978-1-4422-2764-4 (paperback : alkaline paper)—ISBN 978-1-4422-2762-0 (electronic)
1. Communication in museums. 2. Museums—Social aspects. 3. Museums—Educational aspects. 4. Museums—Public relations. 5. Museum visitors. 6. Authorship. 7. Narration (Rhetoric) 8. Museum techniques. I. Title.
AM125.W35 2014
069'.1—dc23
2014022343

Printed in the United States of America

Contents

Acknowledgments   vii

Preface   ix

1 Audio Tours   1

2 Blogs   15

3 Brochures   29

4 E-mail   39

5 Education: Learning Outcomes: Learning Outcomes   49

6 Environmental Graphics   61

7 Exhibition Videos   75

8 Guided Tours   85

9 Lectures   93

10 Magazines   103

11 Newsletters   115

12 Pinterest, Twitter, and Social Media Strategies   127

13 Public Relations   139

14 Solicitation Letters   151

15 Store   161

16 Survey Questionnaires   173

17 Volunteers   187

18 Website   199

19 YouTube   217

Contents

20 Writing Tips   227

References   231
Index   241

Acknowledgments

From my first foray into writing about museums, my colleague Tom Hamilton has been a source of encouragement and information. Patricia Rath Balsamo over many coffees shared her writer's wisdom and insights. Joyce Knauff kept me supplied with museum materials and updates. Craig Sigele, Barbara Cohn, and Lon Ramsey talked museum to me and I continue to enjoy their enthusiasm. Jane Barack, Nancy Gardner, Lynne Gilberg, Pat Herbert Allen Livingston, and Kay Pick drove many miles to visit far-flung museums with me and nudged my scholarship. Special heartfelt thanks go to Paul Wallace for a five- to fifteen-year-old's perspective. Going back before the gleam was even in my eye, three people earn my gratitude: Barb Siebel for telling me that a person could be dropped anyplace in the world and if there were a museum there it would be a fine day; and to Chris Wallace and Ginger Withers for giving me my first worldwide guidebook to museums. I also acknowledge Cornell Wright for patient technology help. Finally, grateful thanks to Jim and Karen Adler for always asking how it's going.

Preface

Two museum directors unwittingly suggested this book. One director led a local history museum in a quiet Midwest suburb. The museum's mission was focused on that community only, to the point that if a washboard came from a suburb two blocks away, it was rejected. Yet, with those strictures and within a handful of rooms, many insightful stories were told. "Your panels are wonderful," I said. "Yes," she replied, "we're fortunate to have a wonderful writer." The second director steered a maritime museum, a larger and more prominent fixture in its Florida city. One exhibition wove sea chanteys into a larger seafaring story. I commented on this and again a director said, "We have a wonderful writer."

When such respect for wordcraft comes from people who daily rub shoulders with visually exquisite objects and tangibly ingenious displays, writing assumes new gravitas. Taking a closer look at the milieu of the museum director, the many ideas the director juggles, and the challenges looming at every turn, I saw words marching into all kinds of situations. I began looking for them everywhere in the museum, in every nook and white space, on every screen and in every communication. My writer's eye was relentless.

Panels expanded into articles; gallery tours developed into blogs; videos explored knowledge on multiple levels. Brochures elucidated so clearly that their information multiplied on web pages. Websites became vast lobbies, the virtual first step inside many museums. Fund-raising letters, in the hands of a good writer, began to sparkle and job descriptions glittered. Visitor surveys, volunteer manuals, and e-mail each steadily elevated clusters of words into powerful marketing tools.

As all these words thread through and wrap around your museum, you begin to see how powerfully they can propel your marketing efforts. Here are some highlights:

INTRODUCTION

Each chapter of this book tells how to put into words the information you need to convey the stories you need to tell. In each chapter you'll find examples from museums of all sizes and types, each a model of strategic thinking and effective communication.

- Audio Tours—Self-guided tours are popular on many levels, and that's because someone has written the tour very wisely.
- Blogs—Here's your chance to document your scholarship, flaunt some knowledge that doesn't make it to the galleries, and spread erudition and professionalism to audiences you haven't reached before.
- Brochures—These stick around for a longer time than any digital communiqué, and there are guidelines to make brochures worth hanging on to.
- E-mail—The oldest of the new media has traditional advantages: control and targeting. You control the message, and select the specific audience you want to talk to—at the right time and with an appropriate message. After visitors have found your website or blog or tweet, convert that interest in an e-mail address, and then keep them engaged by writing lots of e-mails.
- Education—Whether it's integrating museum programs into school curricula, or enhancing a one-off school tour, remember your museum's education mission; that's why schools partner with you in the first place.
- Environmental Graphics—Parking garage to café, environmental graphics shape the spaces that people inhabit. Because galleries scoop out so great a space, and fill it so well, it's easy to gloss over the other places people go. Other rooms, corridors, entries, and exits are part of the visit, and words continue the museum story throughout the building and beyond.
- Exhibition Videos—Of the multitude of new media choices now available to the museum curator—and many other departments—video has the advantage of place: it complements the exhibits at the right point along the visitor's journey through the museum. Script, voice, images, duration, and physical location all can be planned to enhance the experience.
- Guided Tours—Guides and docents tell the story face-to-face and, along with the information desk personnel and guards, are the human faces of the museums. How these one-to-one narrators represent the brand, at the same time facilitating learning, requires a well-written outline that not only delivers the right message, but lays it out in language the docent feels comfortable using.
- Lectures—Before and after visitors see your exhibitions, they will be invited to a full menu of other museum experiences. The names on your mailing lists, along with their friends, see much of the museum via classes and lectures, without actually stepping inside. In many cases, members are

reminded and reconnected only by attending lectures. Different audiences, different mind-sets, different time frames characterize these programs; conscientious writing is required.

- Magazines—Four-color member magazines are key pieces in the marketing and branding life of your institution, and the quality of the published text must equal that of the visuals. Start with the letter from the director, or the introduction, and sharpen the editing pencil.
- Newsletters—E-mail makes it easy to deliver the news, and good writing makes the news worth receiving. This wonderful retention tool needs constant honing.
- Pinterest, Twitter, and Social Media Strategies—Social media is powerful and evanescent, and strategies are needed for selecting which ones to use, and how to write them. Pinterest and Twitter are exemplars of specific social media for niche audiences.
- Public Relations—Many activities crowd under the rubric of public relations, and they all shape your issues, influence the public, and tell your story.
- Solicitation Letters—The "ask" is a sensitive communication tool, and it follows the same rules of strategy and wordsmithing as any marketing piece.
- Store—In many museums, the store is the first gallery visitors see, and the last one they flow through. It echoes the museum, using merchandise as examples of the exhibits in the galleries, and displaying them in a space where it's easy to touch and talk. This bully pulpit needs several kinds of good writing.
- Survey Questionnaires—Visitor research needs new rules for the road. This chapter will show the depth of insights that derive from surveys that use noncliché questions.
- Volunteers—Your volunteers shape the image of the museum: to visitors, members, scholars, the community, and the media. What you communicate to them, they pass along to everyone else, so your words yield profound consequences. Consider all the ways museum volunteers hear the brand narrative, from the Volunteer Opportunities page of the website to interoffice communiqués. Volunteers are ambassadors to the visitors and prospects outside your walls, and they deserve the best writing you can give them.
- Website—This is your virtual lobby, your galleries, your storage facility, your everything. Organization is essential in this Swiss Army knife of marketing tools.
- YouTube—It personalizes, demonstrates, informs, entertains, and endures. With a few pointers, you can become a YouTuber, too.

The pages that follow detail the communications that introduce your museum to new constituents, maintain awareness among current loyalists, and reach out with particular grip to donors, community partners, and the media. These written words speak with the voice of your brand to audiences that will listen.

Hire writers when you can; this book will help you supervise them effectively. However, also have the confidence to write more—and more effectively—yourself. Whether you function as a supervisor of writers, or The Writer, this book attempts to bring writing within the comfort zone of those who haven't indulged in the pleasure before.

For museum professionals with never-enough hours and almost-enough employees, finding budget and time for a writer might seem magical thinking. It's possible. "I've got a great writer on staff" is the desired outcome of *Writing for Museums*; it will enable museum staff to become effective writers.

Chapter One

Audio Tours

Figure 1.1. This sign above the Writers' Museum in Edinburgh, Scotland, quickly communicates what to expect inside. Whether it's your sign on the door, the cover of a magazine, or your exhibition brochures and banners, communicate what kind of knowledge the visitor will find in your museum. *Provided by author.*

Close your eyes and imagine the world around you. Now close your ears.

It can't be done, so it's understandable if people haven't thought about the intricacies of sound, any more than they think about improving oxygen. However, sound is an ally we all rely on to complement visuals. Sound is words given voice, and the voice of your museum breaks through in many ways. Because it encompasses listeners in a private bubble of concentration, it becomes very personal. Nobody with a headset turns to a friend to nod and discuss; audio tourists are wrapped in your words, and rather rapt. They're in your world, so make it a rich one. This requires skillful writing, and whether you undertake this project yourself, or supervise the work of a vendor, this chapter familiarizes you with the steps.

First, realize that audio tours are complex talks, with options at every stop, and you retain control of the flow and timing of the tour. However, unlike mobile devices whose links entice the user to stray, the ideal audio tour permits a minimum of choices, so they have to be very engaging. Visitors buy into the hardware and technology of an audio tour because they want learned information to help them learn. They expect the exhibition to be enhanced. They expect you to give them that rich experience.

THE PLANNING STAGE

The writer of audio tours collects, organizes, and orchestrates ideas like a television show runner. Concept, topics, visuals, words, speakers, timing, pacing, and summation are all part of production. At the start, the team of curator, educator, exhibition designer, person responsible for approving budgets, visitor studies person, marketing person, and writer will meet for the story conference. The team contributes information, advice, and consent throughout the process. However, a framework is needed, and the person best equipped to provide the form and to shape the content—to take the narrative from beginning to end—is the writer.

These are the elements of the writer's story: selection of objects or artworks, selection of galleries or rooms, use of one or more narrators and selection of voices, length of time spent at each exhibit, determination of the physical path from one object to another, and the keyword that runs through the tour. The keyword is the most important because it distills the objective of the story into one word or phrase.

Keyword

The keyword is an aural device that reminds the visitor of the tour's objective at every stop. The keyword at a 2013 exhibition at the Art Institute of Chicago, *Impressionism, Fashion, and Modernity*, was "artist." Whatever the specific artwork, the continuing narrative began with a reference to the person who created it. The keyword could have been "clothing" or "revolutionary fashion design," and been consistent with the theme of the exhibition. The keyword "artist" was selected, and the audio used it assiduously. "Artist" gave structure to an audio lecture with many parts. At each stop, the narration started with words like: "In this painting, the artist Edouard Manet shows a young woman dressed in a fur-trimmed jacket, which would have been the height of fashion at the time." Or, "Here, the artist Jacques Tissot, known for his lush depiction of fabric, shows an elegant woman in an atypical pose." The fact that the woman was his mistress, and that neither of them could afford such an elegant garment, made for entertaining listening, and those points were made in the narration. But the story at that painting began with "artist." In any exhibition, and especially the Art Institute's critically acclaimed blockbuster, there's a lot for visitors to absorb, and keywords keep the ear on track. Imagine if the narrator had started each segment with "this dress" or "what's revolutionary about the subject of this painting is"? A writer could write a good story from either, and before setting off on the long road to a script, good writers insist on a firm starting point. So do listeners, and a leitmotif (the aural icon) holds the journey together.

Selection of the Objects to Feature

You can't highlight every object, and you select them by the facts, or background, or color they add to the main narrative. Get some consensus from your team about which will contribute most to the story. Bring in some visitors to give their opinions. Their comments will help you select items and their questions will help write the words. For example, if a visitor finds something confusing, you can build a whole forty-five-second narrative around the strangeness of an object. If a child picks out something everyone else failed to notice, that might just be the nugget that earns an object a place in the audio tour. Welcome different opinions on what's interesting. A docent can redirect the conversation if an object proves uninteresting. There's no such leeway in an audio tour.

Some objects might be fundamental to the story: use several of them throughout the script, not just at the beginning or end. Other works elucidate a fact or highlight an interesting quirk, and these should also be sprinkled throughout. Think of this tour as a ten-course dinner, and think variety. Large pieces help listeners know where to turn; remember that they are not just listening and looking, but physically navigating through new territory. Intersperse smaller pieces to encourage leaning in. And use familiar or identifiable objects to provide mental relaxation and a pause.

In addition to size, look for different colors, textures, and mood. Some pieces will appear bright or calm, smooth or heavy, easygoing or humorous or complex. These variables don't necessarily influence the decision to use them in the exhibition; they simply help the writer find vivid words for the story. Also, the medley of objects substitutes for the medley of people that get excluded from the attention of an audio tourist. Those earphones tend to shut out the rest of the world, and for many people the fun in museums is the hodgepodge.

The writer plans the story by first looking at the objects, understanding how they represent the themes of the exhibition, and how they relate to one another. A rocking chair, book, and fireplace tell one story. Straw brooms, milking stools, and spinning wheels tell another. A collection of arrowheads found in the garden might not add to the story at all. The writer doesn't select the objects but should have an outsized vote in culling the selection.

Galleries or Rooms

The next part of the plan is the galleries or rooms that will be visited. If every gallery is to be visited, that's a comprehensive story. Moving through selected galleries outlines a more defined tour. Galleries of paintings and sculpture from one period suggest a chronological theme. A tour of works depicting women proposes another story line altogether. The writer knows which story can be told in the most scholarly, or witty, or emotional way. And that tone of voice is another decision point.

Tone of Voice

Choosing narrators, one or more, depends on the size of the museum, and its personality. The Whitney Museum of American Art, at an exhibition I saw about ten years ago, provided a dramatic audio tour with multiple alternating curators telling the main story, and actors adding period color when the button for "more information" was touched. Small museums with more intimate spaces would be wise to take a more conversational tone, with one voice being the friendly guide. I prefer a third option of alternating voices, to give the listener variety. Whatever the voice, it dominates the story, often in ways you can't predict. What sounds to some like a cheerful voice will sound childish to others. What some people would term a cultured voice would come off to others as snobbish. There are no real people to cue the listener, so you hedge your bets by using more than one speaker.

Length

Audio tours should last no longer than a visitor would normally take to tour the exhibition. In a large museum, that walk-through might take an hour. In a smaller museum, the time will vary, and you are the best person to know how long visitors usually stay. Take into consideration the chosen route, and the number of options at each stop. Be guided also by the length of docent-led tours, which customarily last forty-five to sixty minutes. You probably cater to school groups, and they demand a short, clear story. There will be a lot of give-and-take here, a tactical battle between the suggested length and the suggested physical path. Remember that compromises will always be made in the interest of the visitor's brain and back endurance, as well as the museum's mission.

THE STORY

What kind of story you tell visitors is essential to an audio tour because, like it or not, these days anything recorded is perceived as entertainment. We get TV shows and movies on tablets and mobile devices, and even recorded books now have music; viewers and listeners are accustomed to handheld productions. It needn't be an elaborate production; a good story is sufficient. Stories might revolve around the life of the artist, the history of a business in your community, the green systems in your new building, or how the members of a family occupied their time in the historic house.

Stories can also be scholarly. The story in the Art Institute's exhibition told how artists used nineteenth-century fashion to convey revolutionary thinking. That's quite an original hypothesis, and the admirable show narrated how avant-garde artists of the 1880s and 1890s used fashion and fashionable people to represent their new ideal: rebellion from the old ways of doing art and the spontaneity that typified their movement. Thanks to this very clear exhibition strategy, the multitudes of works in a mansion-like number of galleries represented those old favorite artists in an entirely new light. The story's theme also facilitated the trend in exhibitions toward depicting an era through many art forms of the day, and the exhibition included rather progressive quotes from an array of artists, writers, and critics.

For smaller museums, the continuity of the story line is equally important. You have to promise new tales all the time for your local constituents who may think one visit per generation is enough. A history museum could tell a story about the people of the community, or its sports, or its sociopolitical ideals. And should you want to honor a donor of a collection, nothing flatters more honestly than using their collection philosophy as a foundation for a story.

If your staff each wears more than one hat, those busy people will find a story line helpful in composing, approving, and evaluating an audio tour.

When searching for the words to your story, ask the members of your team a simple question: "Tell me about this exhibition." With some variations, the curator highlights criteria for selecting certain pieces and why each meets the criteria; the educator talks about learning objectives; visitor studies professionals cite research about what visitors like; the designer points out visual details that deserve a focus; and the financial person—the one who approves expenditures on installation and displays—frequently, with the best intentions, forces a different way of looking at things. As you listen to different experts talk about their view of the museum, you'll hear a lot of specifics, and that's excellent. Sweeping overviews don't help write a script. When you use specific objects and examples, the story almost writes itself.

MAPPING THE WALK

Travelers through an exhibition, especially those who are walking, listening, and looking at the same time, need a road map. Your own staff is best qualified to know when they should turn, where they should stop, and how far they should walk to the next stop. Docents figure this out by watching their flocks. Your writer has to estimate. Walk through the tour yourself before you finalize what sights to include in your story. And pay attention to height. The trend is toward hanging paintings at eye level, lower than has been traditional. That depends, of course, on the height of the visitor. A recent survey I conducted noted that most works in a given gallery, even ones devoted to family-friendly exhibits, are too high for children under age eight. They can't see them from across the room, and certainly can't see them close-up if they're hung over thirty inches from the ground. Even if you're writing an audio script for adults, they might have a child in tow, and both should be able to see—if not hear about—the work.

How fast the tour moves is an important consideration, taking into account the number of older people who are your most loyal supporters. The John and Mable Ringling Museum of Art in Sarasota, Florida, had a tour for its entire campus; the audio narrative was installed in trolleys.

Think also of people who might be on either side of the listener, taking the same audio tour and crowding in. A rule of retail shopping applies here: according to market researcher Paco Underhill, people who have stopped to inspect an item don't like to be bumped. Stores make sure their aisles are wide enough. You can control bumping by directing walkers to objects that have space around them.

NARRATOR AND VOICE

The narrator of the tour might likely be a curator, because those experts are fluent in their subject and accustomed to speaking convincingly about exhibitions. However, it must be remembered that this is a voice without a face, and disembodied voices are heard differently.

Television advertising people believed for years that male voices were more authoritative and female voices more reassuring. Others believe that the clear tones of a feminine voice are better understood. As for childlike voices, one has only to read the posts on a 2013 YouTube commercial to realize that kid voices are clichéd, unbelievable, and annoying. A generation ago, sounding "American" was familiar and uncontroversial. For a while, any English accent conveyed luxury. Currently, the English has to be RP, or the Received Pronunciation of the well educated or the BBC. Accented speech, of course, now enlivens every video narrative from cooking shows to reality housewives to eccentricity TV. And in a fiercely multicultural world, the one embraced by museums, the question is certainly up for discussion. What is indisputable is that you must, similar to the Hippocratic Oath, "abstain from whatever is deleterious and mischievous." Do not mispronounce foreign names. Do not mispronounce names of collections or their donors. Do not confuse the listener by using a narrator with an inappropriate voice.

I have always pictured a narrator as a cross between Hans Christian Andersen and the actors who introduce public television's *Masterpiece Theatre*. Other people say that a friendly grandfather in an armchair makes the perfect teller of stories. Recently, if someone has a spot on TED, or a well-followed blog, that authenticates them as a storyteller. There are talk show hosts, doctors, and judges whom, at one time or another, people gather around to hear wisdom. In the museum world, you have a broad selection of possible narrators.

A diplomatic way to audition people who'd like to narrate your audio is to give them a fifteen-minute script to read. Reading is harder than one thinks, and both you and the reader may come to a decision quickly. If you can afford a professional actor, that's a wise choice. If you have a college with a drama school nearby, audition its students; they should be paid something, but may be happy to work gratis on a project for their portfolios.

HOW THE NARRATION LEADS

The narration begins by stating the theme and keyword; each stop in an audio tour reiterates that theme. Whether your exhibition is on diamonds or aircraft, the format is similar. It starts with something like: "In this tour, we'll be looking at the dark world where sparkling diamonds begin." Or, "This tour looks inside the earliest commercial airplanes."

For each stop of the audio tour, plan on eighty words of script. Eighty words equal a thirty-second television commercial, so use that as a gauge. At each stop in the exhibition, be it an artwork, aircraft overhead, or gem display at your feet, the script continues: "This is the cockpit of a 1920 airmail plane." Or, "This photograph shows a typical diamond mine tunnel, lit with one dim bulb." Be obvious in your description, because audio tourists have many things vying for attention: figuring out the handset, adjusting the headset, finding the object in the gallery, and getting close to it. A straightforward description uses words such as "this cockpit, with its square and round dials" or "this light brown diamond, the size of a baseball." The next sixty or so words puts the exhibit into the context of your theme. The last ten to twelve words provide continuity as the listener turns toward the next stop. Use phrases like "You'll see this color sneaking into the next painting, as well." At the beginning of another stop you might write, "As we saw in the diamond mine photo . . ." Connectivity from exhibit to exhibit is important, because the visitors are following your lead. While they can choose the next button to push, if you keep the pace moving they'll want to follow your route.

Time the individual narrator to get an accurate timing, because all professionals read at slightly different rates. And then, take another look at your eighty words. You might want to use some of those words to give an alternate title of an artwork, dates of an object, or derivation of a word. There are several guidelines applicable to audio-script writing that wouldn't apply to other formats.

Use pointing phrases as often as possible, as if the narrator were pointing at a detail of the object. Write, "What's so intriguing about that open cockpit is . . ." or "Look at the height of this mine tunnel."

If there's a color theme throughout an exhibition, or a map appears next to every gem, write, "This appears throughout this exhibition." You might put that into a docent script, but it's easier for a visitor to look around on a live tour. Following a tour on tape, where the focus is on each individual stop, one is less apt to notice what appears throughout the exhibition. And pay attention to words on the wall, a technique used more and more to connect multiroom exhibitions. You shouldn't repeat the wall text in the script but, depending on how many wall panels there are, you can refer to them.

Dare to use multisyllabic words, where appropriate, because they flow off the tongue much more smoothly than off a page.

Beware of foreign words that need long explanations, and/or foreign words that have been traditionally mispronounced. Note alternate forms for foreign words or phrases: the Quai d'Orsay Museum in Paris is colloquially referred to as the Orsay. Henri de Toulouse-Lautrec loses the "de" when his last name only is used.

BEGINNING, MIDDLE, AND END

A good tour, whether led by a person or a voice, tells the reader how long the tour lasts. Readers are used to seeing the size of a print book, or the percentage read in an e-reader; movie and theater patrons can read the running time in advance. Digital video displays the length of the video and where you are at any second. Symphony programs list the length of each piece, and indicate intermissions. And any medium divided into acts tells you where you are at any point. However, when visitors take an audio tour, one that moves them around in an open-ended enclosure of sound, they can lose track of time. People don't like that! So structure the trip with an end time, and tell visitors that if they follow the suggested stops, "this tour will take forty-five minutes." Tell them that if they access further information the trip will take longer. At the midway stop, say, "You are now halfway through our tour." Studies have shown that pedestrians are more likely to wait for the light to change when the signal indicates how long they have. A museum director in Sydney told me that when they installed "Your waiting time is . . ." signs at ticket lines, visitors didn't complain. Time matters. And just to complicate this issue, the pace of life varies from culture to culture.

Varying the pace of the narrative is what any movie director does; some objects can be appreciated quickly, and some exhibits take several minutes to digest. For the lengthier stops, consider using a second voice such as an expert talking about aircraft or an actor reading the journal of a diamond miner. Use these second voices sparingly, or the narrative gets jumpy.

How long should your audio tourist stay at each work? Observational research of your visitors should help you determine that. More important is the balance of narration to quiet viewing time, and your audio can encourage taking a few seconds for reflection by saying: "Take a moment to form your own thoughts about this work. [PAUSE.]" After no more than ten seconds the narration continues with "When you're ready, push number 5 on your handset for the next exhibit." Very few tours, live or recorded, ask visitors to pause and reflect, and that's too bad. The goal of an educational tour should be on learning, not teaching.

An advantage of writing for audio is finding out immediately if you're talking too much. What looks like a short caption on the page can sound like an encyclopedia in the ear. You'll be forced to select the most salient information and state it precisely.

End the audio script with a thank-you and one more repetition of the exhibition title and theme. Unfortunately, there's no way in a recording to replicate what a live docent says at the end of a tour: "Any questions?" There are other ways, though, to end a tour without shutting off discourse. The audio narrator can wrap it up with: "And while this is the end of your tour today, think about what you'll remember tomorrow." If you allow photography in your galleries, you could end with: "This is the end of the tour but, if you like, go back and pin, tweet, or post the parts you like most." To prompt reflection and plant the seed of memory, instruct your staffer at the equipment counter to ask this very good question, the one the smiling lady at the Art Institute of Chicago said when a customer returned the apparatus: "How was it?" After so much time with a recorded voice, the human inquiry is welcome. And it's a valuable source of feedback.

SPEECHIFIED LABELS PROHIBITED

The audio tour is not a label re-created in full sentences. Labels are documents and identification cards; narrated tours are chats, and there are tricks to simulate a two-way conversation in a one-way technology.

- Be colloquial. Go over the script, and for every four-syllable word substitute a shorter word.
- Speak in short sentences that direct the eye. "Look at this pattern," "Watch that movement for a few seconds," "Look at that group of people; can you tell who the leader is?"
- Use conjunctions: "so that" and "because" and "as if." They sound more helpful and less didactic.
- Show humility: "I've studied this painting for years, and just recently noticed that . . ."
- Interject nuggets of information. Museum professionals know lots of anecdotes, and can slip in asides such as how the artist Jeff Koons, as an eight-year-old, painted copies of old masters and hung them in his father's furniture store windows. The human voice can say things that don't belong on a label and translate poorly on a panel.

WHAT ABOUT MOBILE?

The interactivity of mobile devices obviously opens a world of exploration that an audio tour can't equal. So you can suggest links in your script. If the tour is about fish, suggest that visitors map the species you've covered. If your visitors are learning about an herb garden, suggest they find recipes for cooking with herbs. Depending on your time, and the age of your target audience, you can suggest websites and apps, or let visitors explore on their own. My experience with college students affirms that they explore better and faster than you do, and will enjoy the academic freedom.

MARKETING WITH AUDIO

Whether you produce your own audio or supervise the work of a professional, you have to decide if audio tours accomplish goals that live docents can't, and if they are worth the time and cost. Be assured, they have tremendous additional marketing value that distributes the cost. First, they help sell expensive exhibitions. Observational research at a recent Matisse exhibition at the Art Institute of Chicago revealed that 50 percent of those heading for the exhibition area stopped first to purchase the five- to seven-dollar equipment. Importantly, these were not casual museum visitors, but destination visitors.

Once inside the museum, they strode directly toward the exhibition gallery; they did not waver as they stopped at the audio guide counter, neither asking about the price nor how to use the device. You could tell by observing that they knew their way around a museum. They are valuable consumers who want a rich experience, spend freely to enjoy it, and return often. Perhaps they are members; at the very least they are dedicated museumgoers. Consider them loyalists and use the tour, with its bounty of information, as a tool to keep them engaged.

Audio tours are also a way to promote your museum to donors and partners. They are the sound track for a slide presentation. They are a recorded memory of past exhibitions, and a vivid way to bring the archives to life when you want to demonstrate the breadth of your programs.

As a link on your website, an edited audio tour enlivens the encyclopedic material stored in your site's pages. Audio snippets of an exhibition are a "sticky" feature that visitors might return to. They are a useful resource for scholars and the media. They are examples of your competencies to make available when wooing administrators.

As museums look to all their content, many components assume new responsibilities. As performance spaces become regular features of new and redesigned museums, they will play a growing role as forums for all contemporary arts, including theater, music, film, and dance. Audio will play a different role than just a gallery enhancer. It might be a lobby activity before the show or during intermission, or an alternative format for the dramaturge's writing.

Audio tours can complement visual presentations on-site and off-site. Think about the lesson plans for homeschoolers, or the presentations for local businesses. If you've ever wondered how you'd find the time to give a presentation to a local organization, an audio tour might make that project easier to handle.

When it comes to academic museums, the possibilities for creativity multiply. Even a small archive of audio tours would provide intriguing pairings of exhibits and commentary. And if students could record a response to an exhibit rather than write about it, they might find the alternate learning style liberating.

And so, millennial opportunities continue. Considering the many current obligations of museums—entertainment, economic driver, civic treasure, national identifier, education necessity, social center, democratizer, and defender of the arts—it's valuable to have a voice at your side. Audio is a strong instrument for shaping the museum experience to so many constituent markets. Enjoy its power.

SCRIPTS FOR THE VISION IMPAIRED

A special kind of writing is needed when recording a tour for the visually impaired. For someone with low to no vision, merely describing an object and its context is frustratingly inadequate. You need to put into words what sighted visitors see immediately.

Size in Height, Width, and Depth

This is easy, as most objects are labeled or registered with specifications of size. But numbers of inches are neither interesting nor quickly digestible. Compare the size with a sheet of paper, or the palm of your hand, or a refrigerator.

Shapes

With artifacts, describing shapes becomes a symphony of description. Round bowls are easy, but soon you'll be verbalizing bottles whose neck is actually two thin necks, that come together to form one large bottle neck. A carved deity is child's play to describe compared to the intricacies of a carved altarpiece. You'll sharpen your verbal skills when you verbally carve out shapes.

Materials

Materials are included in labels, of course, but they take on new significance when you describe an object for the visually impaired. An artwork that on first glimpse has a pattern of blue and yellow is revealed to be much richer when you realize that the colors come from feathers. A sighted person's brain would make the connection: "Oh, feathers! That's what makes the colors so brilliant." That instantaneous mind-match needs to be figured out by the writer and translated into words.

Patterns

It's hard to describe the pattern of woven baskets or ceremonial masks, but all it takes is time. The visualizing writer has to find patterns where none existed before the artisan created them. You'll perfect your observation skills on this project.

Oddities, Political Considerations

Conventional sensitivities also get thrown overboard when describing for people with low sight. In the exhibition *Peru: Kingdoms of the Sun and the*

Moon at the Seattle Art Museum, the figures in the paintings were significant because they had crossed ethnic lines to marry, and the script told exactly how to see this. It pointed out that the husbands had the white skin of Spanish colonizers and the brides had the darker, olive skin of native Peruvian people. Details like skin color that we've been taught to disregard or euphemize now must be highlighted and spoken out loud.

The Display

It's not just about the object. Surrounding the object is its display, which sighted people can scope at a glance but your visually impaired audience cannot. Describe its pedestal, plinth, or mounting; estimate its distance from the wall, ceiling, and floor. Measure its proximity to other objects and the rationale for isolating or clustering your grouping.

The Gallery

How big is the room? Are there one or more doorways to the next gallery? What about the location of labels and panels: does it matter that the labels are all at the end of the wall? How is the room lit? What color are the walls? What texture?

"Visual description of the artwork intended for someone with no to low vision" is how Seattle Art Museum describes its audio tours, but this ultra-descriptive writing benefits anyone who works with creativity. It requires a new mind-set to take all the details that people with normal vision automatically absorb in a blink of the eye and write them down in words. You'll have to carefully see, and then articulate, how creators make their magic. And that's an eye-opening exercise.

REPURPOSING THE AUDIO TOUR

The concept of an audio tour is useful far beyond the walk-and-talk prepared for visitors, although that is the focus of this chapter. It's also a means to introduce board members and supporters to your museum, a catalyst for your departments, and a teaching instrument for staff, interns, and volunteers. As discussed in chapter 5, it's very effective as preparatory and follow-up material for use before and after a field trip. And you can use your audio-tour script as an outline for a slide presentation with a fraction of the effort it would take to start from scratch, which will suggest outreach programs that might formerly have been beyond your reach.

Chapter Two

Blogs

Not all social media are created equal. Each was nurtured and grown by a community that was fiercely loyal to everything that platform promised. When it delivered on the promise, it grew even more. Some social media have famously faded away, no longer meaningful or useful. Blogs have endured because they continue to matter. They have faced the test of time and audience participation.

Blogs and museums were made for each other. Museums have a lot of knowledge to impart, and blogs have the space for it. Blogs give museum experts a forum to share explorations and ideas. Blogs help researchers, from autodidacts to narrow-niche scholars, follow their curiosity. Blogs are one of the last bastions of authority, a media that permits authors of ideas to develop them at length and sign them before the community validates them by adding their opinions. Blogs are focused enough to be provocative, long enough to demonstrate thoughtfulness. Readers of blogs are prequalified to be engaged in your museum and to post commensurately thoughtful comments. Blogs encourage the posts and comments that add perspectives to their ideas, but their long form also inhibits frivolity. There are seven adjectives that describe the way blogs enhance the mission of museums of any genre, any size:

1. Authoritative
2. Timely
3. Regular and consistent
4. Topic specific
5. Brand oriented
6. Multivoiced for multiple communities
7. Narrative

The numerous examples of blogs in this chapter demonstrate these seven features and help you make your own voice heard.

AUTHORITATIVE

Blogs look and act much like journalism articles. They can be as long as the author wishes and the museum deems possible on a regular basis. A regular blog of 150 words lets you introduce many topics to show the breadth of your museum's collection and interests. An eight-hundred-word blog is more like a newspaper column, and demonstrates expertise in your area or participation in contemporary issues. The Cantor Arts Center at Stanford University publishes a blog on conservation, an area of expertise and a significant focus of the museum community as a whole. Its blog on conservation validates the museum's capability and resources in this area. Because blogs are signed by their authors with their full names, they have accountability, a hallmark of a strong museum. Blogs give a museum credibility and gravitas, and they get cited. Blogs are big, bold objects that are found by search engines.

Blogs give your staff a chance to author pieces relevant to their independent inquiries. The personal nature of blogs allows them their voice and the chance to pursue their own lines of inquiry and unique service to museology. Blogging allows your professionals the opportunity to strategize, analyze, synthesize, and write—a boon for your interns and entry-level employees who are just starting their museum careers.

Bloggers write for a wide range of new to established publications, and the best are considered journalists with all the rights and entrée that entails. They attend media briefings and events, and they can practice their profession even outside large metro areas.

TIMELY

Like all social media, blogs are defined by their timeliness. They address hot issues and provide current information. If the fable persists that museums are fusty shrines to the past, the daily blog dispels it. Unlike other forms of social media, blogging allows the writer to have time to analyze a topic of immediate significance.

The Lower East Side Tenement Museum wrote a February 26, 2014, blog on Sojourner Truth, tying the current month to a nineteenth-century Lower East Side resident:

"February is Black History Month!" the blog starts. It then tells its intent "to celebrate one amazing African-American woman who once made her home on the Lower East Side." Timely and appropriate for the mission of the Tenement Museum, a museum dedicated to telling the stories of the people who lived in the immigrant-dense Lower East Side of New York from the late 1800s to the mid-twentieth century. Truth is not one of the residents whose lives are recounted in tours of the Tenement Museum, but her story of escape from slavery and legal action to protect her family is current. And telling that story allows the museum to expand on its mission. By the way, the term "Lower East Side" appears three times in the blog. That helps search engines find it.

REGULAR AND CONSISTENT

Blogs appear on a regular schedule, much as a journalist's column does. Museums want visitors to return often, and frequent online visits build loyalty and engagement just as regular visits do. It also provides a second and third chance for comments by readers who may not engage and post after just one visit.

The blog of the Museum of Life and Science in Durham, North Carolina, has a delightful series from its Animal Department. A February 25, 2014, blog wrote about animals in the snow, a very timely article in the midst of the worst winter in memory across the eastern half of the United States. The Animal Department curators take turns writing about what they see on their daily feedings, and what they've recently read in other publications.

Compare the schedule of blogs with Facebook posts, tweets, and Instagrams. Blogs appear regularly, but not hourly, so there's time for thoughtful consideration of a topic and attention to persuasive writing.

Consistency is essential with a blog. In the cacophony of online messages—updates, alerts, comment, posts, tweets, pins, trends, and more to come—blogs can stand out by espousing a point of view and developing it over time. If you want to essay another point of view, start a different blog.

Consistency also requires that you not use too many synonyms; repeat the words that best reflect your mission and core values. Again, the Lower East Side Tenement Museum does an exemplary job; in an April 2013 blog on basketball's history, the word "neighborhood" appears five times. "Lower East Side" is mentioned seven times. The blogger didn't write "community" or "lower Manhattan." The Indianapolis Museum of Art, in its blog on bees, used the words "bee" and "honey" over ten times, "pollinate" three times. If your department isn't well known, blogs have a wonderful propensity for getting search engines to discover you.

In some media, good writing demands variation of the same noun or verb. Not in the consistent blog, where search engines are constantly on the lookout for the most-used keywords.

Use visuals freely, with captions. A picture, contrary to cliché, is not worth a thousand words. It communicates strongly, but imprecisely, and is worth at least a twenty-word caption.

TOPIC SPECIFIC

Blogs keep you on topic. In the heat of daily writing, it's easy to lose sight of the fact that a museum has a mission, a collecting policy, and a reputation in its geographic and intellectual community. Blogs, with their longer form, force you to talk about what you know best. The Burke Museum at the University of Washington, Seattle, has American Northwest artifacts at its core. In its "About the Burke" statement of vision, it writes that "every object has a story to tell, not just as a record of past life on earth, but as a resource for the future. . . . The Burke [Museum of Natural History and Culture] brings together people, objects, and the stories that make them meaningful." And in a February 2014 blog it writes about a "mask that likely inspired the Seahawks logo discovered in a Maine museum." Masks are important artifacts in the Burke's collection, and when they bring together historic peoples, scholars in Maine, and sports fans, the Burke is fulfilling its mission. If you're a scholar or donor, you will be impressed by the museum's wide-ranging attention to its core values. And who knows, football aficionados interested in the Seattle Seahawks might also find new relevance in the Burke.

BRAND ORIENTED

Well-written blogs go the extra step and create a distinctive banner. It's good branding to refer to your blog by a name, rather than generically. Everybody has a blog; only Cantor Arts Center has a blog titled *Cross-Sections*. *Cross-Sections* also has a tagline: "A look at what goes on in an art conservation lab."

With their sharp focus and sufficient space, blogs support branding elegantly. The blogger has time to select brand-appropriate topics and space to incorporate the museum's brand perspective. A good blog will hew to these branding principles:

Blog Name

Names are singular and very personal possessions. They impute the same individuality to blogs as they do to people. Tate Museums, comprising Tate Britain, Tate Modern, Tate Liverpool, and Tate St. Ives, publishes many blogs, including one named *Tate Debate* and another with the name *Tate*

Shots: Interview. You'd expect a national museum with an international reputation to address big issues, and *Tate Debate* reflects that mission. You'd expect a major museum to query contemporary leaders in art, and *Tate Shots: Interview* fulfills that brand promise with video interviews of painters, sculptors, and photographers.

The National Museum of the American Indian tells its many stories through some wonderfully named blogs: *A Song for the Horse Nation: Horses in Native American Cultures* and *All Things Green.* They both describe the museum's mission of "bringing Native voices to what the museum writes and presents . . . acting as a resource for the hemisphere's Native communities and . . . serving the greater public as an honest and thoughtful conduit to Native cultures."

All Things Green blogs on every use of flora from koa wood in outrigger canoes to blueberries as ceremonial food. *A Song for the Horse Nation* writes about everything from horses captured in World War II Germany by American Indians, to masks made for warhorses to make them more fearsome to enemies.

Visuals and Captions

Visuals reinforce the brand message. The Tenement Museum, Museum of Life and Science, and Cantor all use photographs and videos to make their point. Of course, Instagram and Pinterest also use photographs to excellent effect because they are generated by the community and followed by the community. However, only blogs let you curate images for your specific community, and then relate them to your mission and core values. Captions further target your brand mission.

A caption to a photo of the nascent movie industry on the Lower East Side captures the personality of the Tenement Museum in all its cultural diversity:

> A Yiddish Theatre on East 12th and 2nd Avenue, date unknown. Second Avenue, the center of the Yiddish theatre scene, was nicknamed the Jewish Rialto.

A detailed caption description of one step in canoe building, featured in *All Things Green*, demonstrates the National Museum of the American Indian's attention to the quality of native artifacts, and the importance of the maker:

> *Manu* extending upward on the back end of the *'Auhou*, NMAI's Hawaiian canoe. Protruding below it is the notched extension where ropes would have been attached to bring the rough-hewn hull out of the forest.

The caption on the *A Song for the Horse Nation* blog reinforces the horse story that is part of the museum brand:

> Joseph Medicine Crow, about to enter the dance arena at the annual Crow Fair, holds a dance stick representing the horses he captured from German SS officers in World War II.

Photos and their captions bring a blog, and its museum, to life. Look for images that connect to the brand, because that consistency keeps returning readers familiar with your museum and comfortable sharing their ideas with you.

MULTIVOICED FOR MULTIPLE COMMUNITIES

Bloggers speak in many voices, to many communities, allowing museums to deploy a range of ideas, which in turn encourage a broad swath of respondents to respond with their own array of thoughts. The blogs of Cantor Arts Center, Museum of Life and Science, National Museum of the American Indian, and Lower East Side Tenement Museum all feature a range of writers, each with their own style and format. Some use a how-to approach, with

Figure 2.1.   This blog takes a step-by-step approach to describe historically accurate canoe building. *Courtesy National Museum of the American Indian/Smithsonian.*

illustrative photos; some use video. Some are conversational, some journalistic, some scholarly. The Animal Department curators speak in the first person, charmingly informal. *Stories Yun Told Me*, from another Tenement Museum blogger, is written under the pseudonym of a young Chinese man, an imaginary immigrant who interviews other immigrants. Because blogs insatiably demand more content, you must draw on many people to develop and write them.

Happily, it is the nature of blogs to flow from the pen—they started out as weblogs or diaries—and many people in your museum have the information and the writing habit to create and maintain a blog, usually with only soft supervision from above. Individuals communicate meaningfully with their communities, and, in the social environment, there are infinitely more communities than the niche market segments of yore. Just two NMAI (National Museum of the American Indian) blogs reach out to multiple communities of canoers, boatbuilders, historians, seafarers, cooks, horse enthusiasts, and ceremony researchers, and more "Customers Like You" communities. All these groups contribute a wide spectrum of perspectives, each feeding back their distinctive comments.

NARRATIVE

Blogs restore the reputation of writers, essayists, satirists, and biographers, and they will resuscitate any media on the brink of paper-borne disaster. They have evolved into magazine-quality opinion pieces based on facts, and they have a beginning, a middle, and a conclusion. When they incorporate visuals, chosen judiciously for symbiotic effect, they are multimedia tours de force. Like streaming media content that, with complex story lines, is being compared to Dickens, there's no reason why a blog can't read like a novel. And if your museum has a story to tell, a blog is inestimable: next to the exhibits inside the walls, nothing can tell your story better.

The museums whose stories demand a blog are those that are:

- Short on space
- Blessed with more knowledge than artifacts
- Concentrated on research
- Closed for renovation
- Distant from large markets

BLOG-STARTING IDEAS

There is never a deficit of material for a blog, and once you have a subject posts flow from there. The challenge is to find a singular subject to zero in on. Blogs need be only as long as you have something to say, and you write them as you would say them. They can be informed by scholarship, or simply musings on the day's activities, but they're rather conversational in tone. The schedule of blogs allots enough time to write well—with facts, detail, and charm—but not enough time to bury personality. The following categories of blog-starting ideas contain hundreds of blog subjects.

People

Museums like the Tenement Museum, and the Wing Luke Museum of the Asian Pacific American Experience in Seattle, are based on the experiences of immigrants who have braved ocean passage, faced dramatic obstacles, and created new lives. There's a story in every document held by museums like this. There's a narrative in every dish or cupboard of historic houses. Your curators and registrars have the stories, and a ten-minute interview with them will get the blog going. They don't have to be long, and additional research can add new angles to the original story at any time.

Food

If your museum has cookbooks, recipe cards, or reminiscences, wait until you're hungry and intersperse your own food experiences with those in the collection. That's one angle. If you have time for research, ask the curator or education department how the food was prepared. If you are, yourself, the curator and the education department, just reprint the recipe with a brief description of its provenance. Most museums have the makings for a food blog. It's easy for botanic gardens to provide salads or floral decorations for the table. An exhibition on rain forests or prairies or seafarers might suggest foods of the region. Every heritage museum and historical society has a cache of food ideas in their collective memories. And art museums have still lifes and genre paintings from which to borrow the seed of an idea.

Furniture, Hats, and Decoys

If chairs, lamps, and carpets are part of your collections, single out one piece and describe it. Compare it to today's version. Tell what part of the household budget it would have taken to purchase it. You know these details, and you don't have to write a history on interior design. The same stories emanate from articles of apparel and occupational tools. Little details quickly engender a rich paragraph, and that's all you need for a blog.

Feather and Fin

Details reside in all types of museums. Start your natural history blog with:

Ever wonder why this feather . . .

Or

This fin is different from all others in the river because . . .

Interview the Staff

Stop any worker in your botanic garden and ask:

Why are you doing that?

Or

What do you do when it rains?

People love to explain their jobs, and they do it well. I learned this when I asked questions of the gardeners at the Chicago Botanic Garden, in Glencoe, Illinois, and the horticulturist at the Ringling in Sarasota. The lady at the lily pond, the man crossing the banyan-strewn campus, each instantly became encyclopedias of fascinating information.

The Museum of Life and Science's Animal Department blog is excellent because staffers talk about their jobs and find stories in their routines of dealing with animal meds, the steer that gets excited when he goes for a walk to get weighed, and bathing the birds in water and dust. Museum people often write with the conciseness of scientists, as well as passion for their work. Their daily grind is in fact a stimulating brew. You don't know this until you ask.

Don't Forget the Guards

If your museum's job description is anything like that of the Cleveland Museum of Natural History, you expect your guards to "maintain good working knowledge of the Museum exhibits and displays and be prepared to answer visitor questions regarding these areas." Ask the guards what insights they get from watching visitors. They've seen it all and will regale you with behaviors that you, behind the scenes, never see. Also find out what questions visitors ask guards. My research has shown that visitors have no reservations about asking the guards for information, so even if your guards aren't coached with answers, ask them to share the questions. If your guards want to write a blog, terrific. Otherwise it's yet another good assignment for an intern.

Archives

How can you excavate a regular blog column from your museum's trove of information? Here are some suggestions.

Mine the newsletter. The following blog material was taken from the Winter 2014 newsletter of the DuPage County (Illinois) Historical Museum. It's an example of translating existing information into a blog: "Can a hat tell a story? Does a wristwatch have the power to teach us lessons about our own lives?" The museum says yes, and the rest of the article lists many other accessories, each one of which could form the subject of a blog.

In another newsletter the museum writes about its Folk Art exhibition and the twelve private tours and ten lectures and workshops that supplemented the show. That's a lot of blog material. The newsletter is newsy and brief. It mentions everything from fashion accessories to carved decoys and itinerant portraitists. A blog could delve into each one of these separately. Small museums have the information, and many of your staffers will welcome the opportunity to showcase their knowledge with a bylined blog.

Categorize

Take, for example, a serving piece in your period dining room, and list all the other pieces in the category of table service, or dinnerware. Many will be in your collection; many will be on your wish list. Research the former items as if you were labeling them. Research the latter as if you were justifying a proposal to acquire. Now, write two-hundred-word essays on tureens or goblets or oyster plates. Become an expert on mealtimes. And give the blog a name, like *Dinner Is Served*.

Listicles

Listicles, as a form of journalism, have been a mainstay of blogs and landing page fillers for about ten years. The portmanteau word is formed from "list" and "article," and though many demean listicles as weeds flourishing in the culture of short attention spans, they follow good writing principles of originality in thought and brevity in words.

Listicles are written to a theme, and it must be original. Top Ten Artists is not quite as original as Ten Artists Who Paint Dogs. It's an angle, which is classic journalism. The list is well researched, in the finest tradition of journalists and museums. The listicle form calls for a short paragraph of explication following each listing. The format looks readable, which is a benefit, and it looks like you'll learn something. Also not given full credit is the urge for readers to form their own conclusions. Lists make the reader wonder, "Why these ten?" Lists lure your readers into adding their own list items. The one-through-ten format prompts an internal assessment of priorities, and if you can get a reader to think, "I would have made the Manet the number three artist of dogs," you've created a comment-ready blog and one more engaged reader.

In her article "The Listicle as Literary Form," Arika Okrent compares listicles to haiku, a very short form of literature that also artfully stacks words together. She admits that she first thought the term meant prose on a Popsicle stick, "vertically arranged, quickly consumed, not too nutritious, but fun." Listicles certainly are refreshing. They add variety to the page layout, generate comments from viewers, and jog the mind of writers facing the blank page.

Lift the Curtain

Behind-the-scenes activities are trending. Not all museums can afford to build an open lab or conservation area, but bloggers can go behind closed doors and document preparation.

Romance the Data

The Museum of Life and Science has a blog entry called "Who Weighs More?" Round 2 asks you to choose between Ray the alpaca and Auggie the potbellied pig. The more obscure the numbers, the more interesting the blog: How many people does it take to install an exhibition? How many rolls of tape? Number of boxes in traveling exhibition. Or this from the brochure of Brooklyn Museum's Luce Center for American Art: "Decoding the accession number."

Expanded Labels

The NMAI exhibition *A Song for the Horse Nation* encompassed more information than labels and wall panels could hold. So the blog told the rest of the story. Here's just one paragraph:

> As horses became more integral to American Indian tribes like the Navajo, Crow and Blackfeet, riders became experts in fabricating horse gear for hunting, warfare and ceremony. Along the way, they transformed utilitarian equipment into a unique art form.

The information is there. It just has to be published in the blog.

Play

If your museum has more toys than space, write a monthly column on the diversions of children. They are so frequently rooted in larger stories that this will engage many more people than one usually expects from a blog.

Disaster Stories

Near catastrophes abound in any endeavor, and everyone can recall a favorite. A happy ending usually ensues, so blogs based on a problem are instructive. Shipment goes astray? Write about packing, labeling, and scheduling. Artist demands? This would be a fascinating blog, fathoming the psyche of creative people you've actually met.

Parry the Questions

This blog subject addresses the many questions tour visitors ask. Have tour guides collect those questions so you can answer them calmly in a blog. Have the guide tell the questioner: "That's a fascinating question, but too involved for me to go into here. I'll send you the explanation it deserves if you will kindly give me your e-mail address after the tour." Thus you have not only an idea for a blog, but a device for adding names to your database.

Keyhole Details

Archaeologists and spies know how to gather a full picture from a tiny fragment. You could decipher the war history of an officer from a close-up view of several medals. Details are also highly visual when they're cropped dynamically, as if through a keyhole, often more intriguing than a full-blown photograph.

Play Geography

A docent told me that she started every tour by asking the visitors where they came from. It helps to place them on a map, to appreciate how far they may have traveled, and to compare your museum with ones in their hometowns. A highlight was the discussion that ensued from a contemporary artwork that included a teeter-totter, and what that icon of childhood was called in different languages. There are so many stories in the big world, and they start with hometowns.

Standing Titles

Standing titles don't have to be like magazine columns that appear monthly, year after year; even a short run can build interest. The idea is to invent a discreet, often humorous, category, like the Life and Science Animal Department bloggers did: "Why You Should Always Carry a Camera." They started with "Reason #1" and kept on going. Standing titles give you a theme and a device for finding other stories for other days.

School Tours

I first discovered the value in nine-year-olds' questions from overhearing a fourth-grade museum tour group. Field trips are ongoing sources of ideas, and a blog from their perspective would be instructive. A variation comes from Adam Gopnik in his book *Paris to the Moon*, for the idea of a "Glad Sad" game in which his young son was asked to look at art portraits and statues in Paris's museums and guess what the people were thinking. Over the years I've been regularly astounded by what the child sees.

STRATEGY COMPENSATES FOR LARGE STAFF

Small museums that don't have the staff for regular tweeting, shooting, and pinning might be better served by blogs, which are published at longer intervals. County historical societies and museums also have the particular challenge of documenting their local history, and their documents offer more subjects than can ever be exhibited. But bloggers can select any number of local topics to expatiate on. I envy the DuPage County Museum in Wheaton, Illinois, which has rich archives on topics from early railroad commerce to polo in America to itinerant portrait painters. These are the nuggets that make small museums gleam in a blog.

Small museums can present a larger presence with an active, inquisitive blog, and if your staff is already stretched, consider collaboration with another museum in your community. Two St. Louis museums, although not small ones, got together in 2013 with the goal of writing from two perspectives. The Pulitzer Foundation for the Arts and Contemporary Art Museum St. Louis became the Contemporary-Pulitzer blogs and alternated posts with refreshing differences of outlook. True collaboration comes from partners that aren't alike, that find a third idea from two contrasting ones. That's powerful leadership and renews the authority expected from museums. It's also apt to draw more comments.

Blogs, like all social media, invite responses and comments. The superiority of the incomparable blog platform is its depth and continuity and, as a result, its ability to foster deeper and longer engagement with its followers.

Chapter Three

Brochures

"Brochure" is a grab-bag term used for a variety of small, usually six-panel, folded pieces that fit in a regular-sized letter envelope, or on a rack; a brochure gives a brief overview of the museum. Remember brevity and small size, because brochures are narrow in focus and highly strategic, written for specific purposes. They are first and foremost awareness communications, with just enough information to tell a prospective visitor why to visit your museum and not do some other leisure activity. Think of all the other brochures in hotel racks and convention bureau mailings, and you'll see the strategic positioning of a brochure: it's between a one-page print ad and a many-page catalog. In addition to a general-information brochure, even small museums use two or three different brochures during the course of a twelve-month period. Each brochure creates awareness for an exhibition, or special objects, membership, or even a season of the museum year. Brochures are not booklets because little books are full of information of all sorts; brochures are purposely narrow, targeted arrows of information that get right to the specific subject. They are one-offs, even if they stay in a visitor's suitcase, in a pocket, or on a tabletop for a while.

FOUR KINDS OF BROCHURES

There are at least four kinds of brochures: basic informational; specific exhibition; concept, such as summer evenings at the botanic garden; and strategic. Strategic brochures are written to announce specific goals such as membership, facilities rental, community partnerships, complementary programming, or capital campaigns. Strategic brochures also are used to target specific audiences, such as meeting planners, conference attendees, educators, or research scientists. All follow the same organizing structure as the basic informational brochure: cover; introduction; flap; four to six images with brief captions; three to six paragraphs of information; back cover with directions, times, transportation, map. Good writing is, above all, organized, and once you discipline yourself to the organization of a brochure, you'll be able to write a good one.

BASIC BROCHURE STRUCTURE

The brochure with the longest shelf life is the general information brochure, the one you use most often, print the most copies of, and keep in stock the longest. It's like the table of contents of who you are, what you do, why you're different from other museums, when you're open, and where you can be found.

This is its structure:

Regardless of budget, the basic brochure is an 8 1/2 x 11–inch sheet of paper folded twice to create six panels. Think of a basic sheet of paper that gets folded for insertion into an envelope. Within the six panels is all the information needed by a visitor or prospect to decide whether to visit or, if already inside your door, how to learn more. The brochure attempts no more than quick information for decision making.

Front Cover

The front cover, the part visitors see in racks or inside mailed envelopes, has a big picture, a headline, and the name of the museum. The brochure for the Marine Museum in Biarritz, France, shows a large seal diving into blue water. The headline says, "Take a dive into the Bay of Biscay." On the cover is the name of the museum, its logo, and a small British flag symbolizing the

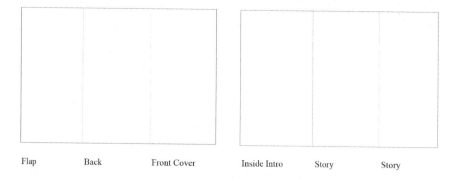

| Flap | Back | Front Cover | Inside Intro | Story | Story |

Figure 3.1. The basic brochure is designed to fit in hotel and tourism racks, meeting presentation kits, and 8 1/2 x 11 envelopes. *Provided by author.*

English-language version. It's instant communication of the name, place, and type of museum. You can tell this museum by the cover. Inside, there are three panels to further explain the fundamentals.

Inside Intro Panel

Note that there is a panel that's on the left when you open the folded sheet. This is the inside intro panel for introductory copy. Here's where you'll briefly describe your museum's distinctiveness. This is the space for your mission or brand story. The New Museum in New York says this in its inside brochure's introduction:

> The New Museum is the only museum with the mission to promote new art and new ideas, and the only museum in New York City devoted exclusively to contemporary art.

There's another paragraph on its beginnings, evolution, and philosophy of experimentation and questioning, all telling a compelling story of why this "daring" museum is worth a visit in a city with hundreds of other choices. Not all museums, of course, have so much competition and such a great need to stand out, but even if you're the only leisure activity in town, your introduction panel should talk about your distinctiveness.

One tip for writing the inside intro panel is to start with the thought, "We are distinctive because." Look for distinctive words. The New Museum uses phrases like: "founded by a curator . . . who had abundant resourcefulness [and] . . . combative ideas . . ."

Another tip for writing this panel: tell a story about your museum. For example, if you were a regional arts museum, you might start with: "We were founded by the daughter of a cabinetmaker who believed that . . ."

A clue to writing a good introduction comes from children: ask any field tripper what he or she liked best. It might be a small detail to you, but it probably condenses a basic truth. And it will be an emotional response, always a good core around which to spin a tale.

Flap Panel

Next on your six-panel outline, look at the panel that flaps over the inside spread. Its positioning allows for a sidebar, a singular, key aspect of your museum that provides additional insights into its distinctiveness. The New Museum's flap panel tells about its distinctive architecture, which provides a structure for some of the spaces a visitor will see inside. Another flap panel, in the brochure of the Deere-Wiman House, says:

Deere-Wiman House, home to John Deere's descendants from 1872 until
1976, rests on seven hilltop acres above downtown Moline, Illinois.

Short and evocative, this briefest of brochure text situates the mansion of a
tractor magnate above the hustle of machinery to an idyllic aerie. Good
writing doesn't have to be grandiloquent; it stirs the imagination using a verb
like "rests" and an unexpected adjective like "hilltop." And then stops.

Back Panel

There are three panels left, and the back panel is reserved for contact information: address, telephone, website, hours, and days. Information about
guided tours, accessibility, accreditation, and partnerships also belong on the
back panel, all in one place. This is also the space to put icons such as
earphones symbolizing audio tours, or national flags symbolizing transla-
tions into other languages.

That leaves two panels for the illustrated story.

Story Panels

The rule of thumb is four to six images and three to six text paragraphs for
the scenes and chapters of your story. You've set the stage and played the
overture, now it's time for the show. The conventional, straight-up-and-
down, grid story panels are the easiest to write and lay out, although younger
readers are used to layouts that flow more organically. Whatever the layout,
pretend that the photos tell the story and organize them first; then add paragraphs of text. Then go back and add short captions to identify photo details
that would take up too much space in the text. Here are some examples of
photos that carry a narrative of a museum.

A brochure for a historic house might show six of its rooms. A re-created
village could depict four houses and two close-ups of demonstrations. A
museum that's distant from the town center will use one photo to highlight its
restaurant or café. And larger museums might show five works and a shot of
merchandise from the store. Some layouts utilize both story panels as one
four-color spread, with large and small images and very little copy; frankly,
this format is a favorite among graphic designers, and is very artful, but it
doesn't give as much information. If your museum's brand is best served by
a highly visual brochure, write concise captions with each photo; visitors
can't get the whole picture from just a few individual pictures.

If you have more information than the above organization permits, information that absolutely, positively must be included, then you probably need
either a larger, more expensive brochure, or an additional one. Time and
budget will determine how many specific brochures you produce, and you
should be guided by strategy. Ask: Why do we need a brochure on the fall

exhibition? What special audiences are served by a facilities brochure? What's the purpose for talking about our map collection at this time? If you know why you need a special brochure, it will help write it.

SPECIFIC EXHIBITION BROCHURE

Your museum spends time and treasure for a special exhibition, so it makes sense to publicize the research and creativity that went into it and the attendant opportunities for educators, community partnerships, and support. The cover is the big change, and it should blazon the name of the exhibition and its identifying visual. The inside intro panel should include the basics of your museum but highlight the special exhibition. This is the place to explain the rationale for mounting a special exhibition, and why tourists and the local community alike should take the time to see it. The flap will contain an intriguing detail to further emphasize the mission of the special exhibition. The story panels will expand the narrative in pictures and words. And the back panel will give the special hours, if any, and perhaps local information such as participating institutions, hotels, and restaurants.

If the exhibition lasts for more than three months, you might want to supplement the special brochure with auxiliary brochures on programs and lectures, family touring tips, or related subjects. With long-running shows, you'll need to refresh their newsworthiness and give additional reasons for local patrons to return. An exhibition on agriculture might add a brochure of home green gardening; an artist's retrospective might add a brochure on other artists of the era; a heritage exhibition might supplement the displays with instructions on crafts, or sheet music, or recipes. These complementary brochures follow the same organization as the basic brochure, but they can be produced less expensively with black-and-white printing on less expensive stock.

CONCEPT BROCHURE

Concept brochures need not be a privilege of wealthier museums; they are a delightful extra that is affordable if they result in extra visitors, store purchases, and awareness. You don't need a special exhibition to develop a concept, just a good theme. Hold the equivalent of story conferences, the kind favored by TV show runners and magazine story editors, and gather together your staff to identify some concepts that overarch your collection, exhibits, and usual programming. Much like the complementary brochures used for long-running special exhibitions, these will refresh your schedule, but without major new installations. For example, a botanic garden might print a brochure for herbalists. A historic home might put together a brochure on "who else lived here," an idea espoused some years ago by a conference at the McFaddin-Ward House in Beaumont, Texas. Crystal Bridges Museum of American Art in Bentonville, Arkansas, produced a brochure titled *Community*, in which it featured six works borrowed from "our fine colleague institutions" throughout northwest Arkansas. This is a concept that reinforces the Crystal Bridges mission of bringing American art to its region, at the same time collegially saluting six other museums.

Again, the organization of the concept brochure follows the same guidelines as the basic informational brochure. And as you organize the details of your concept, as you discover a different perspective, you likely will find new audiences to reach out to.

STRATEGIC BROCHURE

Strategic brochures address issues usually involving numbers and money. This is simplistic, but it's a good rule of thumb for deciding whether a new brochure is worth the cost. Although there are limitless reasons to produce a strategic brochure, here are some of the more common ones: membership; classes, lectures, and performances; facilities rental; a capital campaign; an appeal to legislators. All these activities have financial implications, and where money is concerned, it helps to have well-designed supporting documents.

If your museum relies on a heavy schedule of classes, rather than changing exhibitions, you need a strategy to keep your offerings meaningful and fresh. A brochure listing courses will increase their educational importance and give your museum a fresh look with each new brochure. The Georgia O'Keeffe Museum in Santa Fe, New Mexico, has a fairly static collection, but a rich schedule of classes. Its course brochure is exciting, and heightens awareness of the brand each time a new brochure is printed. The DuPage County Historical Museum has the same challenge as the O'Keeffe Museum. It prints class schedule brochures on its photocopier. The information is just as fresh, and equally interesting, so never let a small budget deter you from bringing out the brochures to bring out visitors.

Niche markets sometimes call for an audience-targeted strategic brochure. For example, a brochure sent to meeting planners in your Tourism Department's packet of information can be rewritten to highlight your museum's relationship to the city. Use the same images, but change the inside intro panel, or the poignant detail on the flap, to emphasize your place in the city's panoply of cultural attractions. Design a brochure that highlights your distinctiveness as a tourism stop. Remember that in this situation, your city is in competition for the meeting. You might want to have your basic brochure translated into another language, which doesn't have to be an expensive four-color print job; the information will be appreciated and adds to the competitiveness of your city's meeting bid.

When targeting major prospects in a capital campaign, or legislators in an advocacy campaign, you might want a brochure to supplement letters and supporting documents. This brochure will recalibrate the image-and-text ratio. It's hard to visualize financial responsibility, or volunteer hours, or any of the facts you muster to make your case. Although there are no rules for strategies that are so individual and consequential, there are two guideposts. One, know your audience, and remember that you are speaking to a small, accountable, focused group of people who might be your neighbors but in this instance are primarily money givers. Two, know the danger areas, which include photos of people (may not be gender/ethnicity/age balanced), numbers, facts, frivolousness, and deviation from the immediate interests of the target audience.

BIGGER BROCHURES

If you have more information, the eight-panel, three-fold brochure follows the organization of the smaller version. It is easily printed on 8 1/2 x 14 paper in any copier. It still fits into a No. 10 envelope, presentation folders, and most pockets and bag flaps. The increased space lets you use the center for larger images, a more comprehensive map or floor plan, one or two additional paragraphs of text, and one or two additional smaller images. It does not give you carte blanche to load the reader with much more information.

BOOKLETS ARE NOT BROCHURES

A booklet is similar to a brochure because it is narrowly focused on a specific event or topic. It looks like a little book, and often is bound with a staple. It usually has longer paragraphs, with fewer images and more scholarly text. It is bigger than a brochure, often with eight to sixteen pages. You might want to print a booklet as a gallery guide to accompany an important exhibition.

A good example is the sixteen-page gallery guide to the Picasso *Retrospektive* at the Kunstmuseum Basel, *The Picassos Are Here!* It's a well-written booklet, with the gallery numbering clearly marked and interesting insights included with every work mentioned. Dates are used frequently, giving a sense of scope, even though many, many events are omitted because they aren't represented in the exhibition. It's easily read, with just enough but not too much detail, and it doesn't overwhelm the art itself. A few illustrations stand in for major works not in the show. Significantly, it's printed in black and white, on plain paper, and the images are small. It's not as promotional as a brochure—it's not flashy—and all the excitement is in the information. If you think you have enough material for eight, twelve, or sixteen pages, you don't want a brochure; you will be writing a thoughtful booklet.

Of course, booklets can be four color, beautiful, and proportionately expensive. The Ringling Museum assembled a lovely piece for a floral exhibition, complete with arrangements and flower-arranging instructions. It was twelve pages, staple bound, very pretty, and deeply interesting. It was not a brochure.

A booklet follows the structure of a book or a magazine. There's a cover, which can be alluring with an image and title, or just informative with a title. Inside there's a clear progression of information, as logically organized as if it had a table of contents. It starts with a brief introduction, followed by clearly delineated paragraphs of information, each with a subhead, or name. The Kunstmuseum booklet simply numbered each paragraph to coincide with the work's number in the gallery and its title. The Ringling booklet starts each page with the name of the flower arrangement.

WORKING WITH THE PRINTER

Unlike this paragraph that you're reading now, and which brings up the rear of this chapter, the specifications of a brochure should be discussed before you plan the content. Discuss with, don't tell, your printer what you hope for: how big; how many colors; size, thickness, and quality of paper; quantity needed; deadline. These details often determine what is said inside. Obviously, if it is to be an expensive print job on quality paper with new photography, you might want it to include a year's worth of information. If it's an inexpensively produced piece, you should be encouraged to update it several times a year. If it's a heavy piece, postage rises and, because of cost, some pieces are destined for rack displays only. If cost isn't so big an issue, mailing direct to a large audience is an option, and that might affect whether you add a cover letter. Brochures are frequently redesigned after a considered talk with the printer. For example, a directional map is recommended for brochures placed in hotel racks; they target audiences that are at the decision-making stage. Direct-mail brochures reach a broader target, those who might not have even picked a city destination, and the space is better used for one more event, or exhibit, to help create interest.

Note to small museums: inexpensive and persuasive brochures can be printed on a photocopier, and once you get used to producing one, try rolling out others for every exhibit and program. You want to encourage every visitor to return again, and a table full of different brochures signals the variety and richness of your offering. The DuPage County Historical Museum displayed, among its other literature, three different brochures. One announced Scout and school programs, one gave a sneak peek at a gallery renovation, and one detailed themed birthday parties at the museum. They proved how vibrant and robust a small museum can be.

Chapter Four

E-mail

One click. That's all it takes to get from an e-mail to four-color, full coverage of your news, newsletter, event, offer, store, and more. Make that one click count. Don't let a little click shortchange you.

Now a standard part of daily life, e-mail is still an exciting and powerful form of communications. Research shows only a 1 percent decrease in marketing usage over the years, and that's because e-mail, like so many life-changing technologies, has stayed relevant. It is tried (not tired) and true. It delivers the goods every time because this is one digital media that allows the marketer to maintain control; you control the message and the recipient of that message. You control the links from the e-mail to your announcement, offer, news, and website. In the social-sharing environment, your control over your own e-mail is a major advantage.

If you need more motivation to write more engagingly in e-mails, consider the clutter in your own inbox. Mind-numbing jumble is the age-old enemy of marketers; it confounded experts fifty years ago when advertising research departments warned their creative people that three thousand images bombard people daily and therefore they needed to stand out from the clutter. Imagine the number of messages we get round the clock today, and vow immediately to write more specific e-mails that speak to your intended audiences with words that relate to your own museum.

There are seven components to an e-mail, all within your control: the To line; the Subject line; message box visual, message box headline, text and links; the tagline; and the Date line. Maximize that control because it's a real advantage in the social-sharing environment where the crowd can adapt the To, Subject, message box visual, message box headline, text and links, tagline, and Date. Remembering the "e-mail seven" will help avoid blasting out e-mails on autopilot, much as you did back when mailboxes didn't contain two hundred messages an hour. You want that click, and there are seven ways to get it and repeat it. We'll save the To line for last.

#1: SUBJECT LINE

This is the first thing e-mail recipients will see and take into cognition. They may not recognize the Sender Museum, so a meaningful Subject line is like a news media headline, or a magazine ad headline. It helps to grasp the power of a good Subject line by reading some weak ones. Here's an example of a weak Subject line: "January edition." The reader may be able to tell by the Sent line whose newsletter is inside, but it takes another second of thought. And if the name of the Sent line is that of the local tourist bureau, or the parent university, the name of the museum doesn't appear at all.

Here's an example of an excellent Subject line: "One Day in Pompeii," from the Franklin Institute in Philadelphia.

The Subject line is like a headline. It communicates a specific piece of news or information to the targeted audience. It can be short or longer, just so it conveys the message. If you keep the message topmost in mind, you'll never waste your time or the readers' with meaningless mail.

"Alfred's Beloved Garden" was a recent Subject line, and each of those three words stood out. "Beloved" is a surefire attention getter, and "garden" targets an audience. "Alfred" is a bit of a teaser, but for members, donors, and former visitors to Ten Chimneys, the historic home of Alfred Lunt and Lynn Fontanne in Genesee Depot, Wisconsin, it completes the message. "Waking Up at 97 Orchard Street" is another appealing Subject line. If you're on the mailing list for the Tenement Museum in New York, you may not know the address, but "Tenement Museum" is in the From line, so it teases, it doesn't annoy. Compare this with "Update" or "Breakthrough exhibition," subjects that all too many museums use.

One hallmark of effective writing is unique language, words that are fresh and specific. They don't have to be erudite, and should never be fulsome; they just have to be particular to the topic being written about. "Update" falls flat. It's a word that applies to detergent ingredients as well as scholarship. Anyone can update anything; there's nothing wrong with it and nothing right. Learn to spot the "update"-like words—"news," "announcement," "this week"—and substitute a better word. Tip: put the Word cursor on "news" and click Shft+F7; it will garner synonyms like "information," "report," "intelligence," "gossip," "rumor," "hearsay," "bulletin," "broadcast," "summary," "flash," "communiqué," and "notice." Not all are appropriate for your e-mails, but they are all more singular words than "update."

Another problem with the "update" format for starting an e-mail: in addition to being a lazy word, it's a lazy structure for creative thinking. If museums only updated their collection or their staff or their prospective donor list, they'd be in maintenance mode, not moving forward. Update is passive, and conjures images of a museum person struggling just to keep up. That might be a reality for many hard-pressed professionals, but it's a dangerous attitude.

Now, as a test, based on the Subject line, would you open these e-mails?

- "Celebrate Our Tenth Anniversary Season With [name of museum]"
- "Join us this spring at [name of museum]"
- "Celebrate fall at [name of museum]—Extended tours through November 25th"
- "A SPECIAL OFFER on [name of museum] Tours"
- "See what's happening this month at the [name of museum]!"
- "An extra week of great American art"
- "All [name of museum] Stage Tickets Now On Sale"

The punctuation is the museums', and I have altered the Subject line only by substituting "[name of museum]" for the real name. In each case, the generic subject should be replaced with a specific event, or inventive writing:

- For celebrating an anniversary: Steve Jobs was born in 1955, and so were we.
- For "Join us this spring" write: Join us for tulip time.
- For "What's happening this month" write: Candlelight tours are happening this month.

#2 AND #3: MESSAGE BOX VISUAL AND HEADLINE

Ideally, the first message one sees is visual. Sometimes it takes two clicks to get there, depending on the recipient's server, but one click usually connects to an e-mail version of the website's home page or landing page. The Franklin Institute has a wonderful one-click visual on e-mails announcing special exhibitions or events. At the top of the screen is the logo banner, with Ben Franklin's image identifying the museum. Below that is the full-screen visual, with the title of the exhibition or event superimposed. Once the striking visual was the greenery of a Brazilian show; another monthly e-mail was fiery orange and brown tones of a movie on volcanoes. The whole story may not be told in the first click of the e-mail; rather, the reader gets an intriguing teaser message, to be explained in full by scrolling down.

Art Museum of Delaware also opens its e-mail message with a powerful visual coupled with a standing headline: "Art Is." It follows with a one-word distillation of the e-mail's message. "Art Is Social," or "Art Is Oh La La."

The full-banner photograph is always beautiful, well lit, well cropped, well thought out. It does an excellent job of marrying picture and words to establish a unique presence in the cultural life of its community. Burke Museum at the University of Washington, Seattle, designs its e-mail so that when you click to open you see the headline of the first article, such as "Short Takes on Dam(n) Science," from the February 10, 2014, e-mail, or a visual of a collection piece, like the cracked pottery vessel with the caption "Seattle's First Coffee Mug," from the April 2, 2014, e-mail.

There are many kinds of good visuals, just as there are many styles of opening scenes of a movie or facing pages of a glossy magazine article. The visual could describe an exhibition, a specific object, a lecture or workshop, a new item on the café menu, or successful community collaboration. This visual, almost always a photograph (but possibly an illustration, map, or chart), must be provocative, without borrowing interest. Do not amuse, astound, delight, or warm hearts with a visual that does not represent your museum's brand. And because it reflects the excellence of your museum, the subject should be photogenic: not all artifacts, store items, or building facades are equally attractive, so select diplomatically for the ones that photograph well. Photogenic, by the way, does not relieve you from taking a good photo, with excellent lighting, clear details, and no background clutter. The visual should be meaningful: not necessarily newsy, but indicative of the focused creativity and innovation that your museum is known for.

If the visual is a video, there's added potential for confusion, as well as impact. Since the first moving picture over 125 years ago, no one has denied the advantages of motion. It's entertaining, engaging, and full of emotion that comes from the emergence of a smile or delivery of a serious subject. Videos offer the opportunity to show off the nooks and crannies of your museum, the flow of a visitor tour, all sides of a three-dimensional object, snippets of a lecture, or behind-the-scenes workings of your lab. However, the very stimulation of a video will change your main message, for good or bad. If the ten-second video highlights the message, that's a good visual. If it's longer than ten seconds, and still interesting, it verges on being borrowed interest, an entertainment and diversion, not an illustration.

#4: MESSAGE BOX TEXT AND LINKS

After the visual, or the headline, or the visual/verbal main message, what follows is explication: a brief outline of the event to come. This is wide-open territory for the writer, so don't let all this space seduce you. Readers can X you away in another click; if they stay around, give them something of import. "Dress up like a dinosaur," says the text of an e-mailed message from the Burke Museum when one first opens it. "Ever since James McNeill

Whistler sued John Ruskin for libel after the critic condemned *Nocturne in Black and Gold: The Falling Rocket*, art and law have been intimately intertwined," says the text describing a lecture at Delaware Art Museum in an October 31, 2013, e-mailed communication.

Problems to Avoid in the Message Box Visual, Headline, and Text

It makes sense to feature your store in the content of the e-mail message because the items are visually appealing. However, the dimensions of an e-mail message are smaller than those of your website, so make sure you put enticing, relevant visuals and headlines at the top of the screen. Don't squeeze a bunch of merchandise items onto one screen. Start with the most photogenic object in the store. Don't write: 10% off all items in the Museum Store. Do write: 10% off Hand-Dyed Woven Jewelry. Don't write: See our large collection of science toys. Do write: Five Fierce Dinosaurs. Remember that any headline that mentions a savings gets read anyway, so you don't have to use large type. And if the reader has opened the e-mail, he or she knows you're a science (or history, or art) museum. In an e-mail, it's best to avoid disaster-size headlines so the reader doesn't have to scroll down to see the pictured item. The same goes for books. You should be proud of your bookstore, and books sell, but some covers aren't very attractive, and others actually misrepresent your museum. You might have a fine collection of decorative arts, but a book with paperweights on the cover might not tell your most important story.

Finally, be aware of posters. Many museums can offer the same posters. And with a film poster, it might perfectly describe the film in your program, but have the wrong look for your brand. This is one case where it makes sense to write your own provocative headline—not the movie studio's—and make it big enough so it ties the movie to your museum.

Once beckoned into the successive links, the text of the new message must pay off. If the links lead to a newsletter, it's especially important to tell the whole story alluded to in the headline. The subject stated in the Subject line is developed logically in the opened newsletter. If it links to a fuller story on your website, that's better, because now you've lured readers to all the enticements of your museum. Remember that e-mail was invented by the government to help scientists communicate their findings; write with the follow-through of a scientist bent on making a point, and you'll hone your content to a sharp point, too. Here, the Tenement Museum scores, time after time. Their excellent e-mails start with a reference to the families that populated the tenement building home of the museum, and whose stories continue to grow its "collection."

The charming e-mails that seem to arrive every week or so from the Tenement Museum are so intriguing that, when a link suggests, "Read the rest of this story on our blog here," it's irresistible. The e-mail that started with the welcoming subject line, "Waking Up at 97 Orchard Street," and showed an illustration of a kitchen in the tenement at 97 Orchard Street, linked to a fascinating story of breakfast across cultures and the hope of a new day in the immigrant world of old New York.

The Tenement Museum's collection and mission is stories—the actual tenement apartments are kept in their original condition, sometimes with meager plumbing or electrical outlets intact, but with little or no furnishings. The illustrator has imagined the original kitchen for you, and words do the rest, nicely connecting the current season with the past:

> [In] these last winter days, we turn to hot tea and coffee for warmth and caffeine. Here at the Tenement Museum, we also imagine how they might have awakened the senses of residents at 97 Orchard Street. . . . In the Baldizzi apartment there's a canister of Maxwell House Coffee. In the Confino apartment, visitors take a whiff of Turkish coffee. And a coffee grinder is now a hands-on object in the "Meet Bridget" program . . . how would the families in our tenement at 97 Orchard Street have consumed them? You can read the rest of this story on our blog here.

Another seasonal story starts: "Batter Up! Baseball on the Lower East Side" and follows with text that relates to the history of New York baseball as experienced by immigrants living on the Lower East Side. This particular July newsletter continues: "Summer is upon us, and it's time for beaches, beer, boardwalks and baseball." In your museum e-mails, the seasonal connection could lead to a museum lecture, event, or new book in the store. The story format helps you connect the stories of your exhibits to current and relevant programs of the museum itself.

"Click here" can lead readers anywhere, and you can control their exploring so that they visit pages that fill out your message meaningfully and enhance your museum's viewpoint. Don't be too generous with external links; don't lead readers astray to sites that detract from your message. Before too long, six degrees of separation occurs, and your visitor is far, far away from you.

#5: TAGLINE

Not all e-mails open to a newsletter or special event page. Some e-mails are just mail, with a message to a donor, educator, community partner, vendor, scholar, or any number of constituents on your various mailing lists. This is where a tagline comes in handy, and a surprising number of e-mails from individuals have their museum's identity—tagline and possibly logo—right under their signature, telephone number, and e-mail address, so it's rein-

Figure 4.1.   The stories these walls can tell! And the East Side Tenement Museum blogs do. The museum holds no traditional objects; it collects stories of the people who immigrated to the United States in the late nineteenth and early twentieth century and lived in tenements like this one. The narratives imbue every e-mail, newsletter, and blog in ways no gallery exhibit ever could. *Provided by author.*

forced with every Yours Truly. This book does not deal with how to discover your museum's identity, or how to develop your logo and taglines; that's a process addressed in my book *Museum Branding*. This chapter simply reminds you to use your distinctive, familiar, and respected brand signifiers on all communications, including basic e-mails. E-mails are ubiquitous; you'd be negligent not to include a little marketing at the bottom of every single one.

#6: THE DATE LINE

Some e-mails appear in mailboxes all the time, or so it seems. In fact, they may only appear occasionally, depending on the workload of museum staffs. However, each time they do appear they reinforce awareness and familiarity. A survey of one avid museumgoer's mailbox showed that the most memorable e-mails appear no more than twice a month. It's the consistency of the intriguing Subject lines, the layout of the visuals in the message, and the text of the message that keep these museums top of mind, so that when they do arrive in your recipient's mailbox, they are welcome and opened. Whatever the timing of the e-mails, it's important to match the subject to the time of year. This relevance tells the reader that the museum contacts him regularly, whatever that regular schedule turns out to be.

#7: STRATEGIES OF THE TO LINE

Unlike a poster in the community, advertisement in the media, or even your magazine available at the information counter, you know exactly who will see an e-mail. Sure, like all digital communications, e-mails can be forwarded limitlessly, but initially they go exactly to whom you intended. Be strategic with these communications. If you send new messages regularly, as the Tenement Museum and Ten Chimneys do to people already on their visitor list, assume that they will be read as reminders, and write them to embellish your ongoing story. Time-specific announcements of special events probably will be best appreciated by members or visitors within certain ZIP codes. These people already know your story; first they want dates, times, and prices. E-mails with offers, or discounts, or special entrance hours are sent to valued members, and should be written telling them just that. Teaser mail like the above-mentioned "Alfred's Beloved Garden" comes from Ten Chimneys in the hopes that visitors will return sometime to this rural Wisconsin museum, and keeps the story alive over a longer period of time. Messages to the broad database of onetime visitors should include events that can be planned in advance. Links to store merchandise are important because shopping and actual buying keep awareness high over time. As your database becomes more sophisticated, you can target the To by whether they attend lectures, when they donate, if they buy at the store or restaurant, and how many guests they bring when they purchase tickets to an event. The guidelines for handling the To aren't hard and fast but, rather, reminders to sharpen messages, mine data more deeply, and connect the two.

Chapter Five

Education: Learning Outcomes

Learning Outcomes

Figure 5.1.   El Museo del Barrio, in New York City, states its education goal where everyone can see it. *Provided by author.*

"A man who carries a cat by the tail learns something he can learn in no other way."

Mark Twain understood learning outcomes, and this chapter will borrow his straightforwardness. Education, of course, is half what is taught, and 100 percent what's learned. For those writing about education programs, all words lead to learning outcomes. When you write about learning outcomes—

as opposed to teaching goals—all constituencies understand the role of education more clearly. Your constituents are numerous: students, teachers, principals, adult visitors, museum administration, funders, donors, professional conferences, governments, and accreditation agencies—all the people you're answerable to. Constituents love learning outcomes because they document your accountability; you'll love learning outcomes because they sell programs.

"Learning outcomes" run the risk of sounding mandatory and boring. So think of a brilliant schoolteacher, standing tall and energetic, around whom happy students are cheering and jumping for joy. The teacher is your education program, which is taught. The happy, cheering group represents what is learned. On the proposal page, the program description comes first, but it is closely followed, supported, by a list of learning outcomes. The description can be written in any style, from witty to serious, flowing to staccato. The learning outcomes are written succinctly, telling what participants should be able to do, starting with verbs like:

- Identify
- Relate
- Discuss
- Dramatize
- Discover
- Critique
- Solve
- Reconstruct
- Create

Even thinking in terms of actions verbs like these, new ideas flow. I'm reminded about the Saturday program I saw at the Burke Museum at the University of Washington, Seattle. Students were cleaning up after making paper antlers to wear on their heads. I never saw or heard the program description, but I saw the outcome—what the youngsters had created—and I discovered an effective way for students to learn about animals of the Northwest forest. Learning outcomes suggest a full-color, joyous discovery that your students will experience.

THOUGHT-PROVOKING LEARNING

This chapter will discuss the effervescence in learning outcomes. Frankly, a bullet-point list looks static. But if learning outcomes are written well, everyone will understand the fizz about to bubble up. Whether your programs are designed for school lesson plans, continuing education programs, or creative adult programs, by emphasizing what is learned, rather than what is taught, they reveal the true gems in your museum, the discoveries and insights that students find at every turn. By looking at your museum's excitements, you'll write better outcomes. In describing how several museums turn their distinctions into learning outcomes, I have, in most cases, rewritten these outcomes in bullet points, so you can see how to distill an activity into learning. In the process, you may find surprising new ways to awaken education experiences of your own.

The following is the college syllabus format for writing learning outcomes. I have imagined a small local history museum, and found it filled with learning opportunities.

Learning Outcomes

At the completion of this program, students should be able to:

- Discover objects that people in the nineteenth century used in their homes
- Explore the jobs, chores, and duties that different people in the community had
- Identify the tools in the average home or business
- Imagine what the people in the portraits or photographs did each day
- Prepare a dinner from what is available in the cupboard, garden, and stores
- Plan a trip to relatives who live fifty miles away and explain why and how you are traveling there

Write no less than three and no more than six learning outcomes. If it's a short program, three is plenty. If the class, field trip, or workshop lasts two hours or more, you'll want six learning outcomes to structure the content. The first learning outcomes are general, the middle ones add examples and in-depth learning, and the final outcomes anticipate that students will apply what they've seen, internalize these sightings, and discuss their ramifications.

The ladder of verbs starts with learning as exploratory, a survey. Then the student delves into the examples, modifications, and more complexity. Finally, there is synthesis as students apply their learning to actual challenges. The progression: new ideas, explanation of facts, repetition, critique, evaluation, conclusions. How static the theory, and how lively the learning!

TEACHING TO LEARNING

There are unlimited ways to coax out and write the learning outcomes that reside in your museum. Here are eleven suggestions.

Suggestion #1: Writing from Research Findings

In 2013, when it was still a brand-new jewel in the heart of the Ozarks, Crystal Bridges Museum of American Art wisely conducted research on how it might attract school field trips to Bentonville, Arkansas, from throughout its multistate region. Joining with the expertise of the University of Arkansas Department of Education, Crystal Bridges discovered that students:

- Observed minutely
- Displayed critical thinking in discussing the art
- Noted diversity in their surroundings, as well as the art
- Were open to opinions of their peers
- Imagined situations outside their experience

Further, a video prepared in conjunction with this research revealed some other benefits of the field trip. Students:

- Unlearned some preconceived rules; they could talk and laugh in museums!
- Gained confidence in their opinions

These findings can easily be converted to learning objectives and adapted for your museum. For example:

At the completion of this program, students should be able to:

- Describe a detail they liked
- Explain one thing they didn't like
- Remember something about the trip that was different from home
- Relate something surprising
- Compare what they noticed with what a friend noticed

The Crystal Bridges research also unearthed an underlying problem that occurred well before the field trip: subtle and creeping disinterest in field trips in general. It wasn't just economics, or parental fatigue after helping their children "learn for the test." It was lethargy, induced perhaps by parental preoccupation, scariness of the unknown, lack of confidence on the part of students, and uncertainty as to the purpose of the tour. Turn these research findings, too, into learning outcomes:

At the completion of this program, students should be able to:

- Discover an object or idea to discuss with your parents
- Identify people and occupations you never knew before
- Draw a story about what you saw to take home

If you are able to provide teachers with brochures, videos, and small souvenirs before and after the trip, they should reiterate learning outcomes as well.

Visualize the programs you offer field trippers in illustrated brochures to be taken home, or an e-mail slide presentation addressed to parents. Help the family discuss the adventure together.

Videos preview the trip for the classroom, showing students what to expect. This is especially supportive in any school districts where museums are far away; the video might show everything from the building and the road leading to it, to the objects inside, and the comfort areas such as the lunchroom and the bathrooms.

Small souvenirs should be a reminder at the end of the trip, a permanent memory of your museum.

Follow-up classroom materials supplement and extend the one-day event and provide reminders of the value of museum learning; this is good pedagogy, and also proof of the value of the field trip to administrators.

Suggestion #2: Writing Big Ideas

The Tenement Museum in New York offers workshops for teachers built around issues of relevance to its early and current community such as commerce, industrialization, immigration, and discrimination. The Wing Luke Museum in Seattle offers workshops on introducing race and social justice, poignantly cataloging the constant struggle for jobs against intractable opposition to Asians. As topics for children or some adults, these may seem ponderous or too sophisticated. Don't underestimate people's desire to tackle big issues; just find synonyms for the big words, and relate these universal issues to more local events.

At the completion of this program, students should be able to:

- Identify the jobs and professions of immigrants to America
- Describe factories and factory work
- Show the journeys of immigrants from homeland to America
- Relate how discrimination was practiced
- Examine the effects of injustice
- Devise laws to prevent unfair treatment of others

Suggestion #3: Writing from Primary Source Documents

Primary sources include objects like student report cards, stamped postcards from your community's far-flung families, catalogs of cattle auctions, laboratory supply lists, train schedules, sermons, and wedding invitations. One such primary source, from the Tenement Museum, shows an 1870 census report for 97 Orchard Street, listing male names with occupations such as "segar maker," "dealer in lace," and "law student," female names with occupations of "keeping house." Countries of origin were listed, all by the census taker, as Russia, Prussia, Polland [*sic*], Baden, Saxony, Germany. Relationships in the household were also listed: head, wife, daughter, son, and boarder. One can imagine the critical thinking that students of any age could apply to basic material like this. All you have to do is write the learning outcomes:

At the completion of this program, students should be able to:

- Describe some of the jobs people held 140 years ago
- Imagine how people used lace in the clothing and homes
- Calculate how long it took to travel from Russia to New York City
- Say "My name is _____" in Polish, Spanish, Chinese, Urdu, and Russian
- Discuss the change in law over 140 years
- Relate children's lives then and now
- Explain the science behind the preservation and conservation of paper documents
- Imagine what it would be like to live in a house with a fireplace for cooking

Suggestion #4: Writing from a Non-Adult Perspective

Ask kids questions and you not only hear significant insights, but you empower them to express themselves and feel confident in their opinions. What's even easier, and a lot of fun, is getting a group of college students to remember back ten years and, speaking as their younger selves, talk about museum likes and dislikes, expectations and fears, favorite objects, favorite bus seatmates, and the first thing they told their parents when they got home. Long memories reveal truths about museum visits that seem superficial but lead to engaged learning. One session I conducted turned up this information about what college students remembered about field trips long past:

- Too much noise
- Liked being outdoors
- Hungry
- Liked being with my friend
- Bus trip fun

You can convert these children's fixations into learning outcomes.

At the completion of this program, students should be able to:

- Describe the sounds of a nineteenth-century town
- Name the trees and flowers around the museum
- Plan a dinner menu for a family of eight
- Imagine what friends would talk about if they lived in the nineteenth century
- Compare the costs of maintaining a horse and wagon versus a car

Museums like the Wing offer many programs that deal with children's experiences in a new world filled with strange sights, people, jobs, and attitudes. Its programs' learning outcomes contain provocative ideas for any museum that offers children's programs. You would reframe your program's learning outcomes as issues for children to ponder.

At the completion of this program, students should be able to:

- Describe things that would have frightened a girl who moved to a new home
- Identify the people they would ask for help
- List the things they would need in a place that's different from their home country
- Explain who they are to a group of strangers
- Speak one sentence, of their choice, in another language

Suggestion #5: Writing from Your Brand and Mission

The tour engages high school students in following the voice and actions of Churchill as a leader, focusing on his allies and enemies through three wars. Students will better understand how a leader gathers evidence from his experiences and uses it to help shape the world's future.

This paragraph explains the learning outcomes of a high school education program offered by of the National Churchill Museum at Westminster College in Fulton, Missouri. Fulton is the location of Winston Churchill's famed Iron Curtain speech in 1946, and the museum contains, arguably, the largest collection of Churchilliana in the United States. The whole purpose of the museum is to demonstrate the leadership of one of history's greatest leaders, and its learning outcomes are a lesson for any museum built around a well-known person.

If your museum honors an artist, scientist, industrialist, inventor, entertainer, legislator, civic leader, sport, or group of heroes, think about what skills and values they embodied and write those values as learning outcomes.

At the completion of this program, students should be able to:

- Describe the daily routine of a scientist
- Demonstrate the use of artists' tools
- Interpret the vision of the architect who designed your museum's building
- Evaluate the contribution of a historic businessperson to this city
- Compare an athlete's regimen to your own
- Recall a famous quote from the person whose ideals are embodied in this museum
- Create the title for a memoir this person might write
- Relate the person's significance to your culture

It also works the other way around. If you are rebranding your museum, look to the learning outcomes of your programs for insights. Well-written learning outcomes often lead to a deeper acknowledgment of what your museum stands for, what each object in the collection demonstrates, and what every acquisition should enhance. These course descriptions from the Fort Worth Museum of Science and History describe an attitude of Look around, see your world, learn from it. Once again, what is stated simply for children applies equally for adults. I don't know if the museum expresses its mission this way, but that's this observer's takeaway.

Explore the history and making of chocolate and learn some science behind this delicious treat.

Will today be warm or cold? Will it rain? Find out more about the weather and what causes it. Learn about clouds, wind and temperature and more.

Take a look at the many kinds of plants and animals that dwell in the desert and learn about their special features that help them exist in the harsh environment.

Suggestion #6: Writing from Work Experience

People's jobs often signify their lives, and museum education programs are well positioned to integrate them into learning. Any genre, any size museum can play. A botanic garden structures a program around what the gardeners plant, prune, and protect. A science museum builds a program around a geologist's maps, backpack, hours, and teams. An art museum designs a program that looks at a conservator's research, and types of damage. A history museum immerses students in the daily life of an era.

At the completion of this program, students should be able to:

- Understand the power of water
- Describe the daily routine of a shopkeeper
- Write a resume for a job as a rural schoolteacher

- Plant seeds
- Perform basic animal care
- Operate a telephone switchboard
- Compare a person's workday with their father's or mother's, or their own

Another work viewpoint is that of the professionals in your own museum's sphere. In describing the work on the Lascaux Cave drawings, exhibited at the Field Museum in Chicago in 2013, one panel asked visitors to view the caves through the eyes of the many people involved. Your museum might include some of these in learning outcomes:

At the completion of this program, students should be able to:

- Describe this farm tool from the perspective of the farmer who uses it
- Identify this tool from a historian's expertise
- Consider this tool with the photographer's eye for composition
- Design a costume as part of a display of this tool
- Demonstrate how this tool would be used if it were part of a short video
- Describe how a conservator might assess this tool for damage

Jobs, real and imagined, current and future, occupy the minds of most young people from the days of their first lemonade stand. It is a framework for all our days, and identification for our place in the world. Whatever your collection and exhibits, they can legitimately be considered as outcomes of many good jobs. Invite the participation of your students by asking them to inhabit those jobs for a few hours.

Suggestion #7: Writing from the Dog's Point of View

Take a look at ground level. As adults, we see the world from at least five feet off the ground. The average American adult woman is 5'4". If you consider a world audience, that average is between 4'8" (Bolivia) and 5'7" (Netherlands). Many of the objects displayed by a historic house, science, botanic garden, art, or history museum can be interpreted and studied from a much lower angle. After all, except for stalactites, everything starts at the bottom.

At the completion of this program, students should be able to:

- Describe the smells of the earth in your garden
- Relate the view of a sculpture from lying underneath it
- Draw the legs of the chairs and table
- Imagine what it would be like to walk on a country road to school

- Tell a story about the stars as if you were a shepherd lying on the ground all night
- Imagine the lives of people from the shoes they wear
- Calculate the number of germs in a carpet

Suggestion #8: Include the Family

National Science Museum in London started thinking about parents when developing its five-year program for teachers teaching science. Realizing that an important aspect of learning takes place at home, part of its learning objectives started with this understanding:

> But it is not just about science in the classroom. In fact, research shows that one of the strongest indicators of whether a young person will choose a career in science is the type of support they get outside of school from their families. We will be working with teachers, young people and their families to help create a supportive learning environment for students.

Without changing the content of your programs, you can reach out to include the families of the students. For example:

At the completion of this program, students should be able to:

- Tell their parents one thing they learned that they didn't know before
- Draw a picture to take home to the family
- Discuss how to present a new idea to a younger sibling
- Select one object that they wish they could take back to their home
- Dramatize how one object might be used by mother, father, sibling, or grandparent

The concept of including the family is implicit in the superlative home-schooling programs offered by the Fort Worth Museum of Science, which allows a whole family to learn at one time, often encompassing a six-year age range. Colleges are including freshmen- through senior-level students in one class to change the dynamic of learning from each other at different stages of exploration, synthesizing, and application.

Suggestion #9: Writing from the Walls' Ears

Actually, it's not the walls that have ears, but the guards who stand stolid like a wall but hear plenty. Just what do your guards hear people say? What questions do people ask them? What body language do they notice? The guards at the Denver Art Museum, Toledo Museum of Art, and Museum of Contemporary Art Chicago told me that visitors actually walk back and forth trying to decide which way to turn first; that women always try the seats that are part of an exhibition, but men seldom stop to sit down; that many people want to know where the exit is; and that one Swedish visitor told him (correctly, as a curator later confirmed) that a little girl in a photograph was the future queen of Sweden. Of primary interest is what visitors notice or care about that you didn't know. Reading body language is especially interesting because it's unconscious and seldom shows up in conventional research; you'd have to spend a lot of time on the floor to gain half the insights the guards do. Only they are tasked with scrutinizing people so closely, and they get very good at deciphering behavior. Based on the above observations, here are some learning outcomes to consider:

At the completion of this program, students should be able to:

- Select details that are personally meaningful
- Design a route through the museum that tells a story
- Notice other people's choices and interpret what others find interesting
- Relate what someone of the opposite sex might enjoy

By the way, if you choose to conduct some observational research of your own, a quiet time to watch visitor behavior might be late summer and early fall. According to the Fort Worth Museum of Science, this is before school field trips start coming in October.

Suggestion #10: Writing an Essay

Catherine Mettille, a lecturer in Buffalo State College's Writing Program, blogs that undergraduate composition classes at Buffalo State College visited Burchfield Penney Art Center and Albright Knox Art Gallery to develop students' critical thinking and synthesizing skills. Art museums don't have to teach art students, and science museums don't have to teach science students. However, all students have to think, critique, relate, and revise—in short, write an essay. Imagine how your programs might be learned through writing.

At the completion of this program, students should be able to:

- Select a theme
- Outline the concepts
- Describe the concepts
- Analyze and summarize the concepts
- Compare and defend their conclusions against those of others
- Argue the interpretation of the program instructor

Suggestion #11: Writing with a Craftsman's Eye

If your museum offers craft workshops, think of these functional activities as learning activities. Museums like Vesterheim Norwegian-American Museum in Decorah, Iowa, and John Michael Kohler Arts Center in Sheboygan, Wisconsin, offer a creative potpourri of courses that encourage participants to identify a challenge, master some skills, select the best examples, and analyze their choices—otherwise known as fulfilling learning outcomes. Whether your workshop labors at cooking, or filmmaking, or rosemaling, take pride in the learning outcomes.

At the completion of this program, students should be able to:

- Describe the tools artists use
- Relate art to the artist's time and experience
- Recognize the different media used by artists and craftsmen
- Differentiate between art styles
- Interpret the work of other students
- Devise new approaches to creativity

LIFELONG RELATIONSHIPS, THE BEST OUTCOMES

Of all the relationships your museum nurtures, none last longer than the ties you build through education. Today's grade-schoolers will, in just ten years, be college students and possibly interns. In fifteen years they could be members and donors. In just one month, today's ten-year-olds may revisit your museum with their families. And every student has at least one teacher and principal who supported the museum program and will advocate for museums in your community and wherever they work in the future.

As students mature, enduring ties are made. Your constituents come to your programs to learn, and in those wonderful moments absorb you into their lives.

Chapter Six

Environmental Graphics

Are we there yet?

Many of the families visiting Crystal Bridges Museum of American Art in Bentonville, Arkansas, probably drove some distance to get there. They would appreciate the empathy of this message on the wall of the parking garage. As they walked along the parking aisle toward the museum, they would be reassured by a drawing of a long-nosed Pinocchio with this painted message:

This way, no lie.

These are examples of environmental graphics: words and images that are part of the built environment, as opposed to graphics in printed materials and digital media. Environmental graphics are the communications—words and pictures—that are painted on walls, hung from the ceiling, and stationed on the floor. They are part of the building, as contrasted with content that is added to the building. Think of color-coded sections in sports arenas, ceiling banners in retail stores, and menu boards in restaurants. In places like airports, theme parks, and big hotels, signs giving directions and arrows pointing the way are part of environmental graphics. Environmental graphics are integral parts of any museum, in the galleries, and also in lobbies, corridors, restaurants, and other public spaces.

If your museum has grounds or multiple buildings, the signs that direct visitors from building to building are environmental graphics, and they are symbols as well as signs. They give information that directly relates to the purpose and content of your museum, and they belong to your brand environment. At the Ringling, the signs throughout the large campus are rather formal lozenge shapes that identify each place as part of the University of

Florida. The signs throughout the Chicago Botanic Garden are painted informally on simple wood boards. Whatever its size, every museum needs environmental graphics that inform and direct. They will use words, symbols,
pictures, or shapes. They can be applied directly to the wall, nailed above
doorways, carved into plaques, paved into walkways, painted, stenciled,
molded, or projected.

The term "environment" encompasses a range of spaces calling for creative executions. The Whitney's sign for the café, a supersize "EAT" in LED
flashing lights, is a witty graphic that's a built-in feature of the museum. The
Huntington Library, Art Collections, and Botanical Gardens in San Marino,
California, paints its gallery names on the space above each one's portal. The
Musée Branly in Paris names the rivers of the world on the floor of the ramp
leading up and into the gallery area; actual videos of rivers are projected
there, too. At the other end of the size spectrum, any historic home that
places "Welcome" on the mat at the front door also lays down a graphic
that's a permanent part of the design of the building.

Remember that visuals such as illustrations, photographs, video, and
maps are graphics that speak as powerfully as words. While most graphics
are devised and executed by designers, writers are part of the team. It is the
writer's discipline that not only sparks visuals, but edits them for clear communication and consistency.

Environmental graphics are designed and placed not to adorn, but to
support. They may look beautiful or fun or novel, but they work hard to keep
your museum standing. Here are just ten of the important jobs they do:

1. Categorization—identifying distinct parts of the museum
2. Information
3. Welcoming
4. Store and cafe
5. Directions
6. Exhibition-specific communication
7. Cross merchandising—especially for visitors who come for one purpose and can be persuaded to try another part of the museum
8. Brand reinforcement
9. Monetize the building
10. Farewell

CATEGORIZATION

Museums are made up of many parts, many galleries, and many spaces, each
having different purposes. New visitors can be confused, and regular visitors

need reinforcement. It's not just the galleries that need identification; so do the store, restaurant, library, theater, and other public spaces.

Architect I. M. Pei understood the value of graphics as part of the environment. In designing the user-friendly spaces for the East Building of the National Gallery of Art in Washington, DC, he even named the restaurants, according to author Neil Harris. At the Brooklyn Museum, Saul Restaurant and Bar was conferred the honor of a bronze plaque at the entrance. It states, perceptively:

> It is my deepest wish that you will have an experience in this restaurant equaled only by the enjoyment and knowledge you receive walking through the galleries of this great museum. —Norman M. Feinberg, Trustee, Chairman, 2006–11.

INFORMATION

Museums amp up environmental graphics all the time, and all you have to do is walk in the front door of museums like the Brooklyn Museum to get some ideas for your information desk. This often crowded, big-city museum has constructed a large LED display above the densely populated ticket area to explain its current exhibitions and announce the ones to come. The display is circular, and as it flashes around the circumference of the center booth, it's a work of design that's art in itself. The concept is simple and replicable: keep people informed while they wait. As the director of a Sydney museum once told me: "People don't mind waiting in line if they know what they're waiting for." On a much smaller scale, something as simple as changeable posters affixed to the wall near the ticket counter indicates that your exhibitions are part of the museum, not just something dropped down inside.

Markers along the paths of botanic gardens combine label information and environmental graphics. The challenge for the writer is to select words carefully and prune often. It's hard to inscribe text on weather-resistant materials, and expensive. When you must change a label, your budget watchers will prefer small ones.

WELCOMING

Think of the first space your visitors see: the garage, the lobby, a small foyer, the store, perhaps the café. That is where you must welcome them.

The huge bookshelf spanning the space above the long information desk at the Whitney Museum of American Art (in its original location on New York's upper Madison Avenue) is an environmental graphic: it is permanent

Figure 6.1.   The first view of a museum is often a parking structure. The Museum of Contemporary Art Chicago welcomes visitors immediately. *Provided by author.*

and as important to the design of the lobby as architecture. It boldly connotes that this will be a learning experience, as well as an emotional one.

The garage at the Museum of Contemporary Art in Chicago has quotes about art all along its walls and staircase. The parking area is separate from the museum and visitors walk outside to reach the museum entrance. The quotes serve as a welcome and a connection to the experience ahead.

The admissions area at the Franklin Institute has a long stretch of display boards above the counter projecting science facts. The visitor gets a taste of the museum's mission even while waiting to get in.

You might be surprised how many lobbies and foyers are not welcoming: no signage, no directions, no words or pictures that proclaim, "You are here" or, even better, "We're glad to see you." A surprising number of museums have forbidding facades of steep steps and high columns, or blank fronts of repurposed municipal commercial buildings. Many new buildings present sparkling faces to the public, thanks to the emphasis on natural light streaming through glass walls, but the view inside doesn't say anything. Some entrances are so small, there's barely room for one person to enter, let alone a sign. Some intake areas are so vast, it looks like the proprietor ran out of money before the furniture was ordered. To all museums, I implore: put up a welcome sign. Freestanding sign holders cost as little as $37. An 8 1/2 x 11 sheet of paper printed in Word on any computer costs nothing. Here is some welcome language:

Welcome to [name of museum]
Today's special events [list two or three]
Tickets are at the reception desk
Questions? Ask anyone at the [name of museum]
Our mission statement:
Today's hours:

As any hospitable host will tell you, it doesn't have to be fancy. You just have to make people feel at home.

The most welcomed welcome sign I personally experienced was at the Toledo Museum of Art, a huge museum in a hard-to-find part of town. On a blazing hot day, crossing the street from a sprawling parking lot to a two-block-long stretch of a building, I saw a large dot with these familiar words painted on the pavement: "You Are Here."

STORE AND CAFÉ

This is the space where memories are made. They start in the galleries, accumulate throughout the visit, and are bundled up and paid for in the store. After walking and looking and perhaps listening to a tour, the visual and aural learning in the galleries is consummated with the kinetic learning of doing something. At the store visitors select merchandise, browse books, touch a fabric, play with a toy, and eyeball other people's actions. Here's a place where environmental graphics can help solidify the memory that takes its final shape in a souvenir.

The Museum of Arts and Design in New York is devoted to things people make for other people to use. It makes this function more palpable with merchandise cards that tell the name of artist and country or U.S. state of origin. Many museums do this, and a further graphic would set this museum, or any other, apart: a map of the country or region; a description of the materials used; a brief bio of the artist. Think of author blurbs in books and translate that to other kinds of merchandise.

The Musée des Arts Decoratifs in Paris was the first museum I encountered that treated its store like a gallery and related merchandise to exhibits with lightly erudite counter cards on store countertops and in vitrines. You can do the same thing, on a much smaller budget, and frequently all it takes is repurposing a gallery panel or label for describing the relevant merchandise. If you don't have time to rewrite a label for every item of jewelry or child's toy—and few museums do—simply state: "Representative of items on display in our galleries." The chapter on museum stores, chapter 15, discusses how to relate the merchandise to the museum through table tents, counter toppers, or hangtags. With environmental graphics, you have a large space to link the store itself to the museum. Use the swath of wall above bookcases to say: Furniture, or Missouri Pioneers. Use banners to say Designs Based on Treasure of the Empire. If large graphics for individual exhibitions are too expensive, print a reusable set of wall-hanging posters that say: "These objects have been selected to relate to the learning in our museum and help extend the experience."

Bookshelf Graphics

There are other ways to bring the books in the store alive: At the New York Historical Society, bookshelf labels describe the categories. "Famous Founders" is one, and a look at the spines shows a selection of books on the Roosevelts. If you have enough space to shelve the books cover forward, they'll speak for themselves. But mostly what will show are the spines, and you have to enhance that. All museums have books, so it behooves you to give your selection of books a little of the museum's personality. One tab at the NYHS said, "Working for Freedom: Against Slavery," a compelling heading to organize some of the titles. If your museum has books on gardens, or automobiles, or river reclamation, try markers like "In the Garden," or "On the Road," or "America's Waterways." It's easy to avoid writing where it isn't absolutely necessary, so keep it simple. Don't try for high creativity because the fact that you're speaking out to your shoppers is creative in itself.

There are other advantages to these shelf markers. They're at eye level. They lead the narrative of your entire bookstore, not just individual books. They attract attention from a distance. Interestingly, many libraries are starting to merchandise their books this way. Even though most people come to a library prepared to peruse, their wise institutions go out of their way to make the search easier.

Your other merchandise may offer opportunities to talk like a museum. If the stationery has designs of the William Morris style, or Asian scrolls, write a short counter card describing those art periods. Again, a lot of merchandise is available at museums all over the country, and your visitors may recognize this. With a little effort, you can distinguish your museum.

Memories at the Table

Like the store, the restaurant is a memory builder, working in a different way. This is where visitors stop to refresh and reflect, and it's essential to realize the importance of that. This is where the out-of-towners read the material and decide their next stop . . . or next trip. This is where parents get to relax and just be with each other while the kids draw. This is where employees—internal constituents, from your community—get to know their museum. This is where children and older parents bond for an hour over a new shared interest. I have observed these visitor dynamics in research conducted for my book *Consumer Research for Museum Marketers*, and they are numerous and thought provoking.

Another example of graphics reflecting the museum itself as well as its content: the nutritional information on the wall of the cafeteria at the Franklin Institute. In this prime territory, where reflection is so important but where waiting in line sometimes comes first, information helps both situations.

Make sure, first of all, that visitors find your café. Of all the signs you want to install, the one leading to the restorative restaurant may be the most important. Restaurants today are profitable enough that, according to a 2013 article in the *New York Times*, 5 to 10 percent of their sales are returned to the museum. The same article states restaurateurs' belief that good dining encourages visitors to return more often.

Even before hungry visitors find a table, you can nourish them. Borrow the chalkboard idea from coffeehouses that post trivia questions of the day, in your case based on museum holdings, rather than java culture. In the café, unrestricted by the size of a counter or display rack, the words can expand. At the Franklin Institute cafeteria, panels above the food counter advise the lunchers in line to "eat like a scientist" and "fill half your plate with fruits or vegetables." At the Tate Modern in London, some years ago, one of the cafés complemented its Picasso/Gauguin exhibition with quotes by each artist about the other. These touches are garnishes that connect the room to the museum.

State clearly at the museum entrance the name, location, and hours of the restaurant, so visitors don't miss the lunch hour. Perhaps place a laptop or tablet at the information desk to make advance reservations. Can a laptop be considered an environmental graphic? In this case, yes. Then come the traditional wayfinding graphics of arrows that direct the visitor to the café. There you post menus on the wall, either as you get closer or certainly in the gathering area outside the entrance. Does this seem obsessive? Not if you have a six-year-old who's hungry. Then you can say, "We're almost there" and prove it. Don't neglect entertaining diners while they're waiting for a table or a friend. The Art Institute of Chicago has art books on coffee tables in the reception area of its third-floor restaurant, Terzo Piano. And when you seat diners at the restaurant, have games at the tables along with reading materials.

A table with food provides the refreshment a visitor needs to stay a little longer, reflect on the experience, and develop a bond. Possibly, the rested body attacks the museum store with more vigor, too. Certainly, the competition is on for share of stomach, as museums of every type discover that whatever their mission, food fuels it. As they start to polish the silver and contract with florists, integrating facilities rental into their budgets, the role of the day-to-day food service expands. Now your simple café is an advertisement for your event capabilities. Many visitors convert to event givers, and their first awareness of your museum as a food-event facility could be at lunch. Link the food to the museum itself with environmental graphics.

DIRECTIONS

It's not just multibuilding campuses, botanic gardens, zoos, restored villages, and sculpture gardens that need directional signs. Even small museums can have an addition that's a distance from the main entrance. Don't overestimate visitors' ability to find their way around but instead abide by the working rule: if there's a fork in the path, someone will turn the wrong way. It's up to your architect or handyman to find the right materials for your climate and usage, but it's the writer's job to stipulate the words. These should be researched carefully. "Keep right" may not be as descriptive as "turn right." Research the wording with as many people, at every juncture. Select a sign style that reflects your brand. There's a big difference in attitude between a colonial village and an environmentally correct garden, between a sculpture garden and a battlefield.

Some museums are so large, with corridors on multiple levels, that visitors could get footsore, if not actually lost. Then you need signage like they have at airports and theme parks, and you probably know that already. But you may have overlooked far-flung or undertrafficked areas where visitors can feel, if not lost, far from the main museum. You need signs to reassure them that they're still in the museum. This happens in areas set aside for facility rentals, or restrooms, or back staircases. In addition to directional signs, use "You're still in the museum" signs. Follow the example of the Field Museum, which displays a combination of exhibition posters, actual exhibits, and large photo images in the long passageways leading to meeting rooms.

EXHIBITION-SPECIFIC COMMUNICATION

Sometimes, the gallery itself communicates the theme or focus of the exhibition. Respected designer Gil Ravenel, at the National Gallery of Art, Washington, D.C., once stipulated rough wood walls for *The Great North* show, intensifying the experience of the Pacific Northwest. In a museum whose mission was to embrace all the country's visual culture, this was considered brilliant, if radical for the mid-twentieth century.

The Baker Museum of Art—Naples, when it was the Naples Museum of Art, designed a gallery with velvet wallpaper and Persian rugs to mimic a much-visited artist's studio of the 1920s, all the better to showcase art of that period. It conveyed a different dimension of art of that period: how people viewed it.

This kind of environmental graphic is left to the judgment of the curator and exhibition designer, and it works especially well for small museums that rely on traveling exhibitions. It's a way to connect a show to your own institution. Words on the wall achieve what an architecture critic called the creation of "so powerful a sense of place."

You can't have a docent in every gallery, but your exhibition should have a voice. It will help clarify your vision for an exhibition. Let visitors see the writing on the wall. Quotes written directly on the wall become part of the environment, so they set the tone for the entire show, rather than didactically explain one exhibit. They don't identify an object; they don't explicate contexts; they talk to you. They are the voice of the show, and nowhere was the intent more charmingly impressed than in the Art Institute of Chicago's *Impressionism, Fashion, and Modernity*. Just a few examples suggest the lighthearted tone of voice of the exhibition, which blended serious research with the undeniable allure of beautiful fabrics and garments:

"There are only two ways to be a Parisienne: by birth or by dress."
—Arsene Houssaye, L'Artiste, 1869

"What poet, in sitting down to paint the pleasure caused by the sight of a beautiful woman, would venture to separate her from her costume?"
—Charles Baudelaire, "The Painter of Modern Life," 1863

"The modern painter . . . is an excellent couturier."
—Joris-Karl Huysmans, 1876

In these well-curated words, the exhibition becomes not just paintings but modernity, not just oil and canvas but poetry. The writers quoted come from all the arts, and Paris becomes a place of wit and wisdom. I love quotes and recommend them highly. Carefully chosen, they make any writer a master of words.

At the Brooklyn Museum, the *Connecting Cultures* gallery was undergoing construction in 2013 and the permanent exhibition was installed differently, with some reproductions. A laptop computer, mounted on a podium in the center of the gallery, ran a thirty-second video of the curator explaining why reproductions replaced several works while construction was under way. When you get into digital signage, you're in a different universe from signs, labels, and panels; this bit of electronics placed a virtual person in the gallery, one who functioned as a built-in docent. The same laptop also contained links to visitor comments, which were like fellow museumgoers helping you understand the situation.

There were many comments about reproductions, and one said volumes. "I admire the commitment to conversation the Brooklyn Museum engages with. I always feel in dialogue with the exhibits, this one included," Laura Marie said on September 21, 2013, at 3:44 p.m.

CROSS MERCHANDISING

Museums, like stores, are retail establishments. The customer walks through a real door, down real aisles, looks at real merchandise, selects a few or many to inspect closely, and then makes some usage decisions. In a grocery store, he or she shops for vegetables, sees bottles of salad dressing on a nearby shelf, and gets the idea that there are even more salad ingredients in other aisles. That's cross merchandising. Museums do the same thing when they put a sign in the lobby for a tour or upcoming lecture, or a counter card in the store that links an item for sale with a concept for study in the galleries, or a rack of exhibition brochures outside the restaurant. The importance of retail is key to museums today, because you want visitors to visit your actual space, and move around to all the elements comprised within it.

One simple sign that leads visitors along a path appears at the opening between galleries and says simply: "Exhibition continues in the next gallery." More time-consuming writing connects an artist or object in one gallery to an object or idea in another gallery via a wall panel: "See more works from this period in the next gallery."

Cross merchandising should be used with facility rental spaces. One museum I visited years ago used art frames as part of the décor of their main venue space. It graphically connected the party room with the galleries. Weddings, college commencements, business conferences—just think of all the potential visitors who visit your museum initially as the guest at an event. Install an object from your collection in the event rooms to make the visual connection between the party room and the serious museum. These objects, more than a handout at the sign-in table, direct attendees' attention to the fact of a whole museum just steps away. See chapter 18 for other examples of merchandising rental facilities.

Some of the best cross merchandising is done in the ladies' room, a room that 50 percent of the population uses as a way station for the next leg of the journey. The Burke Museum in Seattle posts data on a subject near to its heart—recycling—on its paper towel dispenser; the Field Museum in Chicago has display cases of store merchandise for women's perusal while refreshing their makeup.

BRAND REINFORCEMENT

Environmental graphics play a unique role in museums because they are so inextricably part of the building and its physical presence in the community. Whereas exhibitions change, and frequently glow with a personality all their own, and special exhibitions, in particular, are world celebrities that play a venue for a brief while and then return to their home and homes, your institution endures. That is the brand you want your visitors and donors to remember. Signs, banners, videos, and plaques convey the meaning of your brand in built-in ways; they are part of the museum, rather than a part of the show. This applies poignantly to special exhibitions that are shared by more than one institution. The exhibition *Gauguin and Van Gogh: The Studio of the South* was a star alighting in two different museums that I visited, the Art Institute of Chicago and the Van Gogh Museum in Amsterdam, and its identity could have outshone that of either museum. It was a glorious blockbuster in Chicago, and a favorite son returned in glory to his home in Amsterdam, and quite different in both places, thanks to a kind of environmental graphics. There was a compelling story that held the many paintings together, and it was written on the walls of both shows. At the Art Institute, a huge encyclopedic museum, the story was told in paragraphs, on the walls of each gallery that held the dozens of artworks. It was sequential, a series of chapters in the dramatic year the two artists worked together near Arles, France. In Amsterdam the story was told in running script that flowed from room to room of Van Gogh's namesake museum and while it embraced the entire building it also embraced the artist. The former was a book, the latter poetry. Each museum brand was individually reinforced by the graphic, although the art was a constant.

One form of brand identity is so common now we forget that, until Thomas Hoving Jr., hanging banners between the columns wasn't done, certainly not in the grand palaces of culture. The director of the Metropolitan Museum of Art in the 1970s was the first to hang banners, on the Met no less. He believed in advertising his museum inside and out, down to the name of the restaurant and the sign that proclaims it. It was a grand brand, and he wanted it shouted to the four corners.

Another example of environmental graphics forging institutional bonds: the chalkboard signs staked low to the ground at the Chicago Botanic Garden. These are additional to the information about the plants, the exhibits themselves. More informally written, they start with phrases like: "Have you ever noticed the way hydrangea in your garden . . . ?" They're meant to give a little personality to the scientific labels, to humanize the science inherent in botanic gardens, and to connect the garden lover to the garden museum. They help create a brand.

Signs communicate more than directions, exhibit information, and museum requirements. Like any marketing material, if they are good communications, they engage emotions. Not always for the best, however, as a recent situation at New York's Metropolitan Museum of Art, showed. The museum posted a sign at the ticket counter that said, "Pay what you wish." What was meant to make a big institution's generosity a part of the experience in fact seeded a tempest of guilt, moral obligation, and personal financial prudence. How much to pay? How little? The ensuing controversy and media coverage proved that signs matter, and when they're affixed to the wall they become symbols and they matter to the core.

MONETIZE THE BUILDING

Sometimes it's not what is on the walls, it's the walls themselves that illustrate the story, tell the narrative, and, in fact, function as an advertisement for the museum. Three museums embody this concept time after time: Solomon R. Guggenheim Museum of Art, New York, architect Frank Lloyd Wright; the Holocaust Museum, Berlin, architect Daniel Libeskind; and Guggenheim Museum, Bilbao, Spain, architect Frank Gehry. They epitomize many of the new museum buildings in the twenty-first century that sought to raise their profiles, literally, through the steel-and-concrete creations of star architects. The Guggenheim in Bilbao, because it put a whole city on the map. Its spiraling New York cousin tells an exhibition story in a way no other museum can. The Berlin Holocaust Museum was designed to let visitors experience disorientation. Viscerally, this story accumulates weight and tension as it moves in chronological order, and quickly affronts the body as well as the mind. In fact, signage along the way instructs visitors that there is no exit except at the end of this increasingly claustrophobic experience, and if they feel the need to leave, to ring for a guard. Each building earned volumes of media coverage that no advertising or public relations campaign ever could.

At the recently reopened Olympic Museum in Lausanne, Switzerland, which spirals down three levels much like the New York Guggenheim, the director compares his building to cinema: "We planned it like a film," Francis Gabet, the museum's director, says. "We worked with thematic clusters like a storyboard."

As museum writers Herminia Din and William B. Crow say, "Typically, museums can draw strength from their physical places. . . . The smell, size and scale and ambience of a place can greatly expand our understanding of a museum and of the objects themselves."

Your museum may not be planning architectural flamboyance, and it doesn't have to, because your building is your home and it will always speak for you. Sometimes you just need to help it along. Put up signs that relate the building's history, however prosaic. Talk about the people who lived or worked there when it was a bank or factory. Paint a graphic on the floor that shows the original foundation. Draw marks on the door frame that show the heights of the children who grew up there. Make a road sign that shows where the residents of the house moved. For example, at the Abraham Lincoln Presidential Library and Museum, there's an old-fashioned road sign with an arrow that says "975 miles to Washington D.C."

Even if your museum is small, the great architect Louis Kahn speaks eloquently for you: "The room is a place in the mind. One talks differently in a small room than one does in a big room." One thing you can do is make it easy for people to mingle and talk in your small rooms. Again, Kahn: "Rooms, like streets, are human agreements." I'd love to see a sign that says: "In this small room, if you bump into people, talk to them."

FAREWELL

The same parking lot and lobby that form the entrance to your museum are also the exit points. They welcome, and they wish farewell. Good customer relations directors teach the staff of every building to say good-bye to departing customers. At Disney Hall in Los Angeles, the guard ushers you out the door with: "I hope you enjoyed the concert." Write that same thought near your exit door. It could be a broad sign above the door, or a small card near the "push" handle: "The [your name] museum hopes you enjoyed your visit." Or, "Good-bye. Come back soon."

Museums are built environments that are rich with challenge, comfort, exploration, and social interaction. While our daily environments may seem colorless at times, devoid of intriguing signposts, our museum interludes can seem like Oz by comparison. Make the most of that with a few well-chosen words.

Chapter Seven

Exhibition Videos

Motion, sound, voice, dynamics—videos augment the museum exhibition, just as they do every other medium, and visitors accustomed to videos in everything from digital textbooks to the *New York Times* app will appreciate this platform in your museum. As videos evolved from big screen, to small screen, to computer, to mobile, they insinuated themselves into our lives, touching us at every step of the day. Video's omnipresence sends a signal to museums to employ them wisely—they will be compared, consciously or unconsciously, with all the others—and to write them well. That's the purpose of this chapter. If you use videos throughout an exhibition, make them as interesting as the other exhibits. If the video introduces a big temporary exhibition, relate the show to the museum mission. Videos that precede a traveling exhibition would do well to refer to the host museum; there are many newcomers at a temporary exhibition, and you want them to know about your institution, not just the works spending a few months in your galleries. Ultimately, the value of the exhibition video is as an introduction and overview of the museum itself. With any exhibition, there is ample opportunity to lose sight of the entire museum that stands behind, and somewhat hidden by, the bounty of individual pieces. Assembled to fulfill a theme, or gathered from other museums, an exhibition is the sum of its parts, not a summary of your museum. The exhibition video can bring the authorship back to you.

Videos humanize their surroundings. The motion and activity of video enlivens the stuff of an exhibition and the personality of the museum itself. A recent exhibition at the American Museum of Natural History in New York, *Our Global Kitchen: Food, Nature, Culture*, was packed like an egg roll (or tamale, pita pocket, crepe, blini, take your pick) with information; however, the simple video showing sauté pans on a range top, with hands stirring a global range of ingredients, brought the show to life.

The best videos combine photogenic objects (inanimate or animate), a collaborative script, and a strategy. Before writing a script or selecting images, ask these strategic questions: What is the reason for mounting an exhibition? What is its relationship to the museum's mission? What is its value to the museum's visitors? How is it validated by the museum's own experts? This makes the exhibition part of your overarching story, and it reinforces your brand while strengthening learning and buttressing the treasury. Because videos literally move a story along, and spark inert objects to life, they earn a place throughout your museum at every point where your story can reach the eye and ear of a stakeholder. The dynamism and organization of a good video are born of a visualizer and a verbalizer working together, usually culminating in more pictures than words, but always melding the heart and mind of a great museum.

PLACEMENT OF VIDEOS

Once you've decided that videos have a place in your museum, you have several places to choose from: the lobby entrance, the anteroom to the exhibition, galleries, resource or study room, café, store, and the lobby exit. A case can be even be made for videos in the parking garage. In the lobby or anteroom, a video introduces an exhibition or the museum itself; throughout the galleries, shorter videos complement an individual exhibit or grouping. In the resource or study room, videos offer R & R, as well as additional learning. This mid-exhibition space is usually furnished with library tables or computer terminals to search books, your website's microsites, or online information sources. It's also a place to pause and reflect, to expand knowledge with independent exploration, and to rest tired feet without sacrificing learning. The store, filled as it is with related books and merchandise, is a logical place for refresher courses in the exhibition. Refreshment in the dining area often includes conversation with the meal, so why not an extra helping of the exhibition via video? This might be particularly useful as an app to occupy children while parents get a respite. Back in the lobby, a video wraps up the entire experience, leaving visitors with your message.

Location is a strategic decision, and you can situate a video screen at one or many places, depending on your goals, time, and budget. Be assured that whether the video is long or short, bursting with production values or economically shot, it will make an impression. At this point, it helps to open the conference table to include everyone from the curators to visitor services to guards, people who have specific messages to emphasize and who see how visitors flow through the museum. Remember the importance of convincing special-show visitors to return to the museum after the show has left town; videos that relate to your museum will stop them in their tracks a little more often, and remind them where they are.

At the entrance to an exhibition, the video—its script and its visuals—is an overview of a specific topic, whether it's the objects in the show, the creators, the period of time covered, or the techniques used. Think of this introductory video as a stage play, where there is no curtain, where the visitor walks into the theater and gets an instant shot of what's to come. This is what they paid for—in the ticket price, or audio guide deposit, or commitment of time—and now they'll know how to process the experience to come. The exhibition introductory video is enrichment, yes, but also a smart service. Part of the museum's challenge is to make the visitor comfortable, for the moment and for the future.

EXAMPLE FROM THE LOS ANGELES COUNTY MUSEUM OF ART

An excellent example of integrated in-gallery video was used by the Frances and Armand Hammer Building at the Los Angeles County Museum of Art, for an exhibition on Korean scrolls. The scrolls were displayed full length, vertically, which made them somewhat difficult to peruse in a crowd. Scrolls are meant to be visual texts, so perhaps that's why the labels were so brief, but the narrative and context needed explanation, and flat-screen monitors provided just that. They showed details of works and gave supplemental information on Korean brushstrokes, calligraphy, colophons, seals, rituals of the scroll, and uses of the screens. True to the artistry and style of the scrolls, the videos moved at a thoughtful, slow pace, telling only a short story whose deeper meanings could be intuited. The staging of the videos matched the narrative: simple and uncluttered. Some scenes showed the calligraphy artists in a setting, some closed in on a brush in hand, and some focused on the brushstroke and paper. It didn't say much, but it told a lot. The video seemed to be authored by the same kind of artists who create scrolls: its "voice" was of a piece with the rest of the exhibition.

EXAMPLE FROM THE ART INSTITUTE OF CHICAGO

The video for *Apostles of Beauty: Arts & Crafts from Britain to Chicago* previewed this Art Institute of Chicago exhibition in a seemingly simple but elegantly artful style. After an effective overview of the arts and crafts movement, its importance, and the strategy of the Art Institute in mounting the exhibition, the video cut and panned to an excellent range of artworks, just five or six of the pieces, but enough to capture the flavor of the show. The narrator, sometimes on camera, sometimes voice-over, talked about each piece, describing the visual, and also explaining its significance. The words flowed from the visual and, I suspect, affected the actual choice of them. Some objects were more photogenic than others, and some told a better story; both kinds of objects have a place in a video. There was enough zooming in for a close-up and enough cutting between the on-camera person and the object to keep the story lively. No digital special effects were needed because of the story told by the writer, along with the curator and a very visual photographer. The narrator, whether shown on camera or heard in voice-over, lent curatorial authority to the narrative. This is how a video on one exhibition becomes a proxy for the entire museum, showing beauty and intelligence and a desire to engage one-on-one with the visitor. The video demonstrates the museum's authorship of an experience that is, after all, dozens of works lent by other museums; it highlights an individual curator's knowledge, which also redounds back to the museum. It allows for a few enlivening side stories and it can even show works that didn't make the physical trip to the museum. The script for this video was highly instructive in just ten minutes. There clearly was a lot of content to choose from, but the writing was tight and the editing sharp.

Along the way, throughout the galleries, short videos clarify the story. They explain at a length not available to a label. They translate, through images, ideas that aren't evident to the lay eye. Educators understand that learners need visuals, or sound, as well as the written word, and usually in some sort of mix. Videos, because they obviously look at exhibits through a different lens, tell the story from the museum's perspective.

EXAMPLE FROM THE QUAI BRANLY, PARIS

At the Quai Branly Museum, where videos are placed along the ramped corridor that leads from the entrance to the galleries, they instantly communicate different cultures; this museum was, by the way, called the Museum of Man. It's also another example of a film-savvy museum in the nation that practically invented film! How does this museum, or your museum, decide which exhibits and galleries deserve a video? Work with the writer for guidance. You may not end up using the writer's words, but the verbal story line can help select the visuals that tell the story.

At midtour, a video is R & R and a few other Rs, too. A place to conduct research is useful for more scholarly visitors. And a simple library table with a few laptops encourages visitors to reflect and reconnect with the museum itself. It's a point in the experience where you keep a tired visitor engaged, or an engaged visitor stimulated.

At the end of an exhibition, a video summarizes the experience. It reminds visitors of why they came to the museum. It reinforces the museum's scholarship. It imprints the excellence of the museum. It reflects the core values of the museum. It expands visitors' knowledge and sends them home with a feeling of accomplishment: "I knew this would be worthwhile, and it was!" Think of the exit video as an environmental branding device, designed to retain loyalty. The visitor has already seen a lot of images; the one at the exit pointedly engraves them in memory as part of the museum.

Whether introductory or serial, an exhibition video can inform, entertain, wake up, slow down, rekindle interest, speak to a differing mind, or probe the depths with a like mind. Always, though, a video will be perceived as another art medium as well as a font of information. It must be conceived and executed to give clear, unambiguous information. It should be written, or edited, by a writer with a sharp pencil and vigorous disinclination toward big words and long sentences.

So, that's the strategy and some tactical considerations of a video. They are some of the many facets of the total production, and a good writer contributes at the earliest stages. Here are some writing specifics that make any writer a good writer.

LENGTH OF VIDEO

The first step to good writing is viewing the overall road: How long is it? Videos can go on for a long time, but that is boring to the viewer, enervating for the museum staff, and costly to the museum's accountant. Figure ten to fifteen minutes. Make the video even shorter if it will remove the intimidation factor for the person doing the writing!

VISUAL SETUP

Next, decide what you want to show. Although videos are instructional, they are mainly overviews or previews of the exhibition if they are placed at the beginning of the exhibition area. If they are interspersed throughout the show, they might feature demonstrations of one object or concept at a time (how horseshoes are forged), or feature a cameo appearance of a contributor to the particular object or idea (comments from a historian of blacksmithing). Using visual language, whether an overview, preview, demonstration, or cameo appearance, a video's words relate to the visuals. They describe what is being seen. Professional writers often start a script with words like: "This is an image of . . ." Select your objects and supporting props, instructional charts, on-camera speakers, sets, and locations with an eye to their visual appeal. Think like a fashion show producer, a magazine editor, or window designer. Or just employ that old Hollywood cliché, thumbs and forefingers forming a square to frame a movie shot.

To help the writer keep the script clear and on message, without stylistic flourishes, pay attention to the look of the video so that it supports the exhibition. Color, for instance, should be appropriate to the content of the show. Fashion exhibitions usually use a lot of color, and architecture shows are usually monochromatic. History is often best served by subtle colors, and science is frequently brilliantly hued. Whatever the palette, the background should be a neutral color, and uncluttered. Strive for a simple look, because no matter how complex your story might be, the eye can take in only so much at a given time, and you're not competing with the exhibition. To get an idea of what the eye registers, look at a rack of magazine covers and see which communicate most clearly; then imagine how they would look if they were moving along the shelf. Your target audience, ultimately, somewhat dictates the complexity of the look. Younger viewers, raised on split screens, need multiple stimuli to learn; studies suggest that a little multitasking is useful to them. Over age forty, most audiences prefer more simplicity.

A real concern is the production quality of videos, since audiences are now accustomed to a variety of looks, even on the smallest screens. If your video has a small budget, spend some of it for an art director to at least check the initial setup, to give it the same professional look as your museum. Surprisingly, even major museums often settle for videos that look home-made. Don't eschew smart-phone videography; it can be as effective as any camera work. But also don't confuse snapshots with a story. Shots must be planned and curated. If taken indoors, they should be carefully lit by some-one who knows what he or she is doing, especially if the video features on-camera presenters. Be kind to your talking heads who may not photograph well; good lighting will prevent their looking tired, unprofessional, or simply outdated. One final preparation: professional photographers recommend a stylist to assist with hair and makeup.

NARRATOR AND OTHER SPEAKERS, ON CAMERA OR OFF

Video scripts are easier to write with a voice-over announcer, someone who speaks with authority but is never seen on camera. This need not be a profes-sional announcer or actor, but someone who can read a script smoothly, pronounce all the proper nouns and terminology correctly, and sound profes-sional and friendly at the same time. Intersperse this narrator with on-camera presenters, people who interact with the objects, or show demonstrations, or lead the viewer through the building or grounds. The greater the variety of scenes, the better even a short video will be. And plan on at least two or three on-camera speakers, just in case. Some will be experts in their field, but not in front of a camera. Some will use their hands awkwardly, or mumble. Some will simply have "mic fright." Use them all, but for shorter stretches, and be prepared to have their lines read by the voice-over announcer. Keep the purpose of the video in mind—whether it's previewing, supplementing, or summarizing the exhibition—and remember that any communication reflects the museum's brand personality. The speaker's voice should never distract from the museum's core message. The expertise of the on-camera presenters and their strong ties to your museum will be evident if you let them talk about what they know best. If they want to rewrite a line to better convey their subject, well, that happens all the time in film and video. If the face to the camera is a museum staffer, or supporter, you'll have to tread diplomatically, of course. If it's a featured artist, designer, historian, or scientist, a different kind of diplomacy is involved, because you might need to edit their unclear or lengthy words; an interview format works well here, because you can preedit by asking easy-to-answer questions.

STORIES START WITH OBJECTS

Your museum has a thousand stories to tell, and each exhibition contains dozens of tales, each waiting to be extracted. Where to start? Many writers would love your challenge, because you can start with the objects themselves. Each suggests a narrative, and you could literally lay them out on a long table to see how those narratives might link together. Select each artifact for the video based on the story you can elicit from it.

Depending on your museum and the exhibition in question, the story line could cover a moment in time, or an epoch. The narrative could take place in your town, or it could range the world. The video very likely will embrace the theme or guiding vision of the exhibition, but in brief. If you start with the visual—the artifacts themselves or supporting props—the immense encyclopedia distills to a manageable article. Don't try to write the words first and match objects to them. You'll be swamped.

The actual exhibits and objects in the exhibition are the first group of visuals to select from. Be very selective and use only a few. If they're small, like fossils or tools, you can use more and aggregate them into a story; if they're large like an edifice, you should talk about the details of that one exhibit. The stories you tell can take the same approach as your labels: centered on the item itself, providing context to the times, exploring the artist's creative process. What a label can't explore is why one piece was selected over another, and this makes for fascinating scripting. It also leads to a second group that may surprise you with its own cache of stories: the pieces you eliminated from the final exhibition. All good stories benefit from a negative, such as the black sheep of the family, the cinder sweeper who doesn't have a ball gown, the embarrassing first date beloved of Hollywood, or the crying baby who wins a million hits on YouTube. It's easy to weave part of your story around an artifact from your collection that doesn't usually get exhibited. In explaining why it is of secondary interest, or less-than-best quality, you highlight the excellence of the exhibition and the curator's knowledge. And everyone learns better from seeing a range of examples.

Consider the size of objects. The camera might find it in the speaker's hands, or dwarfing the speaker entirely, inside a gallery in what amounts to a set, or outside in a "location shot." Consider these shots when writing the script, because it will take different amounts of time to point to a spoon or walk around a chassis. Objects have varying degrees of detail work, and you select them for the details that are photogenic as well as noteworthy. If you can't script a paragraph about a detail, it's probably not as appropriate for a video as a detail that has a story behind it. Wait, you say, every detail has a story! Great. Write it. That's the value a video adds to a wall label.

What makes an object photogenic? You have to literally look through the camera, or check the video screen, to be sure. Some colors, textures, and details just don't come through the lens as you expect them to. Sizes—large harpoons or small silver forks—look the same when they appear full frame on a small screen. If the object is in or near human hands, plan to add a prop like a barrel or coin as a clue to the relative size of the object.

Videos aren't talks from podiums, so use the camera to move away from a flat surface and explore the space around the objects as they actually appear in the museum, or in re-created usage. Build pauses into the script so the camera, or the speaker, can move through that space. A video should never plop the objects on a table and require the speaker to remain behind it. If the subject is chair feet or dinosaur jawbones, encourage the speaker to kneel down or climb up or, if that is not possible, point to the camera doing so. At this point, the speaker is no longer on camera, and the speaker's voice becomes a voice-over. There's a big difference between an on-camera script and a voice-over. On camera, the speaker is a personality, and conversational, and ad-libbed sentences should be used if they're apt. Because a voice-over immediately connotes authority, use these seconds of the script to deliver facts and opinions. The combination of a conversational voice and an authoritative voice-over keeps the script lively, just as the different camera angles, close-ups, pans, and long shots do.

VISUAL PUNCTUATION

Video is an excellent medium for showing complementary graphics such as maps, charts, and time lines. Video, with its motion and sound, animates the most complicated chart. You can use more complex time lines, more detailed maps, when you have a camera to lead the viewer from point to point. If your museum is lucky enough to have archival footage, use it selectively to add depth. Plan to edit this material, if possible, because even the most historic shots can look dated to young people. Conversely, they are so exotic to young eyes that they provide emphasis and punctuation.

EXAMPLE FROM THE MARMOTTAN MUSEUM, PARIS

One such archived film was a memorable video shown at *Monet et L'Abstraction*, an exhibition at the Marmottan Museum in Paris. The vintage footage showed Monet painting *en plein air* while chain-smoking. The Sacha Guitry film from about 1915 showed how Monet would glance at the subject of the painting, in this case a large hedge, and then turn back to the easel and dab on a stroke of paint. Turn to look, turn back to dab. Everyone knows how quickly a cigarette burns down, and you could see how much Monet put on the canvas in that amount of time. It punctuated and emphasized perfectly the whole point of impressionist painting.

It was fast and jerky, and a little disconcerting, and yet, suddenly the revolutionary nature of his quick, impressionistic dabs became apparent. The speeded-up action of the cigarettes as they lit anew and dwindled to ash proved just how quickly the artist accomplished his feats. What was initially off-putting became essential to the story, and distinguished it as a more conventional series of images never could.

Even without words, this is an invaluable introduction to one painter's work habits and to the technique that became iconographic in itself, the impressionist ritual of seeing a fleeting image of light and color and putting that impression quickly on canvas in a ritual that named an era.

The video was not accompanied by audio, but none was necessary. What is important is the narrative was told in images that enhanced understanding of the artist and his art so masterfully. In the Marmottan exhibition, the video was displayed on a wall amid the paintings, like another exhibit in the gallery. In this case, that was just fine.

TITLE CARDS

As in silent movies, some museum videos benefit from title cards at the beginning of a scene, or captions superimposed during a scene. If you don't want sound, or want to focus on a complex artifact or demonstration, use title cards to set up the action. They should be short, well-crafted sentences, more like a title or subhead than text. If you can't deliver the thought briefly, the image probably isn't right for your purpose.

TEST AND EVALUATE

It's a painful thought, but not all videos achieve their objective. And the only way to find out is to test them with a few people. Ideally, this is done with a rough version, not the finished piece, when there is still time and budget to edit. All videos should have a goal by which to measure success. Some test-market responses to shoot for:

"I learned something."
"It explained a concept I hadn't thought of before."
"Now I'll understand the exhibition better."
"I want to see the whole exhibition."
"My friend didn't want to come, but now he's glad he did."
"I'm impressed by the museum's authority."
"I'm proud to be a patron."
"You're a value to our city."
"I want to come back and see more."

Chapter Eight

Guided Tours

Personally guided tours are powerful ways to introduce your museum to visitors, and every tour should have a script. The script might not be fully written, but it should be carefully outlined. It's worth the time to prepare carefully for a tour because the participants are already inside your door, ready to learn more, and you have their undivided attention. Make the most of it.

That puts a lot of pressure on the guide. Watch any museum tour group— 80 percent will be looking at the speaker, rather than the exhibit, and the guide has to lead their eyes back to the subject at hand. Choose the words carefully to support the visuals on display, not replace them. A good example was the Roy Lichtenstein exhibition at the Art Institute of Chicago, where an excellent docent gave a talk that regularly focused the visitors' eyes on gallery after gallery that exploded with visuals. He gestured to the painting on the wall. He pointed to a detail. He said things like, "Look at her eyes," or "Do you see this heavy line?" He used commanding words to unglue the eyes from his face to the works on the wall.

SCRIPT AS ITINERARY

Scripts are essential if the guide has a large crowd. In this dreamed-of situation, there's scant opportunity for informality, for going with the flow. The docent is a traffic cop with a love of culture, and uses words to keep the group moving. Navigation is a problem for any tour group, and scripts can ease the jams. When groups are funneling from one room to another, the guide can talk about what to look for in the next gallery, or suggest that they linger a moment, take a closer look at the works they're passing, and let the line thin out. Tourers should always be encouraged to look on their own, to follow within reason their curiosity, and then return to the fold.

Scripts are important because they force the group leader to select what works to show on a given day. Experienced docents will select works or details of exhibits they have specially researched. If a guide has many favorites, an outline will help decide which ones to connect on a given tour.

Scripts keep you on schedule. Whether your tour is thirty, forty-five, or sixty minutes, that's what visitors expect, and pacing is essential. The script helps allocate time for each part of the walking story: introduction, examples, summation, questions.

VISUALS TO SUPPLEMENT THE AUDIO

All scripts acknowledge the visual part of the story. Museum tours are much like movies, television, and video games in that the visuals cue the action.

One visual cue: point your finger. When the docent points to a painting, everyone looks at the art, rather than at the speaker. This is the objective of a tour, so docents must gesture toward the wall a lot, and use words to accompany that sweep of the arm. Learn phrases like "Turn over to this work," or "Look across the room," or "Now head for that door to the next gallery."

Make sure everyone on the tour is facing the exhibits. If the guide can't physically point, he should suggest it. Say "this painting." The mere use of the word "this" directs everyone's eyes toward the wall. The spoken word is powerful when it makes people listen for the next sentence. To make sure that everyone looked at the exhibit, rather than him, the Art Institute docent added, "Look at the black lines; see how the dots vary in size." Sure enough, everyone in the tour group looked at the painting, rather than the docent. (If your museum is a historic house or botanic garden, the words "Look at that armoire" or "Look at this texture of the leaves" have the same effect.)

FLEXIBILITY

Scripts for docents and tour guides must be adaptable and, preferably, unwritten. Take everything you've already read in this chapter, and are about to read, to heart, not just to memory. Walking, talking real people achieve relations between visitors and the museum that no audio guide can match. Each has its role, and the role of a person is to connect.

If a visitor asks a question, and interrupts a monologue, the guide has hit gold. It means the visitor is engaged, thinking, and learning. Quite likely, it will make the tour more interesting. Repeat any questions so the whole tour group can hear the new line of thought. They'll be encouraged to make connections and share them and everyone will better understand the docent's information. The reason some museums call their docents "guides" is to emphasize that they're not experts, but leaders. To paraphrase the words of scholar Edward Said, "They might know a lot, but that's all they know!"

ANECDOTES

As in any story, a specific anecdote seasons the stew. Sometimes the description of an exhibit is as brief as a caption, as in a label, but a good teacher knows to do more than just spout the facts. One way to loosen up a well-informed guide is to provide him or her with backstories. It's a matter of researching the artist, or maker. Learn about the period and other creative endeavors afoot at the time. Some tour leaders are natural storytellers with an easy wit, but most are not. Everyone, however, can tell an anecdote. To get into the anecdotal mood, start with: "Here's an interesting tidbit about this artist." With that setup, it's easy to tell the story in one's own words. And, remember, the docent is not alone. He has visual cues all around to refer to.

Figure 8.1.   Tour guides tell the stories in the Harry S. Truman Little White House, Key West, Florida. Their well-written scripts are models of information and delivery. *Provided by author.*

The docent of the Lichtenstein tour was adept with an apt aside, but the stories really came to life when he referenced the paintings on the wall.

With large tours, or outdoor groups, some institutions use a portable amplifier carried by another staffer at the rear of the group. It's a great idea, but a little disconcerting since many visitors will hear the words as if the speaker were behind them, when in fact he's standing far in front. It's counterproductive when the guide says "this work here" and the listener isn't sure where "here" is. If a museum is lucky enough to have such a big crowd, the script needs to change to explain a voice that's coming from two directions.

Good guides stand near the work they're discussing: eyes will point toward the artwork. The guide can always move to the side saying, "I'll get out of your way so you can see this better." This sensitivity to the tourers, this graciousness, can be difficult to summon when the guide has so much information to remember and relate. Put it in the mental script, as a reminder.

INTERACTING WITH THE VISITORS

Tours last only forty-five to sixty minutes, so many things will be left unsaid. There are other galleries to see, other exhibitions coming in the future. The Lichtenstein tour guide at the Art Institute referred to these unvisited works, with a suggestion of what to look for. It was a wonderful coda, encouraging—empowering—visitors to look on their own. That reminder should be built into every tour, because more than 20 percent of the visitors took him up on the opportunity to linger and reflect, the kind of reflection than builds familiarity and loyalty beyond the immediate tour.

You don't have to wait until the end of the tour to refer to other works by the same artist, or movement, or culture. Every time you expand on the topic at hand to a wider world, you reinforce that authority of the museum and, at the same time, the intelligence of the visitor. For one tour guide, an "aha!" moment occurred when a man on the tour mentioned that the theme of the tour reminded him of a program note from the classical concert he'd heard the night before. Add these cross-cultural connections to your script, where appropriate. Mention other museums or cultural events in town; tourists will appreciate broader cultural references and respect the guide's sharing of information outside the museum.

At the end of the tour, many visitors stay behind to ask questions of the tour leader, and it's worthwhile to make a list of them for integration into subsequent tours. Good leadership depends on listening to audiences and adapting to their interests and perceptions.

REFLECTIONS ON THE TOUR

Museums hope their tours will be so memorable that visitors remember their museum experience and return for another. To prompt the memories, at the end of the tour ask the group: "What do you think you'll remember twenty-four hours from now? What will you tell people next week when they ask how your weekend was?" Not enough people think to reflect on what they've just seen, whether it's a light movie or a rich museum visit, and they always appreciate this exercise. Nobody ever complains that you made them think for five seconds, and you needn't take much more time than that. It doesn't matter what they say; the payoff is that the answers often surprise them as much as they'll surprise you. Adam Gopnik, who wrote often about his arts education while living in Paris, noted that the lessons he learned were not the lessons expected, which, he pointed out, "is why they call it an education."

SCRIPT AS SOAP OPERA

The Tenement Museum on the Lower East Side of Manhattan writes exemplary tour stories because there is, in fact, not a lot to see. The brilliant concept of the museum is to convey the lives of the immigrant families solely through their stories, and to tell them on location. The museum is an authentic eight-story apartment building, structurally repaired but essentially the same as it was over a hundred years ago. The bare walls, exposed pipes, steep stairs, and communal washrooms on each landing are the only visual exhibits. The people, their names, and their daily home and work lives remain to be told, and the tales are enthralling. With all flattery to the talented writers who spin out the days of the lives of many nationalities and ethnic groups who lived at 97 Orchard Street, it's a format that bears imitation. The documentary style of day-by-day, real-people narratives can be adapted to many museums, and not just historic homes. If you can't climb the steps of the Tenement Museum in New York, visit your local historical society and read about the people who built your community. Their stories might well provide context for your art, science, or natural history museum.

SELF-GUIDED TOUR SHEETS

In an effort to be interactive, albeit in a low-tech format, a lot of museums resort to self-guided tours. The kind of format in question is a printed two-sided handout or a photocopied sheet of paper wrapped in a plastic sleeve. These are questionable formats for many reasons: false economy, user unfriendliness, and inadequacy for the job are just some of them. Because they are so tempting to print up, let's examine their pros and cons. The benefits are all too obvious, because they are clearly cheap to produce and send the message that the museum is cutting back on docent-guided tours. The fact that many visitors think guided tours carry a fee indicates how highly they are valued. Conversely, a printed sheet doesn't seem very valuable.

And they aren't friendly, either to read or to understand. In too many examples, the paragraphs describing the works on the self-guided tour are long and dense. They sound like a PhD thesis or a fourth-grade primer, each extreme falling short of how most visitors like to be talked to. If it's hard for visitors to move their eyes from labels to exhibit, it's even harder to look up and down from a printed sheet.

Despite the good intention, printed "self-guides" fall short of the desired outcome: intimate, engaged interaction between the viewer and the work. Printed sheets are lectures given by a single voice, with no pause for audience reflection, questions, or interpretation.

Here's how good intentions can fulfill their intent.

You can create a self-guided printed handout that does, quite definitely, save money, sound friendly, engage the visitor, maintain the pace the individual wants to go, and bridge the distance between the institution and the individual by putting it in his or her hand.

Keep the paragraphs short, with plenty of white space in between. Visually, the printed sheet should echo the space between the exhibits. Write the information in an active verb style, so the words move like a docent's hands. Write as if you were speaking to the visitor, so it doesn't sound like a fallback substitute for the human guide.

Keep the piece small, on heavy stock, so it feels substantial and doesn't flop in the hand. Be wary of protecting it in plastic, which dents, glares, and quickly starts to look cheap. Select a readable type font, in a large size, so the eye can move easily from words to exhibit. If budget allows, put a small line drawing, or icon, or photograph of the piece being described; it needn't be an exact representation, just a reinforcement, like the symbols for hotels, landmarks, and public buildings found on tourist maps.

Break the self-guide into parts, like legs of a journey. Here's a way to improve on live docents, who can cover only a limited number of exhibits in an hour. Each part of the self-guide comfortably holds five to seven paragraphs, five to seven stops on the tour. If visitors want to see more, they can pick up another card. By color coding each card to differentiate each leg of the journey, you encourage visitors to sample them all, then pick and choose, in much the same way they navigate a website or push buttons on a handheld device.

Write a short hello at the beginning, to entice the reader into the information. Skip the scholarly introductory paragraph in favor of words that sound more like an invitation. "Welcome, and get ready to take a walk through the biggest, grandest house in the county." Write conversational breakers between the paragraphs, such as "Now you're ready to see the smallest . . ." or "Before you walk through the door of the next room, imagine it's illuminated by candlelight."

Imagine you are talking to a real person who might be an adult or a child, a teenage knowledge hound or a connoisseur, an expert or a novice. The content of the gallery and the concept of the exhibition determine to some extent the kind of visitor you expect, so you can adopt an appropriate tone of voice. Don't be afraid to characterize your audience, and don't get trapped into generalizing. The basis of any communication is, always, an understanding of your audience or, in lieu of that, overestimating them!

Read the sheet out loud, and walk along with it. Reading any written piece out loud will surprise you because, frankly, they usually turn out to be too wordy. In the case of a self-guided tour, the narration has a physical component and, like a script for a play, must be blocked out so the reader can move from exhibit to exhibit in a logical pattern.

Work with a visual person to develop the look of the self-guide. Left-hand margins and same-size paragraphs make a dull layout, and dullness on paper augurs poorly for the tour. Design a visually lively piece and the reader will want to leap into the tour. The same economy that prompted the printed piece will tempt you into eschewing the services of a layout artist so, if you must do it yourself, there are a few design tricks anyone can borrow. Make some paragraphs flush left, some flush right. Change the typeface from paragraph to paragraph. Vary the length of the paragraphs, and use the element of surprise: a two-line paragraph. Modify the size, style, and shape of the illustrations, photography, and icons.

Writing a self-guide can be an easy out or a happy addition. Remember that it's unfair to throw the entire burden of interpretation on the visitor. Don't make a leisure visitor read an essay; write brief text for each object, and you can achieve your goal of interactivity and self-pacing. And unlike a live docent, visitors can take the handout home.

Chapter Nine

Lectures

Start with a podium, a speaker, and an audience: that's the bare minimum of a lecture in today's museum environment. It's a simple, powerful tool for making new friends. Look at the audience out there in the seats: visitors, members, prospective members, community partners, and media. The lecture does more than educate visitors and friends. It builds membership, shows appreciation for supporters, and creates revenue. Lectures are popular for traditional museumgoers who love information, and for younger audiences who are growing up with multiple learning formats. This chapter considers lectures from the perspective of both the speaker and the museum professional who organizes the lecture program. Most museum professionals, at some point in their careers, do both.

To recognize the strategic power of a lecture is to acknowledge the need for a good script, whatever your museum role. If you hire a speaker, you must give a good outline or background for him or her to write from. If you hire a speechwriter, be prepared to direct and edit. If you write the talk yourself, learn how to write and edit. Whoever the speaker, the knowledge remains the first priority, but the second priority is good writing. With all the goals a lecture must accomplish, only the right words will get you there.

Lectures, by definition, are readings that stem from text. Usually they are given by a lecturer with verifiable credentials. Today, we soften the threat of pedantry by calling them talks or presentations, adding visuals, videos, music, slides, and, with extra effort and/or resources, a speaker with a box office personality. Whatever the audiovisual support, a lecture/talk/presentation is, at heart, words—twenty to sixty minutes of well-crafted words. These words inform and even entertain, to be sure, and they also reinforce your mission and further engage your visitor/donor prospects. At their best, lectures enhance your brand and widen your market; at the very least, they remind your community of your vitality. There are many strategic reasons for supplemental lectures, and good writing starts with a strategy.

Writing a lecture is a matter of structure and organization. From good scaffolding, words accrue more easily. The lecturer may be an outside expert, a staff member, or you; you all write from a framework.

As the person responsible for finding, briefing, or being the lecturer, your main job is to set the stage. You can suggest topics, even draft an outline (more about this later), but your real value is in determining the objective, delineating the audience, defining and reiterating the museum mission or brand, selecting the venue and timing, and supporting visual aids.

OBJECTIVES AND WHYS

Once you've decided to consider investing in a lecture program, whether it's a one-off or a series, your next step is asking yourself why. Objectives can be stated in one sentence, such as:

- "The objective of this lecture is to create awareness for our institution."
- "The objective of this lecture is to call attention to our upcoming special exhibition."
- "The objective of this lecture is enhanced learning based on our area of knowledge and scholarship."
- "The objective of this lecture is to reward loyal members."
- "The objective of this lecture is income generation from a list of known arts patrons."

There is a temptation to combine two or more objectives, and that is all right, but it increases the difficulty in composing a talk that the audience will listen to. It makes no difference if you're penning a short talk or an hour-long speech, if you're talking, the audience expects clarity.

AUDIENCE

The audience, as you'll quickly discover, is not a mass of faces looking up at the podium. Each person in the room has a reason for interrupting his or her schedule, whether it's leaving home at night, traveling to the museum during the day, or sacrificing weekend errands. They're coming to hear your words. Good lectures and talks always start with the listener at the other end, and the invitation list should be thought of with a suffix of "ener." You know your market, or your prospective visitors, and keep these individuals in mind when you write the lecture. As you embark on a lecture program to acquire new visitors, think about why they haven't been to the museum before. If you want to engage the casual visitor, think how to make a museum more meaningful in their lives. If the purpose of the lecture is to enrich and thank the members you already have, speak up to them and give them insider knowledge. If your goal is to make more money, treat this lecture as a purchase as valuable as merchandise from the store or a meal in the restaurant, and give them something delicious. Your target audience probably has specific demographics such as age or education level, and more subtle psychographics such as a love of photography, or unfamiliarity with rain forests. Each of these audiences comes to the lecture hall expecting something different, and good writing recognizes that. Professional speakers, and writers, always inquire first about the audience; every speaker, regardless of the scope of the lecture, should be aware of who is listening. This way the speaker can intersperse the lecture with phrases like, "As novices to the rain forest, you'll be interested to know . . ." Or, "I know there are a lot of loyal members in this room, and if I had a museum with your rare manuscript collection, I'd be here all the time, too."

A good lesson can be taken from the lectures given by the Lyric Opera of Chicago to reach out to diverse current and new audiences. A corps of volunteers are recruited and trained to deliver talks throughout the Chicagoland area, at local libraries, schools, and, significantly, senior centers.

Who might the opera lecture attendee be: buff, lapsed, or novice? At the start of the one-hour talk, the lecturer asks how many in the audience have ever been to any opera, to the Lyric Opera of Chicago in particular, and how recently. At the outset she discovered if she was providing a lovely Sunday afternoon gift to Lyric faithful, persuading opera lovers to commit time and resources to the downtown opera house, or raising the awareness of the Lyric to casual music lovers. It makes a big difference not so much in the content of the lecture, but in the tone of the session. You don't even have to prepare special words; you'll naturally assume the appropriate tone of voice.

THE SPEAKER

Once you know *why* you're giving lectures and *who* you want to talk to, it's time to select the speaker. Whether he or she is an outside expert or an inside educator, a local leader or a boldface name, a thoughtful negotiation ensues. Of course, all speakers have schedules they're working around—nobody is readily available these days—but they will be more flexible if you state a rationale for the timing of your talk. And it helps speakers formulate their talks if they understand their place in the timeline.

Good speakers will ask about the audience, and although there is seldom a perfect person for your purpose, there are aspects of that person that suit the job very nicely. It's best, in fact, to assume the speaker isn't perfect, and set the stage so he will be comfortably able to be himself. Find out if the speaker is accustomed to big groups and darkened theaters, or informal settings. Be prepared to give him a tight outline, or a Q&A format, or provide a book signing after the talk. Spend time finding nonsuperficial biographical material you can use to make the speaker more relevant, if need be.

Your speaker will be introduced as superbly qualified to speak to your group. However, you or the speaker has to relate these credentials in believable language. Look for the anecdotes behind the achievements. For every book the person has written, or award won, find some biographical details that are more down to earth.

Before the talk, inform speakers about other presenters on the program, if any, so they can tailor their remarks, if need be. Suggest to the speakers that they come in time to hear the others, so they can build on earlier comments. More than one invitee to a conference has arrived just in time for his or her own talk, only to discover with chagrin that the territory was already alluded to by an earlier presenter. Ideally, the later speaker can graciously reference the preceding speaker; in the worst-case scenario, he will sound a little redundant.

Get there early! Polished speakers will ask in advance about your museum and the goals of the program. To be welcomed as relevant, good speakers will research ahead of time your museum, your community, your sports teams, and your weather. If your speakers aren't old pros at this, and most aren't, help them be early birds.

There are other things you should do to prepare yourself for a guest speaker. What other museums has the speaker visited, liked, or disliked? Find out! What other cultural organization has he spoken to? Speakers need to put their area of expertise in context with your specific museum and your audience, not generalized museums and audiences. Conversely, the people in the seats want some familiarity with the specific speaker, not merely the expertise she struts in one brief hour on your stage.

VISUAL CUES

Slides and props are not supporting material; they are integral to a talk and useful in structuring it. We are visual creatures, getting more so with every new technology, and there is no way to communicate with an audience without showing as well as telling. However, don't rely on visuals alone. What museum scholar Steven Conn says of objects also applies to slides: they alone cannot convey to today's audiences "the full stories and knowledge" of your museum. And many a slide show has sunk if there are no identifying captions to keep the audience awake.

One speaker, who talks to small groups in suburban libraries, brings a few CDs and books on the subject, as well as photocopied handouts. Many of the talks you bring to the museum, or give yourself, will be intimate and informal. Some speakers bring laptops with YouTube clips. Posters and magazine articles provide beautiful images of pieces you could never see in person, with the added advantage of accompanying text. It's OK to appropriate the work of others; you teach a lasting lesson when you show your audience that you don't know everything. The books can be looked at before and after a presentation, which gives the audience a chance to reflect on the lecture, and allows the speaker to interact personally. Handouts have the added advantage of touchability, a proven aid to learning. And as handouts are handed around, it occasions brief interaction between the audience members, another learning tool. Good writers like to work with visual aids like this; they indicate the breadth of the story and provide many points on which to construct a richer narrative.

Sophisticated slide presentations seem pretentious for smaller audiences, so bring photographs, maps, or actual or reproduction objects. For groups over twenty, visuals on a screen are a must. Current practice forswears straight bullet-point presentations. Most slide shows are more like scrapbooks, with large photos and short captions; they allow the speaker's personality to come through. Of course, electronic presentations can include videos, music, recorded interviews, and interactive charts and maps. While the technology is advanced, your usage of them doesn't have to be. One educator insists on letting her audiences wait while she accesses the websites or files that contain the material she wants to show. It is rather halting and decidedly casual, but she prefers this hunt-and-search style to slickness. It lets the audience see the process, and that aids learning, too.

VENUE AND TIMING

Your talk might be in a three-hundred-person auditorium, a gym, or room that holds thirty people. The venue dictates, to some degree, the audience and the style of the talk. Big halls necessitate large-screen videos and a more formal presentation, followed by Q&A. Small rooms allow for wonderful give-and-take with the audience. Audiences coming to your museum theater will be museumgoers or theatergoers, people who know you or know institutions like you; yet those exact same people, if they attended the same talk in a community center, would be a different audience, a more casual group of residents and neighbors. And if that talk were given in an office meeting space, the attendees would be there as high-learning professionals. Daytime lectures attract different people, with different needs, than nighttime or weekend lectures. While no museum can generalize about any of their audiences, it's allowable to conjecture that people who attend a lecture during the day are serious information gatherers. Those who go at night equate it with a movie, or play: a variant of entertainment. Weekenders are in their leisure and family mode; this is a playful and, arguably, less critical audience.

You may not be able to pick your venue strategically, but you can be aware of the effect it has on audiences. You have more say over day and time, and this becomes very strategic. The venue and timing combined suggests the tone of your lecture.

PRETALK SETUP

Before the lecturer starts to talk, the talk has already begun. An excellent public relations coach, Mort Kaplan, says that the minute a speaker steps out of the taxi, he can expect to be seen and noted. Certainly by the time the doors open and the audience moves into the room, the stage must be set.

If the setting is an auditorium or any large room, the audience will gather as soon as the doors open, and they'll turn their eyes to the podium. Give them something to see. If the speaker is using visuals, prepare a slide with the name of the talk, date, the speaker's name, and the speaker's title. This is essential for any media covering the event, and it paves the way for the speaker. If any of the words are non-English, the screen serves as a subtitle, acclimating the listeners. If the speaker won't be using projected visuals, turn off the screen after your introduction, and move it aside if possible.

The introduction of the speaker involves (a) choice of introducer, (b) strategy of introduction, and (c) a few well-chosen words. Match the role of the introducer to that of the speaker; they don't have to be of equal rank, because an intelligent intern might be perfect, but their interests should align. If the speaker is one of your corporate or community partners, it's appropriate for the director or a trustee to welcome this VIP. If the speaker is a scholar, a curator will handle the job meaningfully. I attended a talk given by one of a large museum's many curators, and the young woman who introduced her appeared to be an underling or intern who apparently didn't think she had the standing to say much of anything. But she could have enthusiastically stated her superior's credentials, which were impressive. Pick the right person, with the right personality, to welcome the presenter.

The introduction should name the speaker, the title of the talk, and what the title means. This gist of a talk, unfortunately, is not always apparent. The introducer always (a) states his relationship with the speaker, (b) spells out the significance of the subject, and (c) notes the relationship of the subject to the mission of the museum. Never assume the people in the seats are there because they like lectures; they trust the museum to deliver a meaningful one.

That's all you need to say in an introduction. Sixty seconds will do it. But never say, "Without further ado"; it's a cliché that implies that your previous comments were a waste of time. They aren't; your speaker deserves at least sixty seconds of "ado" for enlightenment and pleasure he's about to deliver.

CONTENT

Good news: although of course there is no standard outline for a lecture, there are some standards that will help any speaker, on any topic, organize his or her thoughts. The first few minutes are a bit of a repeat: the speaker reintroduces himself and reiterates his qualifications for talking on the subject at hand. You'd be surprised how often the introducer forgets to name the introducee. Plus, the speaker can add some human-interest qualifications that never appear on official resumes. These two points, repeating the name, reiterating qualifications, confers instant familiarity; now the audience is attuned to the stranger in front of them. It's going to be a fine lecture!

Speakers, state your theme. Good writing has a point. However you choose to develop your theme, stick to it, and, if you wander off theme, return to it as quickly as possible. Repeat the theme regularly throughout the talk, and recap the theme at the end. Sometimes you will sound clunky; you'll have to stop talking and say, in effect, oops, let's get back to the theme. But that's ideal. It's easy to ramble on in a talk, and your audience will appreciate a full stop, and repetition of the theme: it's easier to follow. At an Art Institute of Chicago lecture on photographer Henri Cartier-Bresson, the speaker stated that the theme would be change. It was an intellectual way to tie together Cartier's long life of widely divergent output and experience, and a degree of intellectualism was appropriate for the audience of engaged museum members who had reserved seats long in advance.

Assume that the audience comprises people somewhat knowledgeable about the subject of your talk, and start with a review of it; people who aren't knowledgeable will get a quick overview. Then immediately give one or two, no more, new, erudite insights. At the Art Institute lecture on Henri Cartier, the speaker pointed out that the artist rejected the hyphenated form of his name as too elite. Audiences love new information, clear-cut snippets that relate to the topic, that they immediately understand and remember. Save the scholarly expansions of a theme for later.

Next, it's time to speak directly to the broad swath of audience members who are not knowledgeable in the subject, who want to learn or, more difficult, are simply attending with a friend. Give a biography or time line or context of the subject, lots of facts. Here's where visuals come in handy because they appeal to different kinds of learners; also, visuals slow you down, giving your words time to sink in.

At this point of a short lecture, it's almost time to wrap things up. In an hour-long lecture, it's a midpoint for pausing and refreshing. This is the point to single out possible segments in the audience. Identify the youngsters in the group and speak to their age and interests. Wonder aloud if there are people "who remember when," and remind the entire group of significant recent history. The speaker can emphasize scholarship for the scholarly, local experience for the residents of the museum's community, or related art forms for those who are regular patrons of many organizations. There are always people in the audience who tag along as friends, or out of curiosity, and this audience is the serendipity every arts organization looks for—the new customers who have ventured through the door and just need to be convinced. Pinpoint this friend contingent—a little humor never hurts—and embellish your topic for them. Here's a good time to act like an expert and aficionado; your passion may ignite the newcomers to becoming regular visitors, and it will certainly resonate with the loyals.

Q&A AND AFTERWORDS

Successful lectures beget questions, and when these aren't forthcoming, good lecturers write them in. Q&A serves the purpose of closure, the satisfying ending to the journey of new learning. Ideally, a few people in the audience will have questions that can be repeated in a loud voice and answered authoritatively by the speaker. This interchange of ideas embraces everyone in the room and proves to everyone that the talk has been successful. Frequently, no questions are forthcoming, so a timid audience should always be anticipated with a set of scripted questions. The speaker pauses a moment, looks around the room, and then very casually says: "Actually, a lot of people wonder . . ." Or, the speaker could pause and say, "You know, one question I frequently get is . . ." The informality is always a crowd-pleaser. This is also a good point for the introducer to reappear and ask a few questions that summarize the talk. Some questions can't be answered by the speaker, and this is always an opportunity, never a failure. Simply ask the questioner to come up to the podium and leave an e-mail address; a response will be sent, by the speaker or the museum, within forty-eight hours. Now the museum has another e-mail address to add to the database, and the opportunity to start a relationship with a constituent. One speaker at a local library, at an informal program where the audience ranged from informed to interested to merely curious, responded to a question within one week with an e-mail full of information gathered from experts back at the institution. An interested audience member was perhaps converted to a ticket purchaser. As an information gathering device, Q&A is peerless. There is no limit to the thoughts swirling in the listener's brain after it has been stimulated by a good talk, and much of this input is useful in future planning.

There are many ways to wrap up a lecture: summarize, exhort, or simply say thank you. The best valedictory is, often, a detail. Speakers leave their audiences with one thought for the day. It could be a future trend, or current area of research, or a personal area of exploration, and it is linked graciously to the sponsoring museum. "And that's why I am so pleased to be speaking at [your museum] today."

FOLLOW-UP

After the lecture ends and the audience stand to go, your job isn't done. The last piece of writing is the follow-up communication: the words that retain your audience for future contact. There are many ways to characterize your audience, and this will determine your follow up.

If you're speaking to community groups, such as libraries and community centers, or organizations like League of Women Voters, the crowd will have diverse cultural interests and be difficult to target with additional specific messages. Call this target the culturally interested. You may not be able to collect their names, but, where appropriate, tell them to keep checking for future presentations or information from your museum.

The lunchtime crowd, which can be individuals or business groups whose companies sponsor enrichment lectures for employees, requires you to have time-switching sensitivity; it doesn't readily occur to them that a weekday break could also be a weekend family activity. But that's a worthy segment to pursue, and you might want to say a few family-oriented words while distributing family discount tickets and perhaps collecting names.

Seniors, individually or in social groups such as senior centers, are stealth audiences, often off the radar but ignored at your own peril. Just because they don't often come to your museum physically doesn't mean they aren't intensely committed. This is a group with money to spend and loyalty just looking for a place to belong. Be sure to follow up talks to these groups with regular mailings that cover new topics. You could mail magazines, although this is expensive, or regular e-mail articles, which offer the space to write thorough, illustrated articles; these lectures in writing will appeal to and further involve older people who also, by the way, have generations of relatives sharing in their activities. Don't worry about computer literacy; current research indicates that older people are practiced users of electronic media.

Members, especially at higher levels, are intensely loyal to your museum brand, and though often too busy to attend all your supplemental activities, still like to be reminded of the robustness of your mission. Follow-up with them will be ongoing announcements of future events, presented in the same spirit as the lecture they have just attended.

OTHER TALKS

Once you're used to talking, you'll find many other occasions to give better-crafted talks: 60-second speaker introductions will be more relevant, welcoming talks at member events will be more persuasive, and full-blown lectures will be welcomed as opportunities to grow your audiences.

One guiding thought underpins all content: never, ever fear the small detail. All listeners, regardless of their background or interests, will understand a specific reference. Good speakers don't speak vaguely about biologists' tools when they can specify mosquito forceps. Interesting lecturers don't pontificate about Lincoln's eloquence when they can quote "better angels of our nature." Don't underestimate your audiences; they have the intelligence to hear a specific and apply it to broader concepts. The opposite of detail is deadliness; to speak only in generalizations is to say nothing.

Audiences at lectures are lifelong learners who are accustomed to working for new knowledge. They appreciate the glittery new nugget of information, even if their minds have to dig a little to get it. Write sharp, sparkling words and keep those loyal, lifelong supporters coming back.

Chapter Ten

Magazines

Of all your communications, the one that stays firmly in print is the magazine. Sometimes it's called a newsletter, although news of immediate interest belongs online. A magazine, however, lives and breathes for hard-copy perusal, careful reading, and saving. Like all good magazines, it's enjoyed at quieter times, and respected for not just information, but background.

There are five parts to a museum magazine: letter from the director, table of contents, editorial content, calendar, and recognition. Each has its role in telling the story and communicating meaningfully with your various audiences.

In each of the five points, certain rules of good writing apply. A good magazine finds a point of view, a philosophy, and sticks with it. A good magazine is timely, whether that's monthly, bimonthly, or seasonally. A really good magazine understands its audience, or audiences, and speaks meaningfully to its readers.

Point of view is simply professional because it structures the writing, inhibits verbosity, and doesn't waste the reader's time or your budget. Are you issue oriented, plumbing topics like "The New Rebecca: A Pocahontas Mystery" (in *American Indian*, the National Museum of the American Indian, Summer 2013)? Or are you exhibition driven, as is the Spencer Museum of Art at the University of Kansas? Perhaps the calendar drives your magazine; the Kohler Art Center in Sheboygan, Wisconsin, organizes sixteen of its twenty pages according to the dates of its exhibitions, workshops, classes, and events. Having a point of view also reinforces your distinctiveness and brand. A unique example of style is found in *American Indian*, where every person named has his or her tribe added in parentheses; this is U.S. government as well as tribal policy, and it embodies the mission of the museum as the voice of the American Indian. It sets the tone for the entire content. Once you have a viewpoint, other attributes come naturally: person-ality, tone of voice, and visual "look." Now, consistency comes into play, and it matters a lot.

With consistency, the magazine, the rare item that appears in actual mail-boxes at the consumer's home, becomes familiar and trustworthy. The recipi-ent will read it with the thoughtfulness you put into it. Lack of consistency loses friends; the minute a reader is confused by something that doesn't track, that's the minute the reader turns the page and aims for the recycling bin.

Timeliness is—no excuses, please—essential to being relevant. You don't have to publish often, as this is pretty hard for a small museum to sustain, but you must address your current programs and the events that are of current importance to your community.

TARGET AUDIENCES

Target audiences are trickier, because most museums have several segments they target. And here's where the five parts of the magazine helps. The letter from the director speaks strongly to donors and supporters. The table of contents identifies each of the target audiences with not only the name of the article or section, but a short paragraph explaining the article or section. Content is everything and anything you want it to be: an article on the person who built the historic house; in-depth explanation of the scientific research behind an exhibition; Q&A with an exhibition designer that answers ques-tions the tourist-visitor might have; an article about the lecture series that a local member would find useful; a preview of the summer teen programs that educators would find important. Balance the articles so each audience is addressed. The calendar also targets everybody, since each event is named, described, and given a venue; you'd be surprised how place helps pinpoint an audience. If a program takes place in the auditorium, it's probably for mem-bers who have heard about it through e-mails to the database. If it's in the workspace area, it's probably for families. If it's in the lobby, it's for visitors.

Budget and time of staff will determine how often you target each group with a publication. Even the wealthiest museums mix up the content of a publication to appeal to all segments. You've seen it many times: a magazine that sets aside a page for member trips, school groups, scholar events, or business partnership initiatives. Just know exactly to whom each article or chapter has significance, and identify them, so other readers understand the context.

If it's a story about a member trip, say in the subhead or first paragraph of the article that it is a special opportunity for members only.

For a schedule of continuing education courses for teachers, make it clear in the subhead or first paragraph that this is an important service museums provide to educators. If the article is a review of a book on the history of the museum, note that it might be interesting to those whose families were involved in the founding of your institution.

DIRECTOR'S PAGE

"Dear Garden Member:"

Thus begins the letter from the director of the Chicago Botanic Garden, and those three words are singular examples of good writing. Surprisingly, most such letters use neither "dear," "member," or even the name of the museum in the headline or first line of the letter. If your museum publishes a four-color member magazine, the first page leads off with the same showmanship as a symphony conductor: a bow to the audience, a sweep of baton to the other players onstage, and a crisp breaking of the silence.

As the lead to the ensuing flow of information, the director's page has an outline: headline, visual, letter, signature. The last item, the signature, is obvious but crucial. The top person is signing off not only on the letter, but on the museum's entire programming. His or her comments represent the mission of the museum, excellence of the exhibitions, respect for the visitor, appreciation for members, and accountability. If the director has a personality, the reader can expect the museum to have a distinctive personality as well. The whole objective of a director's page is to sum up the museum experience, from mission to monthly preview of events.

Consider the director's page as you would a magazine ad; it has a strategy. The words at the top of the ad are better termed "the headline." Headlines announce something newsworthy, timely, or singular. The writer's first job is to write an appropriate headline: "Another History-Making Month at [your museum]." If you want to stress that this page comes from the director, print his or her title in large type under his or her signature.

Don't be afraid to switch around the standard elements of the director's letter. The Spencer Museum of Art calls its page "Director's Remarks." It has a headline that's specific to that issue's content. And the director's signature is centered up at the top of the page, rather than signing off at the bottom. It reads:

Director's Remarks
Art Become Personal—Fast.
[Signature]

The writing is distinctive, with a clear premise and seven paragraphs that develop the theme of encountering art, getting to know it on your terms,

Figure 10.1. *American Indian* magazine follows best practices of museum magazines: director's letter focuses on news; descriptive table of contents; in-depth researched articles. *Courtesy National Museum of the American Indian/Smithsonian.*

finding "common ground" with the artist, and experiencing art, rather than trying too hard to study it. The director, Saralyn Reece Hardy, speaks knowledgeably and engagingly. As part of the University of Kansas, the museum is a bipartite brand, but it has one goal and that is to involve everyone on a personal level.

Now that you're thinking of the director's page as an advert, pay closer attention to the visual. Most magazine ads are 70 to 99 percent visual, and our culture is unrelentingly image oriented. On the Art Institute of Chicago's director's page, the visual occupies about 25 percent of the page. It's relatively small, but still obtrusive, because it shows a real person, in a pose standard in historic portraiture: almost full body, looking directly at the viewer. In each issue, the director stands in front of a different part of the museum; even in a small museum, there's a range of exhibits, exteriors, store displays, conservation labs, or architectural detail that help define the institution. At the very least, you can show the director with a relevant item from the collection. Some people debate whether a photo of the boss is necessary; it really helps individualize the institution if it's a good photo. A good photo is well lit, carefully posed, interesting, and relevant; a head shot does not constitute a good photo. Along with a meaningfully staged photo, remember to write a caption that identifies the scene in the photo and explains why it's relevant to the specific issue; the caption also reiterates the name of the director.

The bulk of the director's page tells the theme of the issue, and there should be a theme. It might revolve around news, or seasonality, or an ongoing exhibition. It might convey a general musing, say, on the importance of scholarship, or contributions of volunteers, or partnerships with the community. Themes are basic to any magazine, and in the case of a member communication, it reinforces the museum's core values. Once in a great while, the director uses this valuable real estate to announce a significant gift. That's fine, if it's once in a while, and the gift is really significant. A more appropriate place is in the recognition section. The letter is the place for vision to shine through. The structure of the text on the director's page is best contained in three to five paragraphs.

MAIN NEWS OR THEME

Kevin Gover (Pawnee), director of the National Museum of the American Indian, uses the first paragraph to concisely state an issue of timely importance, for example, the repatriation of sacred and funeral artifacts. Madeleine Grynsztejn, director of the Museum of Contemporary Art, Chicago, used her space in one issue to relate a current exhibition to Chicago's history; being a part of the community is a key part of the museum's identity. Some directors open with a cogent description of an exhibition—current or future—and act accountably by speaking of visitor numbers, media awareness, or scholarly contribution. No director should waste ink on seasonal musings; there are more incisive points to make. The director is a timely person, on top of the news, in control of the situation, and the source of insider knowledge. All readers of the magazine—visitors, members, donors, community partners, employees, volunteers, and media—want to hear from the person at the top, the one in charge whose name is known and whose signature counts. In the digital world everyone is an author, but we still need authorities; the director is that person, and his or her presence is made available to all in the print world of magazines.

DETAILS OF SPECIFIC EXHIBITIONS, ARTIFACTS, EVENTS

Although many qualified professionals plan, organize, vet, and justify every exhibition, every artifact, every event, external contact, and every follow-up measurement—to name a very few details of running a museum—it is the director's august duty to be on top of them, and not just on the organization chart. Two to three paragraphs of the director's letter should mention details, to demonstrate not just knowledge but accountability.

DIRECTOR'S SUMMARY

It is the director's responsibility to point out the relevance of all museum activities, to account for how the above-mentioned information relates to the mission and distinctiveness of the museum. One director commented on two exhibitions and how both reflect the scholarship and visitor experience of the institution. Some directors use this paragraph of the magazine to touch on financial subjects. Some wrap up their letters with news of the completion of a project and its impact. In her director's remarks, Saralyn Reece Hardy of the Spencer Museum of Art focused her remarks on the viewers' perspective; a pullout quote served as the summary statement: "Allow time for the art to meet you."

CALL TO ACTION

Many museums use the last paragraph to invite the reader to visit and enjoy on-site the environment summarized throughout the magazine. The call to action might be specific: "We hope to see you in the new gallery and throughout the museum this season." It might be general: "As we head into summer, we hope you make us part of your vacation plans." It might be very actionable: "We appreciate your support and hope you'll feel free to call us with any comments at 123-456-0000." Keep this ending short; it's not distinctive to the museum and it doesn't evoke the director's eminence, but without it a letter seems rather purposeless.

Kevin Gover of the Smithsonian's National Museum of the American Indian had a singular call to action in the issue on repatriation, exhorting all readers to educate the public on the repatriation of Native American artifacts.

Keep the letter from the director short, and keep the page clean. This is the space for highlights and insights, from the person with the overview. I've devoted many pages to this one page of the magazine, but don't confuse my fulsomeness with your pithiness. Two things good writers learn early: heaven is in the details, and brevity.

STRUCTURE OF THE REST OF THE MAGAZINE

The other four parts of the magazine—table of contents, content, calendar (discussed here as an element of content), and recognition—emanate from other professionals at the museum. A major skill of magazine writers is discovering the experts who will provide them the stories.

Table of Contents

Just before or just after the director's letter comes the table of contents, which can be a straight list, or a dashboard-style design; either way it serves you, as well as your readers, as an excellent map of what follows. Good tables of contents have a sentence or short paragraph describing each feature. Without this guide you'd be lost, and no writer should start any project without one.

With an outline you can see how to allocate space and priorities, discover if there's an imbalance of stories, or if anything is missing. The table of contents is the keeper of consistency throughout the magazine. The wording in the contents is the wording that will follow consistently throughout the publication, and if you publish a big magazine, where readers might want to immediately find an article, rather than turn pages through to it, consistency is important. If you have a complex magazine, where calendar events are sometimes augmented with an article that appears on another page, consistency or lack thereof is a real problem. Confused readers don't struggle to figure out divergent wording; they give up and close up the book.

If you don't know the range of exhibits, special shows, people, and events that a museum offered, a good table of contents will enlighten you. The Chicago Botanic Garden's summer offerings are listed in the table of contents thus:

Summer Programs: An array of music, festivals, and special events beckons visitors this summer.

An article on an important new addition to the museum reads:

New Display Gardens: Plans are in the works for two beautiful, functional new display gardens.

A scholarly article is described in the table of contents as:

Breaking the Code: Norm Wickett, Ph.D., explores the genetics of mosses through an NSF Tree of Life grant.

Readers can identify articles geared to them just from the Art Institute's table of contents. General readers will see the scope of the summer programs. Donors and patrons will see the expansion plan of the new display gardens article. The genetics article speaks subtly to grantors, who will read of the gardens' success in converting grant money to action.

American Indian magazine writes short paragraphs to describe each article or feature. This magazine devotes more space to articles about Native American culture and issues than to exhibits in the museum itself, and takes the opportunity in the table of contents to summarize its many untold stories. The listing for "Trails of Culture" is followed with a paragraph that describes the travels and movements of Central American peoples throughout history. However, the listings for articles on museum activities are equally detailed. Combining the contents listed on the cover of the magazine with the contents in the table, readers learn a lot of new information before they ever get to the full story itself.

Another way to handle the table of contents is with photos, as *Business-week* magazine does; it looks like a handheld museum of business information, with each listing accompanied by a full paragraph and photograph, illustration, or chart.

Balancing the Contents of the Table

A quick look at the table of contents will tell the editor, as well as the reader, the range and the focus of the museum; it's a quick reality check on whether there is editorial bias. Do the stories represent all aspects of the museum? How many pages are allocated to each article or section? Which audience segments are addressed? Which articles are at the front; do the articles at the back seem shortchanged?

Layout

Some table of contents pages are set in a consistent typeface. Some vary their appearance with several typefaces. Some tables of contents are spread over two pages, with full-color visuals; others are set in one column centered prominently on the page; some are scrunched into a corner. Each layout conveys a message; visual organization communicates as much as the words themselves. I can't and won't judge the rationale for magazine layouts, as that is a matter between the editors and graphic designer, not to mention any staff members who offer advice, and the director who may have the final say. I will suggest that you evaluate the layout as carefully as you proofread the page numbers.

Content

Articles. Standing features. Columns and guest columnists. Photo essays. Calendar. Q&A. This rough outline of any museum magazine leaves thousands of options to the individual editorial staffs. There are, however, a few writerly points to remember about each.

Articles make their point quickly. If they have a teaser headline, they must explain it in the first paragraph. Write as much as you want, because you have a museumful of information to impart; then edit ruthlessly. Keep the article on consecutive pages because readers don't want to learn at what seems to be the end of the article that it's "continued on page 14."

Standing features reinforce your museum's point of view and brand image. Repetition breeds familiarity and encourages readers to wait for the article each issue. It also demonstrates a distinguishing area of expertise. The standing feature works well at the back of the book, because many followers will read every page with the knowledge of this reward at the end. Find a repeatable concept and repeat it every issue, because those who like the focus will love reading each iteration. Those who don't like it may find it worthwhile in the next issue. The structure of standing features makes them easy for interns to write.

Columns provide a similar familiarity as standing features do because they are defined by their columnists. If you don't have a popular columnist on staff, and most museums don't, commission a guest column. If you reach out to scholars in your area, or educators, or community partners, they'll be flattered, and it's a meaningful way to build relationships.

Photo essays are recommended only if you have an archive of excellent photographs. If you do, flaunt it. Just remember the captions. The best photos in the world need the assistance of words, and words add credibility. See page 156 for tips on writing captions.

Calendars are backbreaking, eye-straining work. There are so many details to be researched, fact-checked, and proofread. Spend some thought on whether a linear or grid calendar will best serve your schedule. If your events cluster on weekends, or mornings, a grid might make that point visually. If you have events every day of the week, a linear listing will give you the space you need. Don't waste a lot of space on the day and date. Once you have a system, the reader will quickly see if it's a Monday or a Friday. And all readers have a built-in memory of days in the month. In other words, we all know the relative placement of 4, 16, and 25, and that we won't have to worry about anything over 31. Instead, highlight or use larger type for days of the week, which is everyone's first consideration.

Use your limited calendar space to describe the event. It's not informative enough to list "Gallery Walk" every Tuesday if the walks change. Likewise, "Family Saturday" is not descriptive for moms and dads who will buy into the concept more readily if you specify time, place, and topic right in the calendar.

Q&A is the editor's Disneyland. It's fun and easy. As you near the end of a hard-fought battle with assignments, details, and deadlines, you know there's always the Q&A to give you respite. This is where you fill gaps and put leftover information. Whatever you edited out of a too-long article goes in Q&A. Last-minute news stands out in the short format of the Q&A. Overlooked items get new prominence in Q&A. Audience segments you forgot to address? Speak directly to them in the Q&A. Suppose you're a science museum and have the beginning of an article on stars. You don't know which constituent group would be interested in this story. You have no time to develop it now. So simply write:

> Q: What's the big news in astronomy? A: It's really big. One of the newest stars being studied now turns out to be one of the ten largest ever discovered.

You probably have at least one paragraph on this story and that's all you need for a Q&A entry; the entire Q&A column should contain a minimum of five questions and answers. You'll notice how "Q" and "A" stand out when repeated multiple times in one paragraph. On the magazine page it has a similar effect, substituting for the more time-consuming task of writing headlines and subheads.

Recognition

Because magazines are for news, opinion, depth, and brand building, save recognition of staff, volunteers, donors, and sponsors for a special section at the back. Honoring these people is essential, but it is usually not newsworthy or distinctive. All museums have people to thank. More to the point, many people read your magazine only to see their names in print, so they will find the section; it doesn't have to occupy valuable real estate up front. A special recognition section gives you space to describe the occasion of the honor and its goals, as well as the people contributing to it, and it's worth adding extra pages for this reason. We live in a sharing environment, off-line as well as on, and everyone contributes. Acknowledge as many as you can, and spell their names right!

Special Case: Letter from the Mayor

Some publications that feature special exhibitions or events earn a coveted letter from the mayor. Remember that this letter is not just an honor for you, but a value to the mayor, who gains association with a cultural institution. As a two-way deal, the museum can ask to write the first draft of the letter that will appear in its magazine. Actually, the busy mayor's office might be happy to hand over the job. Here's the format:

"Dear Friends:"
Reason for speaking out from the mayor's office
Name of city and official name of event; date of event
Goal or mission of the city that meshes with the goal or mission of your
museum event
Description of the event, saying why it's so interesting to the mayor
Mention of the world and the community. For example, "Bringing the
world of science to our exceptional city." "Connecting our heritage to
the world." "Honoring a great patriot."
Mention your community's claims to fame. For example, "Our city is
home to five colleges and research universities." "Our city has sent
over fifty men and women to national office."
List cooperating cultural and intellectual events to show collaborative
spirit.
Welcome visitors to the city, because the tourism and convention business helps everyone flourish.
Sign off with "On behalf of the people of . . ." and "Sincerely" rather than
"Best" or "Yours truly."

Magazines fill an important space in museum culture, condensing for a brief while, in a small space, everything you stand for. Stacked on top of each other, as many magazines are on the coffee table, they form an encyclopedia of knowledge and progress. They earn the time and resources you invest in them.

Chapter Eleven

Newsletters

Newsletters have evolved, but they took a wrong turn and are in danger of being the branch of the marketing family that goes extinct. Of course, technology lets you send information further and faster, but newsletters have just gotten fatter. They attempt to do too much, and they've lost their singular raison d'être. The reason for newsletters is news. Newsletters deliver the news, in a timely fashion, through e-mail sent directly to individuals culled from your database. Each of the many powerful media platforms has its own unique benefits and characteristics, and they are discussed in other chapters. The newsletter, which is now more effective than ever thanks to database management, has seven unique benefits that no other platform can deliver.

- Awareness
- Continuity
- Connection
- Development
- Internal engagement
- Lapsed-member retrieval
- Branding

Newsletters achieve these objectives by being not only newsy, but newsworthy. The newsletter platform takes the time to cull genuine news for the most worthy news. This chapter reminds you, as interpreters and educators, that news includes new perspectives, new analyses, and new ways of thinking.

When you write a newsletter about newsworthy topics, that means no promotion about to expire; it's newsy but not worthy. Don't lead with a story about Family Saturday; it's worthy, but not news. News is a story the readers never heard before. It could be as exciting as new research into Egyptian mummies, or as homey as a new angle on the family who lived in the house on Main Street. If it's another Family Saturday or Antiques Appraisal Day, provide a fresh perspective on why this meshes with your museum's singular vision. If your museum has genealogy resources, Family Saturday could have news value. Here's a place where the skill of a writer comes in. Don't write a headline about Family Saturday. Do write a headline and lead paragraph about your genealogy studies, and end the story with a reminder of Family Saturday. Don't write a story about saving money at the store sale. Do write a story about how your buyers select the merchandise, and end with a call to action to buy now. Don't omit standard newsletter topics like the calendar of events, shout-outs for employees, photographs of member events, and solicitations. Do start with a big headline about something fresh, and follow with a story about why it's special.

The Tenement Museum in New York City understands newsworthiness, and without fail highlights a new story from the annals of the Lower East Side, in addition to more quotidian news like speakers, new tours, or a new title in the bookstore. The Smithsonian Postal Museum leverages a storied past to stay relevant. A 2013 issue announced a new exhibition, *Pacific Exchange: China & U.S. Mail*, that positions the museum as a scholar of worldwide communication.

Here's how good writing can resurrect the newsletter and maximize its format to meet the objectives of awareness, continuity, connection, development, internal engagement, lapsed-member retrieval, and brand.

AWARENESS

Your home page, or the front page of the newsletter, makes the first impression, so flaunt it. Large museums, with well-known logos, are well advised to put their logo up top and large. You've invested years of goodwill in that symbol and nowhere is it more important than in awareness marketing.

If you're a small museum, you have to reinforce your identity with each communication. However you design the page, even if it's a busy dashboard, find your strongest visual and stick with it.

The National Churchill Museum in Fulton, Missouri, opened its e-mailed newsletter to a photograph of the famous man. Any image of Winston Churchill creates instant awareness; to prospects of this museum, the wartime British prime minister is always worth reading about. If your museum is connected with a person of accomplishment, your job is easier, because stories about him or her will always have relevance today. The challenge is constantly making new people aware.

A February issue for the Chicago Botanic Garden leads with a screen-wide banner of a bough of red orchids. Growing things are, of course, shorthand for a garden, and in this case they are also timely for the annual February Orchid Show.

The Tenement Museum newsletter features a banner-wide photo of an early twentieth-century Lower East Side street scene. And in this streetscape stands a single person, symbolizing the many people whose stories the museum commemorates.

Many media platforms deliver timely news, but only newsletters reach such a wide, qualified audience with full-screen photos and headlines that keep your name and mission front and center. With newsletters, you maintain control over the story.

CONTINUITY

Newsletters even help you span the seasons and maintain interest over long periods of time. Botanic garden newsletters maintain interest in winter. Historic house magazines, known for their Spring Walk coverage, continue to hold readership throughout the year. Academic museums, through their newsletters, stay open and robust over winter, spring, and summer breaks. Science museums talk to families of schoolchildren after school lets out. Sun Belt museums reach out to members and donors after the snowbirds go home. Newsletters bridge these gap months by reminding constituents that the museum is still here, even if they've gone elsewhere for a while. These loyalists aren't deserting you, so don't desert them. Before "out of sight, out of mind" escalates to "out of the running," stay in touch so they can return to you without missing a beat.

Focus on the familiar aspects of your museum and what's happening there over the break. Don't emphasize your snowy garden paths or too-quiet galleries; talk about your warm January events and the active discussions that characterize your tours. Don't highlight current exhibitions that your members are missing; talk about what's coming up in the months when they'll be back in town. Describe what the museum is doing in the same tone of voice you would for any season, because you want to reinforce their memories; it will be so much easier for your supporters to ease back into your life if they feel they've never left. Newsletters vibrantly emphasize the show going on, so readers will want to rejoin the excitement when they return.

One kind of story that weathers the bad-weather hiatus: school outreach programs. The Ravinia Music Festival outside Chicago, an arts organization that closes its pavilion and park when summer ends, lists these activities that continue throughout the school year: instruments for student orchestras; music education for twelve thousand students; free, year-round family music school for an underserved community; employment of teaching artists to work in public school classrooms. Your museum has year-round programs like this, or knows of some, and you should publicize even the small ones.

Many media platforms deliver information all the time, but only newsletters achieve brand continuity, because you maintain control over the story.

CONNECTION

Most people on your lists may already be aware of your institution, but awareness is a long way from familiarity, and that's what you want to instill. Newsletters do this well because the writer couples attractive news with significance for the reader. Don't just announce a lecture, workshop, or new merchandise in the store. Explain why your museum thinks they're important. A newsletter gives you the space. An upcoming lecture may not mean much to the casual reader whose name is in your database, so good writing is needed to make that newsy event relevant to him. Don't say, "William Smith, professor of biology, will speak on river ecosystems." Do say, "Come hear a clean-river expert shed new light on our current exhibition." Now the reader has a better idea of your museum's mission, and has a citizen's way to connect with it.

Announcing a coming workshop lets you establish a connection because you can describe the goals of the workshop in words the reader can understand. It's wise to also refer to past workshops, so readers can see your range of topics that might match their individual interests. Merchandise in the store is a wonderful way to connect to the shopper in everyone. If the merchandise is truly related to the mission, highlighting it is instructive and lets you explain your philosophy in the language of shopping. The museum store is a portal for museums. Prospective visitors may not have an immediate desire in the science of molecular theory, but they might be enticed by the science in a birthday gift of a "gastronomy kit" of "mint caviar beads and lemon foam spheres." The writer for the Science Museum in London did a witty job of positioning food as molecules, equation watches as math, and Milky Way scarves as astronomy. It is the challenge of a writer to elevate the ordinary to wow.

Many media platforms connect people better than newsletters do, but only newsletters connect qualified people—selected from the museum's database—back to the museum in meaningful ways.

DEVELOPMENT

With the care and feeding of members and donors, newsletters function at their most noble. New ideas, progress, and innovation is essential for people who are asked to join and give, not just for the momentary visit, but forever. They expect ongoing excellence, and the next event to anticipate. Big donors, especially, want to see long-range plans, the same forward momentum they see in their own businesses. When you ask for members and donors, you put yourself in competition with many other arts organizations, and one way to regularly prove your competitive value is through the little victories described in the newsletter.

An obvious way to demonstrate forward movement is with a well-researched, smartly developed exhibition. Your newsletter can expand on the theme of the exhibition, the experts involved, the items amassed through your professional connections, and the exhibition materials written by your respected curators.

A new acquisition definitely authenticates your prowess in seizing opportunities and enhancing your vision. A beautiful photograph of the object will grace the front page of the newsletter. An intriguing headline will nail its importance. An article, of any length, will explain its relevance to the culture of the community and the prominence of the museum. Smart acquisitions are the hallmarks of winners, and many of your supporters appreciate that strength. Interesting acquisitions, on a less muscular level, provide breadth to your collection, and give you yet another point on which to connect to the people who want to be a part of your family.

Insights and angles also strengthen long-term relationships because they build on your expertise, the core of your brand. Building up, delving deep, and stretching out—these are directional activities demanded by people who want to return often and always find something new.

In its depth of coverage, a newsletter is like a magazine. The newsletter is newsier, shorter, breezier, and much less expensive to produce. And because the newsletter also serves the objectives of awareness, continuity, connection, internal engagement, lapsed-member retrieval, and branding, as well as development, here are some guidelines for finding new news and making it worthy.

Ask your staffers to point out something different in a new exhibition. It could be a different kind of display pedestal or label treatment. Let them find the tiny difference and you write a lead sentence that starts: "What's interesting about this exhibition is . . ." Then you can continue to news about the new show.

Ask the store personnel to listen to shopper conversations and pick out one word or bit of body language that's not the usual. You then write about the interesting reasons people love the store, and continue onto the store news.

Ask your tour guides for the interesting questions visitors ask. Then tie that to a talk or workshop you're offering.

Relate an object in the museum to the weather or season. Talk about what the farm animals do in winter. Talk about the summer garments in the wardrobe of your historic house. Then continue to your monthly calendar of events.

Survey your volunteers for an artist, historian, or scientist whose work was motivational to them. Feature these heroes in an article that leads to news about the employee appreciation event.

Enlist ideas from the community. Ask your local librarian for a recent book that's relevant to your collection and write a book review. Then continue to news about the museum bookstore.

If your museum has a performance space, ask one of the actors, dancers, or musicians to comment on the show. Then continue to news about the dates of performance.

Writing newsworthy articles, or even a few paragraphs, takes time, but the value is high when your readers are members and donors. No media platform matches newsletters for delivering the relevance of your news. If your newsletter doesn't combine newsiness and worthiness, it's a blog. And there's a whole other chapter on that.

Academic museums have a ready-made community that's a source of timely, worthy articles. The Smart Museum at the University of Chicago featured images from Chinese opera during collaboration with other arts organizations that made for several visually exciting news stories.

INTERNAL ENGAGEMENT

These writing tips, not coincidentally, help you connect your core values with those nearest you, your employees. Conversely, an insight gleaned by a volunteer or a staffer helps you find new articles with new perspectives. Newsletters invite everyone on the staff to act as participants in the museum mission, giving them talking points to share with family and friends. Of course, there are many media platforms that allow employees to exercise their voice, and you should encourage your people to blog, tweet, and pin. But only newsletters, published under your name, give their voice the honor of third-party validation.

LAPSED-MEMBER RETRIEVAL

As dreaded as mold, as difficult to identify as an unsolicited artifact, nothing humbles a museum like steadfast supporters who stop returning.

The reasons are many and unknowable. It could be genuine dissatisfaction—with the collection, exhibitions, prices, location, or hours of operation. It could be life-cycle issues like career moves, children leaving the nest, retirement finances, or the changing interests of aging. Equally likely reasons for lapses are subtle: new interests developing into consuming passions, a new residence with different transportation schedules, a new algorithm for distribution of philanthropy. You can't make lapsed members change their minds, but you can stand by them, even while they have abandoned you. The newsletter fills that function nicely. If you keep good customers in your database, they'll keep seeing your e-mails. And if/when they want to change their life again, you'll be top of mind. To accomplish that hoped-for goal, there are some tips for making your data work harder, and other tips for making lapsed members see you in a new light.

Database Tips

By managing your database, you can reach old, lapsed members and donors in new ways.

Don't be discouraged by names in your database that have new out-of-state addresses. People with second homes frequently continue to support their main home museum, and it's the newsletter's job to maintain continuity during the hiatus.

Names that stop coming to family events probably have older children. Move these names to your weekday lecture, facilities rental, or workshop list, and let the newsletter connect them to more appropriate activities.

Names that contribute at lower levels, or no level, remain good ambassadors for your museum. Keep them on the list and aware.

New Messaging to Old Friends

Unlike regular supporters who merely stray for the season, lapsed supporters purposely turn their back and walk away. Don't confuse this with dislike; it's just a change in life plan. Newsletters are effective in helping readers see you in a new light and perhaps find a way to fit the museum into their new life.

Write your e-mail Subject lines to adults, instead of parents. Where you once sent e-mails to your database of families with headlines like "Make a Gingerbread House for the Holidays," now you would send e-mails to your general database with the headline "Wok Cooking Classes for China Exhibition."

Refer to your community more often; that will locate the museum tangibly. For people that have moved out of state, include the name of your city in the Subject line. That might resonate more emotionally than the name of a three-month exhibition.

Send newsletters filled with news, not just familiar events, workshops, and store offerings. For data fields that reveal no reason for lapses, keep the newsletters coming regularly, but less often. It's easy for a disinterested ex-

member to delete a barrage of e-mails from the same sender, but less necessary with the occasional newsworthy headline. It will take careful writing
and editing to include the museum name, city name, and news event in one
Subject line, so plan to send fewer newsletters, and to spend more time on
their content. Here are some for-instance Subject line news:

"[Your Name] History Museum showcases Ohio heritage seed"
"Arias at the [Your Name] bring opera to Springville all winter"
"Car Culture on parade from Elm Street to the [Your Name]"
"Video of Hollywood idol media tour at the [Your Name]"

Many media platforms might reach your lapsed members, but it's a one-
in-a-million chance, and only newsletters can identify them and write the
stories that might reengage their interest.

BRANDING

All the benefits of your newsletter—awareness, continuity, connection, development, internal engagement, and lapsed-member retrieval—benefit its
brand. Your identity, mission, vision, personality, and core values are what
inform the selection of stories, writing, and design. Your brand suffuses the
newsletter, and you have the control to make that happen. Here are seven
ways to always reinforce your brand, to maintain and reinvigorate loyalty.

Name

Because newsletters have the authority of a regularly written, edited, and
published periodical, they should have an authoritative name. Not "newsletter" or "update" but a name that identifies them. Authors are never known as
Writer, or Biographer #265. They have the authenticity of a real person, with
real skills and a discernible reputation. So the newsletter of the Smithsonian's U.S. Postal Museum is called *Postmark*. The Old Colorado City Historical Society sends it news in *West Word*. Bessemer Historical Society's
Steelworks Museum, in Pueblo, Colorado, names its newsletter *Bessemer
Blast*.

Mission

Your mission as a museum is to collect, preserve, interpret, and educate.
Your brand mission will be more specific. And both missions require that
you continually reinforce your message. Newsletters are excellent ways to
keep spreading the word and defining it. Why is the International Horse
Museum's mission to show "the relationship between man and the horse
throughout history and the world?" As you read the newsletter, you'll see

why. The brand has a philosophy and attitude that can be reiterated in every article, every event, every employee appreciation initiative. A newsletter, with its spaciousness and its large audience, is the perfect place to put forth your mission, and not just the brief statement, in front of the public.

Tamástslikt Museum in Pendleton, Oregon, is another museum with a laser-sharp mission. It tells the history of three tribes, first documented by Meriwether Lewis. How did these tribes earn an astute explorer's special attention? Readers of the newsletter will learn the "because" in every issue.

Selecting and writing about activities that reinforce the brand requires cause-and-effect writing. Relating a workshop, or acquisition, or new store merchandise to the brand requires, frankly, lengthy sentences. Writers will use a style of writing that includes conjunctions. So start practicing phrases like:

So . . .

Because . . .

In order to . . .

As you'll see . . .

So our summer schedule gives families more opportunities to visit and learn science together.

Because this exhibition is so interactive, we can achieve our mission of making architecture more approachable.

In order to give you a behind-the-scenes glimpse of our textile collection, we've redesigned our conservation studios.

As you'll see from the list of workshops, our heritage is ever developing.

Name Your Events

Make sure your event has a branded name before you blast it to your entire mailing list. Remember that the people in your database likely belong to several cultural organizations, and at event time they can get confused. Don't call it Afternoon Tea. Do call it Kettledrum Tea, as the National Churchill Museum titles its annual fall tea. The name comes from the Victorian era, when this kind of tea was popular and widespread. Actually, anyone can use the name, but the Churchill Museum does use it. If you list an open house on your calendar, name it Friday Meet and Greet. If you offer a lecture series, name it the Expert Series. If your spring bulb sale is a popular event, name it Trowel Days. Your newsletter then reinforces your brand every time it headlines Expert Series Begins Its New Fall Schedule. By giving an event a brand name, it's easier to tie that event to the brand and mission of the museum.

Your events are intellectual property. You don't just create a compelling activity, you devise its format, build the systems for managing it, write the job descriptions for the various tasks, design the marketing materials, choreo-

graph the flow, fabricate the props and decorations for the setting, and research the results. You have an original, so give it a proprietary name.

Full Names of Artists and Exhibitions

More than good journalism is involved here. Artists' names are their brand,
and when you show respect for his or her distinctiveness, you reinforce your
own distinctive brand. When you write the entire name of your exhibition,
you reassert your ownership of this intellectual property and its role in your
brand. Many museums engage their constituents with arts and craft workshops, but the Vesterheim Norwegian-American Museum brands their event:
"Learn to Knit Like the Vikings Did—nålbinding." It quickly reinforces the
museum's brand of Norwegian living heritage. And it pops on a busy landing
page, adding to the brand of the whole newsletter.

Subject Line of E-mail

When newsletters were printed documents, the first page was visible, the
museum logo could be identified, and the name was spelled out. With e-mail,
you have a small space to accomplish the same identification. Watch out for
Subject lines that don't tell the news in the first few words. On some screens,
or forwarded e-mail, ends of sentences can be cut off.

However, don't count on acronyms to save space. The letter "M," for
example, appears in most museum acronyms; spell out your name, or your
brand identity will disappear in the sea of Ms.

The most popular e-mail Subject lines are also the least brand-useful.
Holiday News, Spring Happenings, and Weekly Updates are empty words.
Everybody uses them and they say nothing about your museum.

Updates

About updates. It's newsy and it's worthwhile to update news of an exhibition, or an education initiative, or a social media campaign. But updates also
encumber and dilute the strong brand story as it was originally told. You
must assume that the reader has never read the original story. It will take tight
writing, but try to recap the who, what, when, where, and how of a story,
each time you update it. As a rule of thumb, imagine your readers (a) have
never picked up your newsletter, (b) know little about your museum, (c) may
have received the newsletter as forwarded e-mail from a friend, (d) are not in
your database. Then write to them as you did the first time you told the story.

Observe the Scroll-Down Factor

You know what you design into a newsletter page, but the reader has to scroll down to see it all. Prioritize your material so that your name, headline, and branded copy come first. Save more general information—such as "for more information call"—for the end of the scroll.

Be cautioned by these examples of newsletter mishaps that ignored all the rules of writing for the brand.

Don't:

- Allow an advertising banner to be the first visual a reader sees. One museum newsletter opened with a tower banner ad for a resort vacation in a foreign country. It doesn't just dilute your brand message, it misconstrues it.
- Design the issue number and date in such large type that this nonessential (to the reader) information obscures the lead article's headline.
- Lead with an article about a preschool program. It's worthy and timely, but it's not strongly advised for the objectives of awareness, continuity, connection, development, internal engagement, lapsed-member retrieval, and branding. With all due respect to all the good stories out there, don't write about them unless you can link them to the interests of the A-C-C-D-I-L-B audiences.
- Position as the second article in a scroll-down a promotion expiration date. All brands have sales. This message does nothing for your brand. And the end date limits interest.
- Mismatch photos to stories, like the museum that highlighted an adult education program with a visual of a child.
- Use valuable space for negatives, such as "Our closed gallery is reopening." If the news is positive, devote all your words to what's new and why it's significant to your mission. Hence, "Visit our new Innovation Gallery and see the future of history."
- End the scroll with another ad for the foreign resort. The last impression must be of your brand. Just as you would like visitors to leave the museum with a memory of your brand personality, so it is with a screen.

Electronic communication flies by so fast, you have to guard your possessions carefully.

By heeding your brand, you select words that are distinctive, relevant, and, frankly, interesting to the newsletter reader. In the digital world, this has another value: search engine marketing. According to SEM expert Dan Quinn, every new issue of your newsletter is full of new keywords that search engines look for. More new words, the higher on the list your entry appears. So a well-wrought newsletter, with words relevant to your brand, invigorates search.

Communication creep is starting to waste precious time. Museums, especially, cannot afford to spend resources on messages that aren't strategic. The newsletter is one marketing tool that thrives on strategy, and if you remember the goals of awareness, continuity, connection, development, internal engagement, lapsed-member retrieval, and branding, newsletters will work very hard for you.

Chapter Twelve

Pinterest, Twitter, and Social Media Strategies

Take a look at the bottom of any museum website: the "f" and "t" in a box, and "P" in a circle, are the most commonly used icons out of all the social media platforms available to institutions that want to share news and ideas with their publics. Yes, they've been winnowed down to just a few. You've got to be choosy, because when you stamp any one of those familiar symbols on your website, you join familial cultures with their own cultish habits that must be obeyed. You can—underline can—benefit from the unique advantages that each offers, but everyone from the largest art museum to the smallest house museum selects only a few, and marketing strategy is required to select which one. Depending on your goals, the audiences and communities you want to reach, and the aspects of your museum that you want to promote, each platform plays a designated role in a multipronged marketing effort; each is more effective when you write to their individual strengths. Most people live by Facebook. Many swear by Pinterest. There's a large following for Twitter and a devoted group for many others. Well-established audiences watch YouTube like they watch television, and readers who once flipped pages of newspapers and magazines now head for blogs.

This chapter gives you an overview of Twitter and Pinterest as examples of different platforms' targets and tools. Of course, there are many other platforms, and there will be more. Once you're aware of the differences, you'll be able to discern the benefits of new ones as they emerge. As you work with the most knowledgeable social media expert on your staff, keep the strategic differences in mind; they will help you ask informed questions.

To begin getting a handle on the many platforms, here's one easy classification, based on word count:

- Few words—Pinterest
- One hundred and forty characters—Twitter
- Sixty to eight hundred words—Blogs
- Four to six minutes of words—YouTube
- Infinite number of words—Facebook

Pinterest requires the fewest number of words necessary to communicate because its format is visual. Twitter limits the writer severely. Blogs let you write as much as you want, but you don't need more than a short paragraph if you post regularly. YouTube videos are best at four to six minutes, up to five hundred words, depending on how fast you talk. Facebook lets you say as much as you want, and the variety of messages is harder to write than just one focused post. All social media feature the equivalent of a headline and text: the headline communicates the main message briefly and the text elucidates at more length.

You can also characterize the five frequently used media platforms by their market segments:

- Facebook—supersize and mass communities
- Twitter—loyal followers of a person or idea
- Pinterest—lovers of visuals, organizers, club people, personal event planners
- Blogs—Curious learners and autodidacts
- YouTube—Information seekers, fans of the YouTuber

For museums, whose missions are based on the collection, preservation, interpretation, and dissemination of information, the most critical categorization is by authorship and authority:

- Facebook has many authors, who edit by "liking" you and commenting on you
- Twitter and Pinterest exist to be shared; whatever you write will be commented on, forwarded, "favorited," retweeted, and repinned by many others.
- Blogs and bloggers own their messages; they can be commented on later, but initially they are signed by an author and given the respect due an author.
- YouTube also owns its message, and it is the most obviously authored because you see a real person on the screen who with thoughtful creativity illustrates his or her distinctive message.
- Twitter and Pinterest see their messages constantly reframed, but despite the blurring of their original thought, a careful writer has ways to keep your name front and center.

TWITTER

Twitter is celebrated for its waterfall of communiqués, tweets cascading all over the landscape, inundating any Twitter participant who logs on. But what makes the fame of Twitter is the strategic advantage of followers. When a museum, or any organization, posts messages on Twitter, they are found by communities of people who then commit. They commit to the actual sender of the message, or to a group of like-minded people connected by a current interest or cause. Followers are an important category for museums; you don't want just visitors, but loyalists.

"Want to ID Tree Pests & Diseases?"

The tree-pest tweet originated at the Natural History Museum, London. The goal was to first spread the word about a 2013 citizen research project, an environmental science study, and then, more importantly, to enlist the aid of amateur scientists throughout the UK in collecting evidence of everything from air particles to tree roots. Although a consortium of UK institutions contributed to the data gathering, NHM seemed to have the Twitter presence and its 140-character requests for help were irresistible.

The writing suited the strategy. They asked for help, not visitors. They engaged a community of people who cared about the environment and enjoyed productive spare time activities. The words reached this community pretty efficiently, without meandering through other viewers, by stating their project and its goal. Kickstarters and crowdsourcers have used Twitter with enviable success because they follow that format: name your cause and your goals right off the bat. The tweet in the example leads with one action verb and two strong nouns: "Want to ID tree pests & diseases?" And it ends with "Our tree scientists need you." Because you have word limits, strive for the unexpected word, particular to your museum.

The point of Twitter is getting devotees. It's not what you tweet, but what gets retweeted. So you've got to get people talking. A tweet has to be provocative, conversation starting, and timely. To be provocative you need action verbs and unexpected nouns that say something other people might want to talk about. To start a conversation, you have write words that invite rather than opine. To be timely, you have to understand the zeitgeist and listen to what's topical in the world of your readers. Museums that tweet don't have to pour out messages every hour, every day, but timeliness suggests a certain regularity. The addition of hashtags to home in on specific topics is more than just a Twitter feature; it signifies focus and a strategic genius for starting conversations other people want to join.

Here's a neat example of topicality and visual nouns:

Welcome 2014! Confetti has fallen, our resolutions are in place, now check
out the artists to watch for 2014! http:// ow.ly/rRgme #newart (116,138)

This retweet comes from the Speed Art Museum in Louisville, Kentucky.
I love the word "confetti," which comes after only fourteen other characters.
The tweet announces a topic—new artists on the horizon—that is of interest
to museumgoers, one that also invites comments and reader input of other
artists. Notice how characters add up as viewers retweet, and how crowded
the text is getting. Since that's the whole goal of Twitter, keep your headlines
short so that your name and topic stay prominent.

Twitter Communities

Twitter reaches out to many well-defined communities, each topic reaching
people with discrete interests. Those interest range from sports stars to politi-
cal causes to museum exhibitions. Good marketing writing demands tweets
that have distinct communities in mind. In the following examples, it's the
community of teachers of science.

My year 7 class would like to know how cold it would have to be for a polar
bear to freeze.

If the Sun was as tall as you are, the Earth would be about the size of your
thumbnail.

These are some of the tweets and retweets flying through the digisphere
during Ask a Curator Day @AskACurator, from, respectively, @cowgeogra-
phy and @airandspace on September 18, 2013.

This campaign from England united a group of museums under the hash-
tag #AskACurator. It was open to any museum, and any interrogator,
throughout the world, and museums from New Zealand and Australia to
Poland and the United States asked and answered. No question was too large
or too small and with 140 characters limiting their responses, the curators had
to answer with simplicity. This is social media at its finest because it con-
verses with those whose interests mesh, and helps distinct communities reach
out and grow logically. Traditional media might reach mainly schoolchildren, or their teachers; in this case, curators are targeted, and they have an
unusual opportunity to learn from each other. As the *Guardian*'s Mar Dixon
points out, "It's a great way for the sector to share learning and knowledge
too."

Twitter, with its accessible shorthand style of writing, helps museums get
down to earth with people who may find them intimidating. If you're a
science museum, you can join the Ask a Curator campaign, and if you're
another kind of museum, you can frame your own challenge to a community

of your choice: "Stump the Gardener"; "Why I Loved My Field Trip"; "Name the Baby Giraffe"; "If I Lived in a Lighthouse." Also, announce this event in your other media. For example, the thinking behind the event is appropriate for a longer blog article. It could be the subject of an e-mail, a piece of news that keeps your database aware of museum activities. If you're writing a grant proposal, a campaign that garners responses is an important documentation of your audience.

Create a Celebrity to Follow

Twitter works because people follow leaders or ideas. The most-followed leaders are well-known heroes from the worlds of entertainment, sports, and politics. However, celebrities can be created, and the Art Institute of Chicago did just that with Jean-Paul Brunier (@jeanpaul19), an outgoing, boulevardier dressed in the top hat and black frock coat of the men in the paintings of Manet, Renoir, and Seurat featured in *Impressionism, Fashion, and Modernity*, the blockbuster 2013 exhibition. Impersonated on the streets of Chicago by a local actor, Jean-Paul finds himself in a strange city in the wrong century, commenting with joyful fascination on what he sees as he ambles through Chicago's neighborhoods. He is bemused by American cheese and Chicago weather, and his tweets resound with enthusiasm for his found city:

> It would seem that I left my Umbrella in the nineteenth century. C'est horrible. [Sept. 9]

> What a relief! I will not be the only one wearing something attention getting @ChiJazzFest tonight. [Aug. 29]

> . . . I did not know one could wear one's shirt outside one's pantaloons. Truly American is the land . . . [Aug. 29]

People followed him. And they could follow your museum's tweeter if you created one. Here are some suggestions if you have a:

Historic House

A historic house is peopled by dozens of characters worth following, from the prosperous head of household to the servants to the townspeople who pass it daily, and it is part of the museum's job to bring them to life. You already do it in labels, panels, educational programs, and tours. It would be very enjoyable for a wider audience to follow any of these historic folks as they tweeted—pithily and wittily, of course—on their daily lives. I'd love to read the reactions of the people who, over the years, received their U.S.

Passion for Fashion

A museum-wide celebration of style inspired by
Impressionism, Fashion, and Modernity

ART
INSTITVTE
CHICAGO

Figure 12.1. The passion for fashion, described in this brochure for the Art Institute of Chicago's 2013 exhibition, *Impressionism, Fashion, and Modernity*, crossed many platforms, including a delightful Twitter campaign penned by a fictional nineteenth-century Parisian boulevardier suddenly transplanted to the streets of Chicago. *Courtesy Art Institute of Chicago.*

citizenship at Thomas Jefferson's Monticello, an idea suggested by this tweet:

> First new citizen to speak! #welcomenewcitizens #monticellojuly4th http:// Monticello.org/July4Live

Science Museum

A science museum might find a famous inventor in its archives, and bring that person's thinking to life. Another tweeter might be a current curator, intern, or educator talking about his or her daily routines. A running recount of weather tracking, or a daily nutrition tip, are two topics of enduring interest.

Tweets from Thomas Jefferson

Thomas Jefferson was profligate in his talents, but his tweeters excel at penning 140-character tweets from Monticello, the historic home in Virginia that embodies many of his accomplishments. The Twitter feeds from Thomas Jefferson's Monticello had gold to work with and didn't waste time getting to the nuggets that describe Monticello's events. It gets to the point in less than fifty characters in these examples:

> Map of where the 80 applicants for naturalization are from.#July4th pic. twitter.com/BGOPCDoai7 [Monticello @ TJMonticello July 4, 2013]
>
> Design innovations of @TJMonticello hailed in the August issue of @Southern_Living "South's Best Historic Homes," http://bit.ly/14RecQD [Monticello @ TJMonticello July 26, 2013]
>
> Graduating from TJ's University deserves a meal on his lawn! Join us Friday 6-8:30pm: http://bit.ly/K9WrwW @UVA @uva2013 @HoosNetwork [Monticello @ TJMonticello May 16, 2013]

To get quickly to the point, avoid starting a tweet with "Join us on . . ." or "Read about . . ." In the waterfall of Twitter conversation, Thomas Jefferson and his home emerge pristine. Again, here are examples of topics rich enough to be given fuller treatment in a blog on citizenship or a Pinterest board on gardening. Museums of all sizes must remember that no one platform can do everything, and the skills of a tweeter can and should be used in other media platforms.

Familiarize yourself with the demands of Twitter, or any other social media, including the tight editing. There's never a benefit to wordiness and experienced writers know to avoid it. Writers always expect to edit themselves, to select and revise and cut, and that's as difficult as the research and writing. It's tiring work, of course, so here's advice from a very reputable source: *New York Times* columnist David Brooks recommends writing for only three hours a day.

PINTEREST

Viewers come to Pinterest carefully, selectively, because they like flower arranging, or crepes, or architecture. And here's the joy and trauma of Pinterest: searching for any of those interests, the flower/crepe/architecture aficionado might end up at a board for weddings. Museums might want to feature their facilities as wedding venues, and include images of flowers, breakfast buffets, and sunny courtyards, but their images will be pinned and repinned by people enjoying pictures of anything from lilies to breakfast to masonry. So, when you put a photo on your own board of your Italianate terrace, you will reach architecture buffs and travelers, as well as facilities renters. Very uncontrollable! But if you write captions, you can start to take advantage of the Pinterest form. If your board features a photo of your beautiful terrace, perfect for outdoor weddings, write a short heading that says "Italianate terrace perfect for outdoor weddings." You'll be identified for several communities, not just the wedding planners, and a viewer who happened upon your photo looking for #architecture might repin your photo on her #museumweddings board. Pinterest isn't the best platform for targeting specific audiences, but it opens you to many others.

Pinterest demands a keyword-heavy style of writing to fulfill its strategy of reaching multiple narrow niches. Both the heading of the board and the individual captions under your pins are loaded with words that other pinners look for. Here's how the High Museum of Art, Atlanta, seeds its board with keywords for its 2013 exhibition, *Girl with a Pearl Earring: Dutch Paintings from the Mauritshuis*. The underlining is mine.

> Who's that <u>Girl</u>?
> One of the most famous <u>paintings</u> in the world, <u>Johannes Vermeer's</u> "<u>Girl with a Pearl Earring</u>," is making her <u>Southeastern</u> debut this summer at the <u>High</u>! The <u>Girl</u> is depicted throughout the world in a variety of different forms, from <u>Legos</u> to <u>iPad drawings</u>. "Girl with a Pearl Earring: <u>Dutch Paintings</u> from the <u>Mauritshuis</u>" is on view at the High from Jun. 23–Sept. 29, 2013. Check out our special website for this exhibition: http://www.high.org/Girl-With-A-Pearl-Earring.aspx

The captions to each pin also contain words that resonate with several themes, each one of them a niche community. The underlining is mine:

> Blue <u>mosaic</u> of the *Girl with a Pearl Earring*

Lego portrait of *Girl with a Pearl Earring*

ArtNews weighs in on the changing face of the *Girl with a Pearl Earring*

Bottle cap art

The Art Toast Project: Johannes Vermeer, *Girl with a Pearl Earring*

The *Mona Lisa* with the *Girl with a Pearl Earring*, a.k.a. the Mona Lisa of the North!

It doesn't take too many clicks to discover niche markets of people who collect themes such as the *Girl with a Pearl Earring*—made of balloons, bottle caps, and pixels—Lego art, art of the brick, spool of thread art, and girls parodied as Daisy Duck and Marge Simpson.

Pinterest themes represent niche audiences, not necessarily target audiences for your museum, so Pinterest is not nearly as direct a strategy as Facebook or Twitter. You won't necessarily reach people who already "like" you. You won't reach people who already follow you. Pinterest reaches people who appreciate good visuals. Pinterest visuals, the ones you repin, have arresting concepts; they're beautifully photographed, professionally cropped, and carefully curated. Pinterest images are discovered by a community of people who appreciate originality in art and design. And museums, which ooze design from their facades to their objects to their exhibitions, resonate with this group. Use Pinterest to achieve a strategy of multiple niches; you may be found by audiences you never thought of.

Because a photo on your museum's board could end up anywhere as a repin, captions reassert your authority wherever it goes.

Here's a repin of "*The Letter Revenge*, Frederic Edwin Church, 1844–47, at Allen Memorial Art Museum, Oberlin College," which was pinned to the J. Paul Getty Museum Pinterest board. On this museum's board it joined with many other photos under the rubric:

J. Paul Getty Museum
Los Angeles, California
In which we consider the many stories of art. Join us.

Suddenly the reader has a reason to follow the Getty, rather than the Allen. If a museum is doing its Pinterest job correctly, this appropriation will happen all the time. So put a caption under your photo that will travel with and identify you as clearly as the old travel stickers on a steamer trunk.

You can also theme your own board, to give your museum a degree of ownership over all the photos you collect from your colleagues. Here's an example from the Metropolitan Museum:

#The Dog: Emblem, Performer, Friend

The Met gives its hashtags and individual boards descriptive headings so when viewers happen upon an image of John Singer Sargent's *Woman with Collie*, they know where to find other works that celebrate man's and woman's best friend.

The Ogden Museum of Southern Art, New Orleans, lets the first line of the caption state the theme, as in:

> "When You're Lost, Everything's a Sign: Self-Taught Art from The House of Blues" on view in New Orleans at the Ogden Museum of Southern Art until July 24, 2013.

The topic is in the first line. Pinners searching for sign visuals will find them at the Ogden. The topic should always precede the news in a pin. Don't start with empty words like "Last Days" or "This weekend is a perfect time to . . ." Pinners interested in collecting themes search for keywords on the theme, not dates. And they will continue to see your name long after the show has ended.

MARKETING TRUTHS FOR SOCIAL MEDIA

As you strategize your writing for social media, remember the marketing verities that underlie a new and growing discipline.

- Verity #1: The genius of social media is its ability to connect with, in columnist Jim Rudden's words, "an audience that cares."
- Verity #2: There are many audiences and communities who share common interests at any given time.
- Verity #3: Media, from wall painting to Twitter, is an intermediary. It carries messages between the person with something to say and the person who reads or hears it. Media doesn't create content; it connects other people's content.
- Verity #4: People choose to receive and listen to media. Therefore . . .
- Verity #5: Relevance is key. A communication won't get picked up unless it's of interest to the target audience.
- Verity #6: Social media transmits via networks and channels built by communities of like minds.
- Verity #7: Depth and richness matter. Don't believe the fogeys (old and young) who say young people can't hold a thought or decent discussion. Young people today dig deeper into life's subjects than any previous generation on earth. They do so by linking, commenting, and sharing.

- Verity #8: Social media is personal—individual to individual talking to each other. Blogs, posts, and tweets, whether written by a named author or the voice of the museum, each speak as a human. They all have personalities.
- Verity #9: There are as many kinds of social media as there are traditional magazines, TV shows, movies, and museums. Each platform has its own market and strategy. Just as marketers buy commercial time on *Monday Night Football* for different reasons than they buy a page ad in *Good Housekeeping*, you use Twitter or Pinterest, You Tube or blogs differently.
- Verity #10: There are disadvantages to any media choice, and if you want to control your message totally, develop your website. That one you own.
- Verity #11: Social media is meant to be shared. It's many-to-many, as opposed to one-to-many; a conversation, as opposed to a spiel. If your message doesn't get liked, retweeted, or repinned, it's not doing its job. It might start out as a one-to-many announcement, but it doesn't stay one sided for long. Look again at the message box on Facebook that says, "Write something." That doesn't augur deep thought. For every gain in audiences you lose the advantage of authorship.

MOVING INTO AUTHOR MODE

As you budget time, resources, and goals for your museum, you will decide when to place your strategy on the most shared and re-mediated social media such as Facebook, Twitter, and Pinterest, or take ownership of your intellectual property—your collection, interpretation, preservation, education plans, employee knowledge and dedication, and scholarship—and write blogs and YouTube videos. If those little icons were heralded at the top of your web page, rather than footnoted at the bottom, which ones would you focus on? Think twice. Instagram is hugely popular, though a little instantaneous for some marketers. And Vine is regaining the appeal it had originally, perhaps because its creativity is tempered with a six-second time limit. For now, if you want to send communications that are carefully strategized, thoughtfully executed, and 100 percent owned by their authors, museums need blogs and YouTube.

Chapter Thirteen

Public Relations

The mother-daughter tea flopped. Yes, the moms and girls turned out in force, gobbled the cookies, and networked like crazy with each other. Yes, they loved the museum venue. But the party cost a lot of money, ate up staff time, and stole the spotlight from the museum itself. Could good writing have saved this event? Yes, because the minute you wrote, "Dear Friend of the Museum," or "Dear Mom," or "Welcome to Our New Neighbors," you would have identified whom the party was for. This event had invited everyone, and they came because of the party, not the museum. The minute you target your public, you're on your way to a worthy public relations event.

Public Relations: Relationships with publics. That's the first definition I ever heard and the notion that there could be many publics—plural—opened my eyes to the importance of targeting what community you want to relate to.

Good PR writing uses the who, what, when, where, and why of journalism—a field where many PR people get their start—and who comes first. That's how you decide the nature of the relationship. In the case of a mother-daughter tea, for example, once the museum and the writer pinpoint whom the event wants to engage, the writing can make it succeed. Here are the audiences the museum could have targeted for its lovely party:

- Moms in the community
- Parents
- School-age children
- Little girls
- Families who aren't members
- Members who don't have family memberships

When you list the possible publics, you realize the objective of the event. And when you know that, you can write effective invitations, web page announcements, news releases, event-day handouts, the welcome speech from the director, captions to the event photographs, and follow-up materials. Of course, you can't predict who will accept your invitation, who will like the event, or whom they'll tweet and send photos to. But now you have a strategy to guide their judgment.

Unlike advertising, which is paid media, or your own website, which is owned media, PR is earned media, and it has always had to earn the attention of the communities it reaches out to. Those communities, those audiences, are people you talk to, not at, because after your message is sent, the receiver will share it on blogs, and every post and comment will widen your audience. Also, you're not communicating with citizen bloggers and posters, but professional journalists and editors who have special expectations. Digital journalists crave relevance and facts as they winnow through the stream of content. Communities may have specific agendas to pitch to journalists, but these communities are so huge, and share so much information, that only sharp, factual, pertinent writing can cut through the clutter on editors' desks and desktops and earn their attention.

There are six situations in which PR writing contributes to strong community engagement and a relationship with a public.

1. Events—fund-raising, thank you, or awareness—for members or prospects
2. Announcements—including news, news releases, announcements, launches
3. Seed and branch ideas
4. Business and cultural partners
5. Government relations
6. Community management

EVENTS

Events are publicists' dreams because they are so high profile; everyone notices the event and the client gets an infusion of excitement. Never mind the cost of caterers and decorations, photographers and videographers, handouts and media briefings; the flurry of attention results in increased museum goodwill. Or does it? The museum must reap awareness, lovability, and treasure or the event is just eventful, not meaningful. Whether you invest in an event for awareness, thank-you to members, or raising money, you need to link it back to the institution.

When the mother-daughter party scenario was confided to me some years ago, I thought it was simply a branding problem, inappropriate for a small-city history museum. That's too glib a response, and many good ideas are lost because of seeming inappropriateness. Smarter to get back to the nub of the idea and write about why it seemed like a novel idea in the first place. Then write that reasoning into all media messages. Talk about the joys of mom and daughter learning; have the moms in the museum write moms-in-the-museum blogs; write tweets that start with words like "Mothers bring your daughter to the museum," and pin motherly relevant exhibits on Pinterest. Before you write a lead paragraph of your news release, talk to mothers of all ages about the benefits of showing your museum to their daughters, and construct your headline accordingly. I asked one mom why she liked to take her kids to the local art museum. She reminisced that it wasn't her sons she took, but her nieces, and she loved listening to them explain the art to each other. There's a story there that will add humanity to the event, and meaning to your museum. But how do you write the headline? Fair question. Take dictation from a child. A lot of headlines come from that source.

In addition to news releases and social media posts, add the event to your website, where there is space for a short paragraph on the significance of mother-daughter learning. Use the same headline you wrote for the news release on any brochure you create in advance. And don't forget these other communities who will be interested in your event:

Volunteers: Provide your store volunteers with a short script that can be spoken whenever a children's book or gift is sold: "If this is for your daughter, please come to our mother-daughter tea. It's a wonderful way to learn more about our museum."

Educators: Use your database of educators to communicate with teachers who are also mothers of daughters: "And here's a special treat just for you and your daughters. . . ."

Family: Create a Mother-Daughter Learning Guide to hand out at the event. This relates the fun of the party to the pleasure of learning at the museum. And on the bottom write: "Please take this home and share it with the rest of your family." You might even add a discount for admission, or purchase at the store or café. Because so many of the adults in this group might be grandmothers, aunts, or other caregivers, you have ambassadors to a whole network of potential visitors.

Closer to the event, put signs or flyers around the museum to announce it. Instruct all guards and information desk staff about the event.

For the event itself, provide an "escort" for the photographer and/or videographer, as well as some suggestions on what to shoot. When the shots are planned, preface them with: "This will make a wonderful picture for our mother-daughter learning at the museum." That kind of context helps photographers do their job. And at the end of the evening you might want to give them some passes so they can bring back their daughters. By the way, add passes to the tip you give the caterer.

Whether your event is a party, preview, lecture, workshop, or trip, the same kind of writing applies: Connect the event to the venue. This connection is especially powerful when you realize the reach of the informal attendees—the serving staff, photographers, and caregivers.

ANNOUNCEMENTS AND NEWS RELEASES

The classic admonition about public relations is how uncontrollable it is. You simply cannot tell a journalist what to write, as these unfortunate headlines demonstrate:

Cut Adrift by Its Would-Be Rescuer, Seaport Museum Seeks a Lifeline

N.Y. Maritime Museum Afloat in Troubles

Exec Who Managed Modern Wing Capital Campaign Departs

The ongoing story of New York City's South Street Seaport Museum got off to a bad PR start in the news in early 2013 when water metaphors and puns inundated stories about the museum's money problems. The situation was a lack of major funding, a long recession that hurt all not-for-profits, and Hurricane Sandy, which critically damaged many Eastern Seaboard businesses. Hence, there were headlines like . . . swamped, capsized, bailing out, submerge. There's no squelching the gleam in the eye of a journalist who suddenly has a lot of sea metaphors to play with. But the first job of a news release writer is to write a positive, informative headline. Finally, a headline told the story straight: "A Plan in the Works for Seaport Museum." One can't know if good wording in a news release got this positive headline, but facts are hard workers when it comes to wrestling jokesters. It certainly seemed like the news release must have been heavy on facts and told with a positive attitude and businesslike tone of voice, totally forswearing eager writers from using shipwreck prose. There's a time for wit in writing, and there's a time for seriousness. You can't prevent journalists from spinning a news release any way they please (yes, journalists do a lot of spinning), but no-nonsense writing will help.

In the case of administrators leaving a museum, a more positive headline will read: "Exec Heads for Houston," which is where, in fact, the abovementioned CFO was going; and he was going there to head the capital campaign for another major museum. Once again, the full story made for a more interesting story and, regardless of which museum sent the release, cast both in a favorable light.

Most news releases announce proud achievements rather than problems, and exciting arrivals rather than departures, but a well-written headline is always needed. We're not talking spin or exaggeration; we're talking facts and vibrant nouns and verbs. "Announcing New Curator" and "Museum Acquires Farm Implement Collection" contain dull verbs and nonvisual nouns.

Here, from one news release headline, springs a combo of intriguing verb and soaring noun:

SFMOMA Unveils New Grand Stair Design

When you consider that San Francisco's lovely museum is closed for expansion until 2016, such a dramatic headline is both unusual and necessary. A more prosaic headline could have resulted in a news story, online or off-line, that started with "Though Shuttered . . ."

The museum also used two good adjectives in its releases announcing the expansion:

SFMOMA Appoints Two New Deputy Directors during Its Transformational Expansion

SFMOMA Museum Store Offers Creative Gifts for the Holidays

Good writing transformed the closing to "transformational" and ho-hum holiday gifts to "creative."

Sometimes good writing is just selecting the more interesting of two facts. The Burke Museum of Natural History and Culture in Seattle published this news release in October of 2013:

Old Man House Collections Come Home

The story was about the collection's new home, the Suquamish Museum at the Burke. The writer could choose between two excellent proper nouns for the headline, and selected "Old Man House." It's easier to read and pronounce than "Suquamish," and instantly evocative of the cultural heritage that is part of the Burke's DNA.

Another path to headline writing winds through the body of the news release. Here's the headline of a news release from Old Sturbridge Village, Massachusetts, in September 2013:

Early American Music Historian David Hildebrand to Speak at Old Sturbridge Village Oct. 3

It's excellent, but there are others to choose from in the body of the news release. Would you substitute any of these thoughts for the existing headline?

Expert on the Star-Spangled Banner and patriotic music . . . how music and poetry became musical extensions of patriotism . . . one of the most familiar patriotic anthems in the world, according to Old Sturbridge Village historians . . . set to the tune of a popular British drinking song . . .

It's normal for professional writers to warm to their subject as they write through it, thereby finding their headlines as they write, reread, rewrite, and edit. Of course, museum people don't have that luxury of time, but you can actually save a lot of time by putting all your thoughts down at length, and then selecting key thoughts to try out as headlines. In the long run, this way of selecting headlines is much quicker than muddling around in your head for just the right one.

At the end of a news release is the "boilerplate," your institution's description, a tightly written paragraph that summarizes your size, location, scope, area served, vision, even your brand personality. It is standardized, so all media get the same message. It is factual so that it will be picked up intact, and not mistaken for puffery. It's a quick reference for journalists that need to know exactly what they're writing about. In the best scenario, a journalist will write, in her own words, the kind of statement that Hilarie Sheets uses in her article about Skidmore College's Frances Young Tang Teaching Museum and Art Gallery. Ms. Sheets says:

The Tang is . . . distinguished for its large-scale interdisciplinary shows . . . [organized] every year in partnership with various Skidmore faculty members who go on studio visits, write catalogue essays, and help design the exhibition layout.

It's great public relations when a magazine writer describes your distinctiveness, and you boost that possibility with factual writing. We have no way of knowing what the Tang news release or boilerplate said, but journalists find details interesting and they respect facts.

SEED AND BRANCH IDEAS

Sometimes you have to dig around a little to discover a growable idea. The extensive Ringling Museum in Sarasota, Florida, did so with its sixteenth-century restored Italian theater, the Asolo. As a museum it was elegant and so small that it was open mainly by appointment. But it was a theater, and when it partnered with local film and arts organizations, it branched out to the community in ways that complemented the other Ringling museums. The

Ringling also comprises one of the world's largest art museums, and its James Turrell site-specific work, "Joseph's Coat Skyspace," has transmogrified from a singular work of art to a contemplation place where one is encouraged to bring a yoga mat. That's another community branched out to.

Crystal Bridges Museum of American Art, in Bentonville, Arkansas, holds sheet music in its collection, and can provide sing-alongs for community groups. All types of museums find nuggets of possibility. Old Sturbridge Village, a living history museum, counts among its holdings examples of Nathan Lombard furniture, and that led to a partnership with ten other Massachusetts museums to honor the legacy of Bay State furniture. Whoever takes the lead for welding these multipart concepts, it's the job of public relations writing to show its relevance and suggest a range of written formats. Think of the key terms: furniture, Massachusetts, interior design, antiques, and travel. From these the website can showcase the partnership and its significance. There's a blog on furniture just begging to be written. A news release to travel writers can highlight the touring trails, complete with local restaurants and inns. The State of Massachusetts Department of Tourism might also be interested. Now that you've identified communities beyond the traditional museum visitor audience, the writer's job is 80 percent completed. How about a workshop on antiques preservation? It's the function of public relations to discover some seeds that could branch out endlessly. By the way, since PR people are trained as writers, when you interview them consider adding writing to the job specifications.

Livestock breeders, heritage seed farmers, and wetland management experts are three of the communities in the Garfield Farm Museum address book. The Campton Hills, Illinois, institution reaches out far beyond its patch of prairie to bring people with shared interests together by connecting with agribusiness, scientists, and universities. This kind of public relations grows from years of attending conferences, sending and responding to mailings, making and keeping contacts, and staying attuned to the needs of the communities it serves. There's an adult focus that parallels the more typical grammar school field trips, and it educates with workshops for professionals and internships for college students, two communities that many museums could cultivate. In fact, if museums didn't give these groups a forum, they might not have one at all, and this kind of uniqueness is a godsend for writing distinctive copy. Garfield Farm invested time and money in an event for animal breeders, a rare breed show. This specific audience and subject has many more facts and anecdotes to write about, and is much easier to publicize than a mother-daughter tea.

Any history museum of any size that holds objects like antique tools, quilts, or sheet music has just identified three communities—at minimum— to which they can expand their reach. The PR release can start with a headline as simple as "Hello, Fiddlers," or "#JacobsLadder Is Calling All Quilters." Or, "Apple Coring Demonstration at Fall Festival Days." It's all about seeing the people at the other side of the exhibit case, and writing for the way they would interact with your exhibits. To get better writing ideas churning, prime your thinking with phrases like this: "People like music because . . ." Or, "Who gave quilts their name?" Or, "How do you use an apple corer?" PR people should remember their journalism training and ask questions. The written words will come quickly.

BUSINESS AND CULTURAL PARTNERS

Inviting local businesses to team up with your museum is flattering to them because it is so effective. The guiding concept is that their standing in the community lends you a solidity and belonging that's invaluable in appealing to new audiences.

For example, if there are food-oriented businesses in your community, any size or genre of museum can parlay an artwork, botanic, or historic concept into a food event. The Art Institute of Chicago stirred its 2013 exhibition *Art and Appetite: American Painting, Culture, and Cuisine* into the Chicago world of business in three particularly good learning moments.

The first corporate tie-in was the more conventional: a congratulatory letter in the exhibition catalog from the lead sponsor, ADM, the food-processing giant that markets to the world from central Illinois. The letter gracefully linked its company's product—agricultural ingredients—to abundance, wholesome eating, Chicago, and Midwest culture. Presumably the Art Institute's strategy was to enlist as lead sponsor a brand that reflected the objectives of the exhibition; the Art Institute is, after all, a wise marketer. The writing wisely reflected that strategy, and I bet that the public relations department of the museum helped outline, write, or edit it; it hit all the right points.

The second tie-in, with Chicago restaurants, was rather radical, printed in full color at the entrance to the exhibition: a sign listing participating local restaurants and, in the racks where visitors usually find brochures, postcards with a painting from the show on one side and recipes from "Chicago's leading chefs" on the other. The postcards were headlined with witty invitations to eat: "It's Five O'clock Somewhere," said the headline above Gerald Murphy's *Cocktail*. On the card depicting Wayne Thiebaud's *Salad, Sandwiches, and Dessert*, a reassuring headline reads, "The Diet Starts Tomorrow." And accompanying Norman Rockwell's iconic family dinner, "Let's Talk Turkey."

The same recipes, and many more, were featured on the Art Institute website, accompanied by videos of the chefs talking about their food. This is a grand-scale expansion of the traditional museumgoing community to several overlapping communities, including not only art lovers, but also food lovers, food experts, and restaurants.

The third tie-in was a four-course tasting-menu dinner in the museum's smaller restaurant. Where the postcard flyers engaged the art-loving audience with reproductions of the artworks and saucy headlines, and the web pages reached the broader community, whose constituents like the Art Institute in particular and voluntarily visited the site, the dinner reached a rather select audience who not only visit the Art Institute and love to eat, but who also choose to pay $35 for a meal. Each course of the dinner, by the way, is described by the server, complete with historic references. And outside the restaurant is a selection of packaged foods for sale, with a simple card stating: "Take these great local products home today! All featured local products were produced in Illinois, Indiana, or Wisconsin."

GOVERNMENT RELATIONS

"All politics is local," said Tip O'Neill, late Speaker of the House of Representatives, and government relations means understanding the goals of local officials and helping them understand yours. This kind of engagement is a linking of arms in mutual advocacy: museums need government support and

Figure 13.1. Salt Lake City Library. Museums large and small are starting to emulate museums in everything from exciting architecture to their curated selections of books. *Provided by author.*

governments need the citizens that museums attract. In making a cogent argument for your needs, and each museum's is vividly different, there is one rule of thumb to remember: organize your talking points. Whether you're writing proposals, requests, or invitations to speak, succinctly state your museum's advantages and abilities to government bodies.

Advantages and abilities must be singular, worded in a way that shows them to be clearly the product of your museum, distinct from other museums or cultural institutions, and relevant to the government's goals. Tell the truth and use specifics:

> We provide supplementary educational modules to over 250 homeschooled children every year.

If that sounds generic, add "from October 15 to May 15." That's giving you an advantage.

> Our twelve-month visitor total in 2013 surpassed 50,000, a 10 percent increase over 2012.

You could append to that: "a 15 percent increase over 2008." If you simply want the mayor to address your annual benefit, write:

> Our museum reaches over 50,000 people each year, over 80 percent of whom visit from the three ZIP codes surrounding our building.
> Or,
> Our sponsors of this wonderful benefit represent the education and business communities in [your city], and we are proud to partner with them.

Talking points declare not only facts and statistics but provable references such as visitor studies, a facilities assessment, information from scholarly research, or media quotes. They should include size of museum, hours of operation, and number of employees (including salaried and volunteer; each consistency is of interest to governments). Talking points could expand occasionally to sample bios of the constituents you serve, examples of your educational programming, and specific objects in your collection. Attach a number to any of these talking points wherever possible; that helps government officials assess their value.

Use details and positive verbs and nouns. It's good writing and effective persuasion. The following talking points, taken from the American Alliance for Museums website, are part of a science-community request to Congress to fund STEM (Science, Technology, Engineering, Math) research in general, and science museum research as a concomitant. It uses specifics to support its summations.

Talking Points:

- "In 2009, the National Research Council of the National Academies re-
leased a report entitled *Learning Science in Informal Environments: People, Places, and Pursuits*, which found each year, tens of millions of Americans, young and old, explore and learn about science by visiting informal learning institutions, participating in programs, and using media to pursue their interests."
- "Do people learn science in nonschool settings? . . . The answer is yes."
- "Designed spaces—including museums, science centers, zoos, aquariums, and environmental centers—can support science learning."
- "People of all ages and backgrounds engage in informal science . . . [and museum] environments [and can] learn to be more comfortable and confident in their relationship with science."
- "[This is significant for] individuals from non-dominant groups who are historically underrepresented in science."

Talking points organize facts and references—the 2009 National Research Council report—and are worded conversationally. They don't opine or orate, but rather stimulate sincere conversation. They engage the community, relate to the public you seek to persuade, in this case a government.

COMMUNITY MANAGEMENT

Used to be, if a museum didn't want to buy media-placed advertising, they turned to a public relations firm. Those were the two choices. They knew they had to pay the PR firm, but somehow it didn't seem like the same kind of money one used to pay for advertising. It wasn't the same money then and it isn't now. PR firms have always persuaded rather than pontificated. They didn't send out headlines from the one to the masses. They gathered a circle of appropriate journalists, or a small coterie at a specific event or conference. Even when the interaction was with people walking down the street, it wasn't random: it was in a specified ZIP code, at a certain time of day. PR professionals discovered and fine-tuned guerrilla marketing (always spelled correctly; PR writers spell perfectly or get fired). They developed buzz marketing or whisper campaigns by enlisting genuine advocates of a product or cause to talk up the product to their friends of like minds; these volunteers got paid in product, sometimes, but the key to the relationship with the public was sincerity; those who buzzed did it for love, not reimbursement.

It's the same today, although with the unlimited possibilities of social communications, relationships with the public involve even more precisely delineated publics. Note that public relations still doesn't seek the mass messaging of advertising; they target their audiences very narrowly. A community could be as small as a neighborhood fighting a zoning law or as large as mothers against genetically modified baby food, but they are still niche populations. And so there is new language in the land, and it's based on community management.

As Elizabeth Merritt wrote in a newsletter article for the American Alliance of Museums newsletter, "When the Worcester Art Museum hires Adam Rozan as Director of Audience Engagement and the Oakland Museum of California engages Lisa Sasaki as Director of Audience and Civic Engagement, it signals a subtle but profound shift in organizational focus." And, I would add, in organizational attitude.

The most recent PR textbook I read says: "Public relations is engagement." It was a quote by Daniel J. Edelman, the late founder of a generations-old public relations firm. He was ahead of his time, and social media thrives because of this insight.

Community, engagement, facts. Over the years, public relations found it necessary to defend itself and its ethics. In fact, the profession of public relations has always taken the positive position of (1) knowing its publics, (2) engaging them with relevant writing and planning, and (3) working only from facts. Anyone writing public relations materials must withhold their fingers from the keyboard until they understand all three.

Chapter Fourteen

Solicitation Letters

Dear Friend,
Join now and get a 10% discount at the museum store.

There has to be a better way to ask for money! When you invite people to join your museum family, whether at the $30 membership tier or multi-thousand-dollar donor level, you're asking them to open their hearts, not just their wallets.

This chapter is not about fund-raising itself, a weighty matter best left to development experts who understand the wide range of legal nuances of "a gift." This chapter deals with emotion-based strategies that acknowledge the many shades of giving, and sharing. Start with the fundamental assumption that people like your museum and want to be part of it, and you can learn to write Ask letters that work hard and smart.

It can be argued that beginning members are more important than large donors, because they are likely to grow with you, whereas large donors can be fickle. The standard template of listing fifteen mediocre benefits available once one joins your museum isn't enough: it's too logical and pretty cheap logic at that. You want emotion. Traditional solicitation and membership letters lack distinctiveness and competitiveness because so many other museums and cultural organizations offer something similar. A free subscription to the museum magazine seems to offer a distinct gift, but you must admit that many museums have magazines, and then you must redouble your efforts to distinguish yours. See chapter 10 for help with this topic. Free tote bags, umbrellas, or garden hats are smart for advertising, because others will see members using them, but these gifts are common not-for-profit benefits, and will have to be of high—read: expensive—quality or design to be distinguishable. The ability to bring a friend, free, is beneficial but not original, and should be positioned as a gift of friendship, not a two-for-one deal. The real advantage is that you introduce your museum to a new prospect; be sure to follow up with the friend.

Although it's not wrong to offer, for example, 10 percent discounts on store purchases—in many states equal to the sales tax—there's a big difference between "not wrong" and "right." And for those who want to evolve toward right, there are many better ways to show the value of a museum membership; good writers will help you create better money-raising programs, in addition to better ways to ask for that money.

The following five strategies aim for people's loyalty in a highly competitive arts environment where many suitors—museums, theater, music, dance, and education organizations—vie for members' devotion.

1. Connect to community
2. Provide news
3. Relate to the season
4. Write a creation myth
5. Refer to friends' testimonials

STRATEGY #1: CONNECTING TO YOUR COMMUNITY

All museums, large and small, are part of communities, which themselves can be large or small. The museum-community bond is an emotional one of long standing. New York's Neue Galerie shows emotion-based strategy in a warmly evocative membership brochure that can be found, among many other delivery systems, in a tray at the front entrance of its grand nineteenth-century house. In the competitive New York environment where hundreds of arts organizations ask for one's affection, Neue Galerie does a commendable job of wooing. Here are the words: "This is an opportunity to become part of a community." Suddenly the curator-led tours and Thursday night parties seem warm and welcoming rather than standard-issue perks. Everyone wants to belong; they already have plenty of transactional membership deals to choose from. There's more to Neue Galerie's two-fold brochure than pretty words, of course: enticing pictures. Whereas many organizations suddenly forget to put on their best clothes when they come to your door asking for money in the equivalent of jeans and a T-shirt, the Neue Galerie dresses up its brochure with rich card stock printed with four-color photos, large enough to be seen. One really gets the sense of old Vienna, the brand identity of the museum.

Small museums have more easily identifiable communities, but they can learn from the example of a national museum. The National Museum of Women in the Arts reaches across the land, and still connects perfectly with its community. The Washington, D.C., museum begins its recent solicitation letter with this little fable:

> For too long, the most famous woman in art has been the *Mona Lisa* . . . [and] museum-goers line up for hours . . . all the while thinking, "What a great artist that man Leonardo was."

If one is at all inclined to support women artists, this opener hits the mark.

The Field, Chicago's natural history museum with very big fund-raising requirements, sent a membership mailing mirroring an experience of many small communities. It leveraged a local historic event, the Columbian Exposition of 1893, by mounting a fair-related exhibition, *Opening the Vaults: Wonders of the 1893 World's Fair.* Then the Field wrote a strategically smart sentence: "[The fair announced] . . . the return of a world-class city risen quite literally out of the ashes of a fire barely 20 years earlier." With those words the museum associated itself with its world-class city, in all its innovation and vigor. It's a funny thing about stating your pride in someone or something else: the excellence of the other redounds to you. The Field, also, is an institution of world class, loaded with innovation and vigor, and you understand this because they recognized it in another. It's the same with your museum; by dint of the soil it stands on, the DNA of your city is part of your DNA, and you become part of the shared memory of its history. All you have to do is write about it proudly.

You also connect with your community when you introduce members to museum professionals, invite them to events with like-minded members of the museum family, and affix their names to the donor wall. These are not just benefits, but signs of belonging.

Note to historical societies throughout the land: Your history, your artifacts, and your people ooze distinctiveness. Whether the pride of your museums is silver mines, railroads, whaling, folk songs, or ethnic groups, you must get those community specifics into your solicitation letters. It's not enough—it's much less than enough—to state that "our museum provides a rich insight into the history and culture of an important era in the history of the state." That's the kind of cliché verbiage and crushing generality that obliterates distinctiveness. Make sure your membership mailings point out your community's individuality in the first sentence. For example, "The Springfield County Historical Museum tells our fur-trading heritage in every artifact, exhibition and program. You can help us save, preserve, and interpret our history by . . ." And if you happen to live in Springfield, Spring Green, Spring Creek County, or Spring Hill, you can see the need to claim your own fame, loud and clear, at the beginning of every letter.

STRATEGY #2: NEWS—SPECIFIC, NOT SPECIAL

News doesn't have to be special, but it must be new. Your mailing—and by the way, a mailing can be digital as well as through the postal service—is like a letter to a friend, telling your friend what's happening in your life. When asking for money or membership, a specific new reason is an important justification. Why else should someone give to or join a museum that's always been there? In solicitation letters, as in letters throughout history, great letter writers take pen to paper because they have something new to report. And their recipients open this mail because they want that news. (Read the Dear Friend letters between John and Abigail Adams for splendid examples of promoting a great institution—in their case the United States of America—through the conveyance of everyday news.) For museums asking for members or money, news is a relevant way of saying we're smart and important. News is sharp, singular, and quickly understood as a good reason to ask for money. News is shorthand. A news headline conveys in three or four words the concept that your museum is robust and worthwhile. If you want to use the occasion of a new exhibition to ask for support, tell why the exhibition is so special; don't just offer it up as a membership deal. If you've scored an important speaker, announce what that notable will talk about; don't just sell the book-signing session as a member perk.

Even if your news is small—say, a new parking lot—there's probably a newsworthy reason why you're expecting more cars; it is very easy to write about paving if there's a story behind the project.

When it comes to the specificity of news, and the value of that approach in fund-raising, take a cue from social websites sites like Kickstarter.com. This fund-raising drive, for a local arts organization community, exemplifies a newsworthy event and a specific need:

> 2014 Atlanta Film Festival—Bring Artists to Atlanta
> When artists meet audiences in person, it's magic. Help us bring more film-makers—and more magic—to Atlanta in 2014.

Crowdsourcing or crowdfunding sites like Kickstarter.com, GoFund-Me.com, and GiveForward.com, offer copious examples of concise, purposeful writing. Each small campaign is competing for funds and must state its case carefully to prove its distinctive raison d'être. Good writing applies more than ever because you have so many amateurs competing for attention.

Remember to tell the story of your proposed project. Don't lead with how good everyone will feel, or how grateful the museum will be. That is understood. Just state up front the fund-raising objective—not the dollar goal! If you're raising money for new air-conditioning, say so and quickly segue to a story about how (if for example you're a historic home) nineteenth-century furniture wasn't built to withstand dry heat. If you need funds for a new paint job, tell a color story. If the goal is a new research space, write about what the people there actually research.

Ask questions of the people involved in your news. As with many writing assignments, the first job of a writer is research. If you aren't getting good stories, ask the interviewee this simple question: "Tell me how you got involved in this project." When people talk about themselves, they speak the language of the storyteller.

Know the audience for your news. Learn some lessons from the crowd-sourcing people. You have a significant potential audience in the folks who are emotionally involved in ad hoc causes. They aren't just younger, or digitally oriented; they're the cohort that cares and gives, the group that specifies on birthday party invitations (even to their children's birthday parties) to bring a gift for charity. They're the group that sometimes doesn't actually throw parties for birthdays; they meet instead at the local food pantry. Recent research, *The Millennial Impact Report*, conducted in 2013, shows that the millennial generation derides websites that don't have contemporary information, a generation that prefers their information based on causes, not institutions. For museums, that means relevance, something all museums strive for, but perhaps need to talk up when they ask for money. Millennials not only want to give but give often; over half express interest in monthly giving. This commitment is invaluable, the stuff of loyalty, and the emotional connection is manifest. Write stories about your news that are detailed and factual and also appeal to the heart.

Some more lessons to adapt from crowdsourcing or crowdfunding sites (actually, Kickstarter.com says established 501(c)(3) organizations are welcome to sign on with them):

- Keep your campaign focused. Aim for small-money funding, as well as large. It's a way to attract younger members.
- Appeal locally and draw on your many small communities within larger ones.
- Reveal insider details about the project because, after all, you're asking people to become insiders themselves by supporting you.
- Enhance this inside information with insights. Learn to use the conjunction "because." For example, "We've identified a new kind of display case that allows us to exhibit our more fragile maps, because many early papers cannot be shown in contemporary lighting for very long."
- Here's another word to add to the writer's vocabulary: "Why?" As in, Why do we need new administrative space? Why have we added a Family Science Day? Then answer the questions with "Because," and tell a story.
- Be open and honest. Say how much money you hope to raise, exactly how it will be spent, and how long the project will take. This is exactly the kind

of information you'd write into a grant proposal, and the people you're asking for money deserve the same transparency that foundations and the government require.

- Finally, remember pictures. Again, a lesson from social media. Users of those platforms speak and listen in photographs. And everyone, whether online, on apps, or on paper, responds to the visual message, so learn to curate your images wisely. Then write captions, because even the most photogenic of new projects—striking architecture, desirable acquisitions, or celebrated guest speakers—need explanation. Captions tell your story concisely. Cull your stories for the most intriguing words or phrases, and construct a one-sentence paragraph to position near the photo.

STRATEGY #3: SEASONALITY

Botanic gardens talk about the seasons. Charleston historic homes hail spring garden walks. Most historic homes hark and herald Christmas-decorated parlors. And those are just a few season-specific events that signal a reason to support your ever-refreshed museum.

Merchant's House, described as New York City's oldest preserved family residence, in fall plays on its distinction of being haunted. Ghost story tours, readings from Victorian-era Gothic tales, and a reenactment of the death and funeral of the home's patriarch perfectly coincide with the Halloween season's reason to cajole membership. In 2013, after some renovations, Merchant's House reminded prospects that construction "stirs things up," and the ensuing creaking floors were a nice combination of seasonality and news. It goes further with membership levels by giving black armbands to members at a certain level to wear at the funeral ceremony; other members earn the privilege of serving as "pallbearers" on the walk to the nearby historic cemetery.

The Art Museum of the Americas always uses images bravely and powerfully, and they work overtime in the holiday season. A December e-mail looks like a holiday card, with a large painting of an angel greeting the recipient who opens the mail. The "Happy Holidays from AMA" seem to be sung from on high and, such is the nature of beautiful art, one wants to scroll down to see the whole image; it's only at the bottom that you'll see a brief message to "join us today with a 2014 museum membership." It lets the visuals do most of the talking.

The four seasons are available to everyone, and it's even easier to take advantage of the innumerable holidays popping up on the calendar. Summer solstice in June encourages you to keep the doors open late for members. Summertime at the Museum of Contemporary Art Chicago mean a weekly farmers' market in conjunction with the City of Chicago on the museum's plaza. April 15 Tax Day offers you the role of community sympathizer, and another way of making tax deductible gifts very timely. Fourth of July is a drum-beating way to parade the importance of history museums and their inextricable link to their community, their culture, even their weather.

Writers need only say:

This Mother's Day, give Mom the gift of . . .

Celebrate the Fourth of July by . . .

Remember Administrative Professionals Day with a gift of membership to . . .

Often, good writing starts not with a brilliant sentence but with a bright idea.

Seasons provide your members with a different pathway to reaching their contacts through gift giving, and not just at the holidays. Have your members think about their doctors, children's teachers, or the dog walker. Tell your members to think about the people they admire, and suggest how they can share the museum they love. The Chicago Botanic Garden captures this sentiment in a caption in one of its membership mailing pieces that says: "Garden memberships make great client, office and teacher gifts." And while you're expanding your member horizons, expand your calendar to include the cultural holidays and celebrations of the rich diversity of people living in your community.

STRATEGY #4: CREATION MYTH

Sometimes called the founder legend, the creation myth is the story of your museum's foundation and fundamentals. There's something about earlier times, not to mention the humility of being just a human once, which makes everyone love a museum's creation myth. If you don't have news, like an event or a new exhibition, occasionally remind your prospects of what you stand for. With this objective, you'll begin your letter not with a price tag, but with your brand, the person whose vision blazed the path that you follow daily. It's easy to talk about yourself when you tell the founder legend, because it's a good story, and everyone loves to tell it and listen to it. Start the way any basic story begins: "In the beginning . . ."

Or begin like a fairy tale: "Once upon a time there lived in Fulton County . . ."

You could start with the date: "In 1894, a family named . . ."

Or even take the once-upon-a-time approach from a current constituent's perspective: "I remember when I first came upon this impressive building, walking down Main Street with my aunt and cousins. . . ."

Then just talk. It will help get a handle on the myth, and/or the legendary progenitor behind it, if you ask several people on your staff to write from the above templates, or their own perspectives. Each will have his or her concept of the museum, which will emerge with the telling. They can write it out longhand in a group workshop, or just speak from memory and knowledge. Some people will take a subjective, rational point of view and tone of voice. Others will range from laudatory to sentimental to ironic. You'll quickly hear the personality of the museum emerge, and when it does you have your first paragraph of a solicitation letter.

It is now common knowledge that stories are the one true way to connect with an audience, but they've always been used by the smartest marketers. Warren Buffett, thirty years ago, revealed the power of stories in his annual "Letters from the CEO." Two Buffettonian examples (it's hard to stop at just one) show the range possible when telling a story about a creation.

> In my early days as a manager I, too, dated a few toads. They were cheap dates—I've never been much of a sport—but my results matched those of acquirers who courted higher-priced toads. I kissed and they croaked.

> American business will do fine over time. . . . My own history provides a dramatic example: I made my first stock purchase in the spring of 1942 when the U.S. was suffering major losses throughout the Pacific war zone. . . . Even so, there was no talk about uncertainty; every American I knew believed we would prevail. . . . Of course, the immediate future is uncertain; America has faced the unknown since 1776.

The emotion in these examples ranges from jollity to inspiration; it doesn't matter whether people laugh or cry at your creation myth; as an artist friend once told me, just so they show some reaction.

One of the first marketing stories I ever heard came from a burly farmer at a green market conference. He talked about the family farm, and the roadside stand, the college agribusiness education, the growth of a farm store to a mail-order food business, the marketing value of farmers' markets. The through line was the love of green things. It was a delicious story.

STRATEGY #5: FRIENDS

Testimonials are not new, but social media has put "likes" and "friends" in a new light, and that's misleading. These friends aren't so much ambassadors as gatekeepers. To take maximum advantage of friendship, follow the strategy used quite visibly by public television, when *Masterpiece Theatre* episodes were introduced by patron Donna Shiley, who talked about her love of drama, PBS, and the boon of philanthropy. She looked like any arts lover who has the discernment to give wisely and well. On a local scale, Goodman

Theatre in Chicago publishes first-person testimonials in the theater's magazine, *OnStage*. In the stage bill for the 2013 production of *Pullman Porter Blues*, by Cheryl L. West, one sponsoring donor wrote:

> Blues legend Big Bill Broonzy one said, "Blues is a natural fact, is something that a fellow lives." . . . *Pullman Porter Blues* is . . . one more example of . . . enlightening life stories . . . diverse voices heard through the arts and . . . enriching "Sweet Home Chicago," [sponsor's] hometown for more than 80 years.

Three rules of good solicitation writing are found in this short testimonial by a donor: news, specific example, and community. The news is the current production; the specificity is the example of Broonzy's quote; and community emerges in the jazz-tinged nickname, Sweet Home Chicago.

There's no downside in enlisting your friends and supporters to extol the museum. Just prompt them with the words "Tell me why you support our museum," then sit back and take notes. You'll discover new perspectives on your museum; you'll gain insights into your customers; you'll flatter your supporters; and you'll have your solicitation letter practically written.

Membership is an affair of the heart, and people join a museum because they love its collection, honor its ways of expression, and get a thrill of anticipation when a new event appears on the horizon. Membership should feel like family togetherness, and being asked for money should sound like a good idea. Supporting a museum is not a transaction, but a pleasure, and that's the strategy.

Chapter Fifteen

Store

When you consider the revenue generated by your store you'll value the writing that connects merchandise to learning. Your customers choose from a worldwide bazaar of items, provided by vendors skilled in marketing to museums' exhibitions and missions. Make the connection crisp and clear by adding a scattering of little white counter cards with a few sentences of interpretation.

Ideally, every book, piece of jewelry, child's toy, or *objet* should be purchased with this sentence in the buyer's mind: "This item relates to an exhibit in our museum because . . ." And that, in so many words, is how you lead in to the basic store label. This chapter will show how to leverage your store to many audiences through the power of the store label, counter card, shelf talker, sign, information sheet, or thank-you card.

My research has shown that customers haven't come to the museum instead of playing; museumgoing, for them, is another kind of play, especially at the store where the game includes the challenge of finding the right purchase. Well-written labels help them score.

Just as there is a story behind every artifact, there's a story behind every merchandise purchase; just ask the buyer. To coordinate the narratives of the buyer and the curator, call a meeting of the two as early as possible in the planning stages.

SHOPPER TYPES

There are several categories of shoppers, even in the already narrow segment of museum visitors. There's the field-trip shopper: "The kids would go in and they would just clean the place out right up to the limit of whatever their parents had given them to spend." Other types of shoppers, depending on a museum's size and location, are status acquirers, learners, or just plain impulsive. You don't write separately to each type, but think about them as you do. You are talking to people who want to relate their purchase to their visit, and you can help them. They want to know: "This item relates to the exhibits I have just seen because . . ."

Museum stores are designed along one or more of the following lines, each reflecting the museum, expanding on the learning, and speaking to different types of shoppers:

1. Gallery: a display of ownable art
2. Bookstore: a library of their own
3. Toy store
4. Marketplace
5. Shopping bags
6. *Objets d'art*—learning by collecting
7. Souvenirs
8. Website

GALLERY

The store is where museums sell the art of the walls, plants from the field, and the equipment at cut-rate prices. Many people start their learning experience in the store because they can't control the urge to shop. They will scout the store first and in so doing get a preview of the learning to come. At least they will if you help them. So give the visitor a real introduction of what's ahead with signs and table tents, counter cards, and hangtags that link as many items as possible to the actual objects in the museum. Tell them what to look for in each piece. When you write:

Black pottery from Mexico

add

Look for these distinctive markings and shapes.

These store counter cards, which act like labels, achieve several goals: looking carefully, thinking, creating a stronger bond with the museum, and motivating a purchase at the end of the tour. The most important objective is strengthening engagement; visitors are easily engaged with the store, and you can leverage that to familiarity with the museum as a whole.

Also write a summary or thank-you card that you can enclose with the purchase at the end of the visit:

Your items represent the mission of the museum, and we hope you enjoy them.

Our merchandise is carefully selected to continue your love of nature long after you leave our museum.

We hope your purchase helps expand your exploration of American art. Thank you for visiting the museum.

BOOKSTORE

Books deserve more respect. Of all your profit-making items, books are the strongest expression of your not-for-profit mission. They're easy to stock, and observational research shows that they leave the store by the armload. Books are the items that keep visitors browsing in the store and sometimes settling in for a prolonged read. Their covers serve as posters for special exhibitions. Just because books are already filled with words doesn't mean they couldn't use a few more.

Use table tents and shelf talkers to connect these desirable objects that are taken home with the untouchable objects in your galleries. The Chicago Botanic Garden store uses a small slate board, like the ones used in the garden itself, to call out a page in a botanical print book that mentions the garden. At another display, a fabricated garden stone, with a slit on top, holds a card that says "Staff Picks." Bookshelves in museums everywhere cry out for message holders that say: "Our eighteenth-century decorative arts curator likes this book" or "Our lighthouse scholar has selected this book for his gift list."

The area of the store devoted to books doesn't just sell books; it encourages reading, an endangered pastime in a multimedia world. At the Museum of Contemporary Art in Chicago, the books room and the merchandise room are separated into two floors, and the reading room is the one with a sofa for reading. Visitors who have just enjoyed one period of time reading labels and wall text will be on a roll for more reading, and the bookstore is the place to indulge them. "Reading, in its quietness and sustained concentration, is the opposite of [the barrage of] information that comes our way, [so] that more than ever to immerse yourself in an involving book seems socially useful," says author Jonathan Franzen. "The place of stillness that you have to go to . . . read seriously is the point where . . . you can actually engage productively with an otherwise scary and unmanageable world."

While a museum doesn't intentionally upset people, it does intend to shake up their minds, hoping to invite some reflection. In the bookstore, you can nudge reflection, with signs on the shelves and nearby seating areas to stop and "think further." Write short instructions to your invited reader, pointing out which copies are available for perusing and providing shelf talkers that preview the books. Preprint a supply of 3" x 5" cards with the header, "[name of museum] recommends," to reinforce the museum brand.

Just as cookbooks now find a home in shelves in cookware stores, a wider variety of books might sell well in museum stores. This is more than a boon to your bottom line, it's a way to fill some gaps in your community and assume a broader information role. Some bridge writing is required, either on table tents or longer handouts, to describe the topic of the book and why your museum qualifies as its messenger. A book I loved, as a social history and architecture guide, was Bill Bryson's *Home*, and it's a natural for many museums that cover houses, England, sociology, architecture, and history. A simple card on the shelf might read:

> Our docent loves the chapter on "The Porch," because it describes how she starts to think about structuring a tour.

Or,

> Here at the Smyth-Ramsey House, we learned a lot from the chapter on "The Kitchen."

The many excellent biographies of U.S. presidents belong in any history museum, as well as local museums of the towns where they lived. The New-York Historical Society uses shelf talkers to call attention to its books on Theodore Roosevelt, who was police chief of New York. But all presidents influenced American life, and associations are not hard to find. Harry S. Truman was the first president to use airplanes to meet his coast-to-coast constituents. Thomas Jefferson collected antiques, designed buildings, and nurtured new strains of plants; and Abraham Lincoln, the most written about man on earth, could inform museums on any subject from mental health to dressmaking.

To get ideas, look at the Notable Books List, published every December by the *New York Times*. Then ask your volunteers and docents to select a favorite for the store and explain their choice. Then write a label that says:

> We asked our volunteers and docents to select a favorite book. These are their choices.

You might add some additional labels that continue:

> Peggy liked this one because . . .

> Jon chose this one because . . .

> For Jill, this book perfectly captures . . .

For all the different kinds of shoppers, and all the reasons that people buy museum books, it pays to heed the words of Philippe de Montebello, former maestro of the Metropolitan Museum of New York, who believed that anyone who comes to a museum is elite by definition "because you are here wanting to learn something and improve yourself when you could be doing something else." Interpretive counter cards respect that need for learning, and fulfill it.

TOY STORE

"Museum store visitors love to explore and challenge themselves. Make them think; help them play; learn through crafts; teach with media. Read, sing, make, watch, listen . . . learn. Your products are the tools." This message to vendors on the website of the Museum Store Association could serve as a wall panel in the toy section of any store. Obviously, you can fill your purchase orders from a broad selection of toys appropriate for your mission and exhibitions. Translate the connection for every adult whose child begs them to buy something.

Science museum stores have the opportunity to connect their merchandise to exhibitions because, unlike jewelry, tableware, and books, there's no functional use for a two-inch model elephant, butterfly stickers, or geodes. The petite elephant deserves a small paragraph, the pretty butterflies will engender flights of fancy if given names, and the break-at-home geodes sparkle sooner if a card explains why all that beauty is encased in a gray rock. Some suggestions:

> Elephants live anywhere there's enough food and water, and flap their ears to keep cool.

> Meet Frosted Elfin, Early Hairstreak, and American Snout.

> You'll never guess what's inside and how it got there. . . .

Some of the items could be merchandised to teachers or homeschoolers. They are inexpensive learning tools that inventive teachers—or more likely their students—would have no trouble devising learning stories about when given some prompts:

> Put the elephant someplace in the room you think she'd be happy.

> Name the butterflies and explain your reason.

> Describe the difference between these geodes.

Don't neglect your higher-priced items. Children love the chance to sprawl on the floor, and you can take the opportunity to teach them about the larger items stocked at ground level. Provide a laminated sheet of instructions like:

> See if you can find these five places on the globe. . . .

> Rocking horses were homemade toys 200 years ago. Here are some other toys fathers carved, cut, and painted for their children. . . .

> Real bears are not as nice as this one. Read on, if you dare. . . .

Of course, many students come to the museum for learning workshops with their families on weekends. Where appropriate, coordinate the workshop activities to items in the store that let them follow up on their curiosity. A child drawing butterflies and pasting them on maps of their habitats might find a book on butterflies in the store. Coordinate between education and store and prepare a handwritten card to place by the book on butterflies:

> This book tells more about the butterflies in today's workshop.

MARKETPLACE

Think of the marketplaces of yore, with farmers selling sheep and grain. Perhaps there were peddlers with pots and pans, buttons and cloth. Maybe portrait painters and cabinetmakers enriched the scene with the luxury of specialized goods and new ideas.

Museum stores can be seen as small malls of function, beauty, local news, and crosscurrents from everywhere. Two museum stores stand out in my mind as bazaars of contemporary things and thoughts. The first time I saw a major museum selling local artists' work was over ten years ago, at the Cedar Rapids Museum of Art, where the bazaar-like store was ablaze with a potpourri of items; it offered an appropriate extension and reinforcement of the museum's mission of exhibiting the work of Iowa artists. As a counterpoint to masters like Grant Wood, Marvin Cone, and Elizabeth Catlett, the store offered a contemporary mélange and a lot of knowledge of the regional art scene. No wonder so many museums now feature local art. More recently, I visited the quieter souk at the Asia Society in New York, where the merchandise was equally abundant, but on denser shelves and in darker tones. This marketplace included nonlocal designs, and its ambience, also, was appropriate to the mission of the museum. In both cases, expert information was available from the store assistants.

Research Needed Here

It's become popular, nay, trendy, to boost the local talent, and there's a real danger of becoming arts and craft fairs. When entrepreneurship takes off it is soon followed by everyone; it sometimes looked like me-tooism and laziness. It's commendable to go local, but that doesn't substitute for interpretation and education. To continue forging links to the community, without becoming an upscale pop-up store, write. Do a lot of research into the artist and art, and write about the connection to the museum. If the objects are worthy, they deserve scholarly description. The insights of a curator, or other experts, rather than the designers themselves, are needed to tease out why this necklace or that cruet represents the best in design. Also, you should justify the connection of the artist to the museum.

For a good model, look to the San Francisco Museum of Modern Art. At the time of this writing, the museum and its store were closed for major reconstruction, but being shuttered didn't stifle speech on its website. It offered an opportunity to make the connection between local creators and a world-class major museum. In describing the local designer of napkins and tea towels, the museum writes:

> . . . born and raised in Los Angeles, California . . . received her B.F.A in painting from Sonoma State University in Northern California and her M.F.A in studio art from Mills College in Oakland, California. All napkins and tea towels are screen printed in San Francisco with waterbased inks.

There are many ways to connect an artist's work to the region. You can write that the artist:

- was born in the area
- lived on Oak Street
- went to college here
- uses woods found in . . .
- draws inspiration from our local cultural scene
- loves the weather here

If there are no links, the artist isn't really local, and this diminishes your mission, not to say credibility.

Whatever locally designed and made products you display, remember that they are functional or decorative. Other information useful to a museum of any size might include how the item is used, or how it has functioned in different periods and by different cultures, or what it enhanced. These are artifacts that are merchandised to consumers as useful or wearable, and relating them to the lifestyle and opinions of their community helps underscore their value.

A word about value. It's central to a retail operation. Obviously, there has to be a perceived worth relative to price, otherwise the item won't sell. More critical to a museum retail operation is value to the brand and mission of the museum. Inside the galleries, aesthetics are taken for granted; inside the store it's your writing that gives pretty things their gravitas.

SHOPPING BAGS

Do people shop at a museum store just to get the attractive little bag? Museum store shops are beloved for their unique merchandise, and my research revealed that many customers buy museum items for their quality, status, and gift acceptability. As one shopper put it: "I feel pride in just carrying the shopping bag; I know people notice it." Long past the visit, shoppers keep shopping bags for hauling and protecting other things, so they're constant reminders of the museum. Many years later, one can still be charmed by the shopping bag from the National Galleries of Scotland shops, with its familiar silhouette of the ice-skating parson; the paper bag from London's Courtauld Gallery that's printed on both sides with the motif that appears on its impressive iron gates; and the colorful paper envelope that protected postcards, from the Ullens Center for Contemporary Art in Beijing. Shopping bags revive memories. Well past the visit date, people save merchandise bags to transport plants, loaned books, and home-baked cookies. Many believe they'll start a conversation with the right people; if they don't, they always prod a personal memory trip. No matter what your museum's size or budget, negotiate for one-color, inexpensive paper shopping bags; or print your logo on stickers to affix on stock bags. Send your name home with the purchase.

Here's where the writing comes in: you'll have to decide just what words to put on the bag. I wish the UCCA store in Beijing had written its name in full; it's hard to remember names of museums in faraway places. I wish the National Galleries of Scotland had identified the silhouette as *Reverend Robert Walker [1755–1808] Skating on Duddingston Loch*, by Sir Henry Raeburn. I applaud the Lower East Side Tenement Museum for including its website's URL, and also for insisting that the graphic designer include the words "Lower East Side" in the name; in small spaces, many visual people cut down on the typography. As for a tagline (Tenement Museum, on its website, uses "Revealing the Past. Challenging the Future"), should your writer argue for including it, consider that option. Most museums don't, and I wonder why. Your store's merchandise represents the museum, and so does the bag.

OBJETS D'ART

Museum store buyers have access to a world of tasteful merchandise, and each one can be educational as well as beautiful with a well-researched and well-written counter card. For an example, look at the online catalog description of a figurine at the Frazier Museum of History in Louisville, Kentucky:

> Here at the Frazier Museum, we are the exclusive home [of] the Royal Armouries, USA and as such have strong ties to Great Britain. Some of the collection here was previously housed in the Tower of London—the same place where Queen Elizabeth [I] was imprisoned by her sister, before her ascendency. This fantastic little figurine is a humorous portrayal of the queen who guided England through the Renaissance and stood as the last ruler from the House of Tudor. A great anglophile gift, indeed.

Many visitors buy *objets* for collections—collections of miniature chairs, teakettles, birdhouses, and architectural models—and here museums as a group have a goldmine. Remember, though, that they're also collecting three-dimensional books, tangible illustrations of vast areas of knowledge. Stores that feature an array of items in a category, with a counter card to explain the category, are really offering a seminar on a subject. The Frazier Museum of History, in Louisville, has the beginnings of a lecture series in their item description.

I have seen equally informative cards at the Museum of Decorative Arts in Paris, and the Phillips Collection in Washington, D.C., and in each case the interpretive labels in the store reinforce the museum's mission and brand. The Decorative Arts Museum store has index-size cards in clear stands describing pieces, their designers, and their materials. Some of the cards tell how the art or craft is made, prizes it has won, reception by the public, and what makes it unique. Writing about your exhibitors' excellence makes you excellent, too.

Store counter cards summarize the research already done by the curator; they distill the interpretations of the educators into a verbal snapshot for shoppers. Many people shop the store for special gifts without visiting the museum, and for these customers, a little interpretation is highly recommended.

With the growing sophistication of museum store vendors, there are ways to leverage what starts as a small thing of beauty into a small lecture or workshop. There's a lot of learning inside a teapot. You needn't write a card for every item in the store; a few well-placed ones will do.

Merchandising opportunities abound when you connect *objets* to your museum. Museum store vendors, through their national organization, are learning the advantages of sponsoring museum events; you might want to look into a sponsored lecture or workshop based on the collection-appealing items that your visitors return for again and again. The counter card or information sheet at the checkout counter would read:

> To learn more about the museum's collection of early American birdhouses, sign up for our upcoming lecture at the checkout counter.

If you don't have time to write and print counter cards, follow the lead of retailers like Sur La Table cookware stores, which uses the books themselves to identify different sections of the store. For instance, books on Asian cooking would demarcate the area in the store that sells woks. Says general merchandising manager Jacob Maurer, "These books almost serve as signage for products in our stores."

SOUVENIRS

Souvenir is the French word for memory, and it applies to every item gazed at and purchased from your store. Focus group research that I conducted revealed the depth—and length—of memories that museum purchases held.
Some of the comments I recorded were:

> I was lucky to take this trip, and I wanted to share it with my sister.

> I wanted to give my grandchildren something meaningful.

> I was going to give it as a gift, but each year it kept bringing back good memories, so I kept it on top of my dresser.

Good writing adapts these responses to counter cards or shelf markers:

> Share your visit with your family.

> Curl up on your couch at home and learn more about contemporary architecture.

> For your fashionista friends.

> For your history buff friends.

If the items are household or functional, like table linens or vases, try these lines:

> This memory of the Southern Home exhibition will unfold at your table for years.

> For flowers from your own garden.

If the items are stationery or calendars:

Remember your visit every time you write a thank-you note.

Remember our museum every day of the year.

Reminding people to remember isn't easy—ask any college teacher—but there's one writing tip that works well: a capital letter term or name or phrase. So name the Specific Exhibition or the Subject matter it interprets. Use the informal Name of your museum. Mention your Town.

Remember the Civil War exhibition with these true to life toy soldiers.

Remember your trip to Portland with a gift to yourself of reading.

Remember your day at the Zoo with these bird whistles.

To make memorable lines even more familiar, give your checkout staff a few words, such as:

This vase is beautiful. Who's the lucky person that gets it?

Then, slip the museum's card in every shopping bag. This is important for museums of any size because right next to the miniature chair or silk scarf visitors also carry home your museum's brand.

Containing boutique-like selections or mall-ish assortments, stores unfetter the human need to acquire, and they provide an activity that supplements the contemplative tone in the galleries.

WEBSITE

Chapter 18 covers the advantages and opportunities of the online store, and it's important to put the virtual and actual in perspective. Shopping is so integral to the human experience—and a museum's health—that no shopping occasion should be left unattended. Websites extend the physical reach of small museums and serve as proxy visits for people who are too far away to visit in person; they also serve as an advertisement for the real store in the brick-and-mortar building. If awareness is created by the excitement of the online store, reprise the items that made people sit up and take notice at home. If you don't stock the item on premises, mount a photograph of it as a reminder. Since you can't have in-store photos of all your online merchandise, print a list, perhaps even with thumbnail photos from the website. Or provide a laptop for ordering, just in case shoppers don't find anything in the store they want. Print a sign that says:

If you don't see an item you liked on the website, just ask.

Then there's the matter of size and price. You may not want to stock many of the large, expensive items sold online, nor squander space on the inexpensive things. So next to your display of the $800 floor lamp, list some of the other one-of-a-kind pieces that can be ordered from the website. And next to the hanging toy rack, list some of the other "stocking stuffers, party favors, and fun things" than can be ordered online. The same procedure works beautifully for small museums with limited space. Even if you only have a counter and a laptop, you will reward visitors with the joy of owning a memory.

EXIT LINES

Museum stores might be no larger than a counter, but there's one label that should be affixed to every cash register. I adapt it from words spoken years ago by a staffer at the checkout counter of Terra Museum of American Art when it was a stand-alone building in downtown Chicago. The store was little more than a nicely merchandised counter in the small lobby, but the staffer knew something about a big presence:

"What memory of the museum are you taking home with you today?"

Chapter Sixteen

Survey Questionnaires

Survey questionnaires are popular because they're relatively inexpensive. This chapter deals with the expensive part of survey questionnaires: getting to Why and So What.

The low cost is associated with the distribution: questionnaires reach a large sample of the target audience through cost-effective delivery systems such as online surveys like SurveyMonkey, mailings to your database, and sheets available at the information desk. They reach a more selective, but still broad, audience when handed out after tours, in event programs, at the store checkout counter, or with the restaurant check.

The expense piles up when you take the time of staff to debate the purpose of every question and then, with the results in, ask, "So what?" about every answer. Professional researchers also recommend a pretest, perhaps a focus group, to evaluate the questions, double-check that they're understandable, and prioritize their order in the questionnaire. It involves a lot of critical analysis.

Surveys snap a picture and give a surface view of what consumers are thinking. They aren't as deep as focus groups but have the advantage of quantity; the quick answers from hundreds of people provide museums with a quantitative overview of specific issues. Here's what surveys don't do:

1. Give insights
2. Probe for nuances
3. Wonder about variables
4. Draw conclusions

Questionnaires can tell you that 60 percent of the respondents "like" the new exhibition. They can't surmise why 40 percent didn't "like" it, or 30 percent found it only "satisfactory." They don't question if "like," "don't like," and "satisfactory" is the right way to scale the response.

However, good writing can turn the low-cost survey into a high-value research tool. Good writing can help you write survey questions that elicit insightful answers. Good writing can help you probe for nuances. Good writing can cover some of the variables. And good writing results in answers that jump from the survey page to help you draw conclusions.

DRAW CONCLUSIONS

Let's start from the end. Think about your objectives for the research and what you hope to gain from the answers. Here are some typical survey questions, ones you've seen dozens of times in other cultural institutions. You've probably asked similar questions yourself. This time, follow each survey question with a question for your staff: Why are we asking this?

Question to respondents: How often do you visit our museum?

- Several times a year
- Once a year or less
- Hardly ever

Question to staff: Why do you want to know their frequency?

Alternate question:

- When was the last time you were here? _____
- When did you visit another museum? _____
- What do you do instead of visiting a museum? Check all that apply:

  Shop
  Participate in sports
  Visit theme parks
  Enjoy the outdoors

Question to respondents: How satisfied were you with your visit today?

- Very
- Somewhat
- Not very

Question to staff: What do we mean by satisfaction?

Alternate question(s):

- Underline or circle what you liked best about the visit: exhibition, tour, cafe, showing out-of-town friends
- Underline or circle what you like least: parking, ticket price, food

Question to respondents: How likely are you to return?

- Very
- Somewhat
- Not at all

Question to staff: Why are we putting visitors on the spot?

Alternate question: What would encourage you to return?

- Exhibits
- Showing out-of-town friends
- Café
- Store
- Tour

Comments_____

Question to respondents: Why did you visit today?

- Friend suggested it
- Sightseeing for out-of-town guests
- Read about the exhibition
- E-mail
- Member mailing

Question to staff: What insights would these standard answers give us?

Alternate question: If you were writing a review for Yelp or TripAdvisor, what one aspect of the trip would you recommend?

_____

Question to respondents: Are you a member?

- Yes

• No

Question to staff: Why do we care if they're members?

Alternate question: What aspect of our museum makes you feel at home here?

_____

Question to respondents: Please rate our exhibitions:

• Wonderful
• Interesting
• Sometimes interesting
• Difficult for me to appreciate

Questions to staff: What will we do with the answers? What will we learn about the aspects of the exhibition that are "wonderful" or "not interesting"?

Alternate questions: How many stars would you give our museum on a website such as TripAdvisor, with five stars being the best? What review would you write?

• One star _____
• Two stars _____
• Three stars _____
• Four stars _____
• Five stars _____

Question to respondents: What other activities do you attend or participate in?

• Theater and stage shows
• Movies
• Sports
• Dance performances
• Music concerts
• Nightclubs
• Other (specify) _____

Question to staff: How will this information help us understand our visitors' needs?

Alternate question: What aspect of the museum did you like as much as other cultural activities such as theater/stage shows, movies, sports, dance performances, music concerts, and clubs?

_____

Question to respondents: What is your age?

- Under 18
- 18–25
- 26–35
- 36–45
- 46–55
- 56–70
- Over 70

Questions to staff: Why do we segment by age? What does that tell us?

Alternate question: Which of the following best describes your lifestyle?

- Student
- Busy with my first job
- Balancing job and family
- Busy, but take time for a "me" day
- Thinking about traveling more
- Enjoying time to explore new ideas

Comments _____

Question to respondents: Annual household income:

- Up to $24,999
- $25,000–$49,999
- $50,000–$74,999
- $75,000–$99,999
- $100,000 or more

Questions to staff: How does this information help us provide a better experience for our visitors? Does it help us price items in the store or on the menu? Does it give guidance in workshop or lecture speakers? Is it important in deciding about admission fees? Will it guide us in setting membership levels?

Alternate questions:

• What is a good price range for items in the museum store?

  _____

• How much do you think the museum restaurant should charge for lunch?

  _____

• What program would interest you most: a nominally priced lecture or a free weekend workshop?

  _____

• Would you pay a higher price for fast-track admission to a special exhibition, and why?

  _____

Comments _____

PROBING FOR INSIGHTS

As you can see from the preceding questions, some were multiple choice (closed ended) and some allowed for opinions (open ended). There are advantages to both. Many researchers believe respondents won't take the time to write an answer, that they'd rather check a box. Others believe that respondents dislike being boxed in, and that only open-ended questions elicit a valid response. You can decide for yourself, and it's easier if you know why you want the answer. If you want to know your three main competitors for visitors' leisure time, closed ended is best. On the other hand, if you want to hear the range of options accumulating on visitors' wish lists, leave the answer open ended.

Open-ended questions render insights. It takes sensitivity to nudge insights from answers, but they're there. You can probe for the insights by listing multiple choices above the comments. Don't worry about slightly altering the format of each question. A certain consistency is essential to prevent confusion, but if it starts looking robotic, respondents lose interest.

The average level of education in the United States is a high school diploma, and the average reading level is eighth grade. So watch your language and don't use "paleontologist" if "scientist" will suffice. However, beware of simple words that are unclear. Here are examples of questions that offer such simple choices that they confuse the respondent and yield vague-to-useless insights:

How often do you/have you visited a museum in the past five years?

- Never
- Occasionally
- Sometimes
- Often
- Regularly
- Always

Here's another example of simple choices that, in this case, are intimidating as well as less than helpful:

Over the past five years, how many times have you visited a museum?

- One
- Two
- Three
- Four
- Five

A more constructive way is to ask the question open ended. It doesn't put pressure on the respondent's memory but, rather, encourages some reflection:

How often do you visit a museum?

_____

The problem with memory is that if a respondent gets frustrated by even a simple memory question—how many times have you visited a museum?—they might not finish the questionnaire. Rather, ask your staff what insights they need from this question. If you want to know how you can entice repeat visits, try the third-person approach:

Describe someone who is a regular museumgoer:

_____

If you brought friends to the museum, what aspect of it would entice them to return on their own?

_____

NUANCES

You can probe for insights, and you can also listen patiently for them to emerge. Open-ended questions allow the respondent to answer conversationally, and in that mode of discourse, unplanned answers burst forth. Ask a series of open-ended questions that allow the respondent to act as the expert:

Who will you bring with you on your next visit and why?

What would your neighbor think of this exhibition?

What would you tell a young child about this museum?

If you came back to the museum on your lunch hour, what colleague would you bring as a free guest?

What would you say to a friend who likes to visit a museum alone?

Here are a few nuance-inducing questions in a survey fielded by the Delaware Art Museum. Because it is a survey, it attempts to quantify insights; but it also aims to discover visitor thinking that goes deeper than number of visits made, the importance of price, and overall satisfaction.

PART I: UNDERSTANDING HOW PEOPLE INTERACT WITH ART

Please describe the following statements on a scale from 1 to 7. 1 being "does not describe me at all" to 7 being "describes me very well."

1   2   3   4   5   6   7

1. I feel comfortable looking at most types of art.
2. I like to know about the story portrayed in a work of art.
3. I like to know about the materials and techniques used by the artist.
4. I enjoy talking with others about the art we are looking at.
5. Art affects me emotionally.
6. I like to be told a straightforward insight to help me know what the work of art is about.
7. I like to view a work of art on my own, without explanations or interpretations.
8. I am comfortable explaining the meaning of a work of art to a friend.
9. I like to connect with works of art through music, dance, dramatic performances, and readings.
10. Some terms used in art museums are difficult for me to understand.

These questions could transition intact to a focus group script or one-on-one interview, options that frequently follow the tabulation of a survey in the overall research process.

VARIABLES

Human nature being what it is, there will always be variables to skew results. With an on-site survey, like the ones often handed out in the lobby, the variables include time of day, for example lunchtime, which affects visitors in a hurry because it's their lunch hour; wrong recipient, which happens when the person getting the questionnaire is not the target audience, but say, the friend who got brought along; presence of children, which distracts visitors; weather, which inhibits length of stay; poor quality of paper the survey is printed on, which to some recipients makes the questionnaire look unimportant; interviewer bias, because you never know how recipients perceive and react to the person distributing the survey.

The sheer number of questionnaires fielded will smooth out some of the variables of time, place, facilitator, and personal reasons. You can overcome some of these variables with multiple surveys at different times of day, and to different respondent samples. Some variables are avoided by delivering the survey online. Some variable can be controlled by surveying a preselected segment of your database such as people unaccompanied by children, or an audience waiting for a lecture to start.

Making the survey more enjoyable overcomes a lot of unknown problems. There are several textbook guidelines to follow.

Avoid double questions such as:

Thinking back on the tour you took today, how satisfied were you with the length and the way the docent described the exhibits?

- Very dissatisfied
- Dissatisfied
- Neutral
- Satisfied
- Very satisfied

What is the respondent supposed to evaluate: the length of time the tour lasted, or the way the docent talked? Ask one question at a time.

Open with Your Best Question

Questions that are fun and easy to answer motivate the respondent to finish the job. For example:

Here are six paintings from the exhibition you saw today. Please rank them in order of preference with 6 being the favorite, 5 the next favorite, and so on, with 1 being the least favorite.

___ Boy on horse
___ Lake at sunset
___ Women in garden with child
___ Peasant dinner
___ Room with mirror
___ Fruit and wine on a table

This reminds the visitor of what was covered on the tour—no art historian memory required.

Save Sensitive Questions for Last

Put sensitive questions at the end of the survey. You don't want the respondent to be intimidated; if they feel challenged, their nervousness may color successive answers. Then pose the question in the third person.

Don't ask: "Does the ticket price of our museum keep you from visiting often?"

Replace this direct question with an inquiry that asks the respondent to imagine what another person might say: "Do you think the ticket price of museums keeps people from returning more often?"

Don't ask: "Did you enjoy the objects that the docent discussed on today's tour?" Do ask: "How do you think the visitors on your tour liked the objects discussed?"

Don't ask the direct question: "How often do you attend a lecture at the museum?" Do ask: "Thinking of the people you know, how often would they attend a lecture at the museum?"

And check one more time for accessible language. It's difficult for museum professionals to relinquish their educated vocabularies for the eighth-grade reading level, but simple language reads faster, and may even occupy less space on the page, both advantages for a visitor survey.

SURVEY DELIVERY SYSTEMS

Good writing can't compensate for a less-than-optimal format. The first decision to be discussed is the relative advantages of online questionnaires versus those delivered in person, on-site, mailed, and telephoned.

Questionnaires distributed at the information desk, restaurant, or museum store solve the problem of prequalifying respondents: if people are inside your museum, they're museumgoers, and that is the target you may want to question. You never know for sure who's taking an online or telephone survey. However, if you do employ on-site questionnaires—the ones on nice paper that look important and worth the respondent's time—write only a one-page list of questions. Unlike an online questionnaire, these must be structured for people whose scheduled time you're impinging on. If you must have more questions, use two sides of one piece of paper. Multiple pages are daunting and hard to hold. And if you must go to multiple pages, print them on 11" x 17" paper and fold it so it handles like a booklet.

Online surveys are filled out at leisure, by respondents who willingly choose to answer your questions. You can make these questionnaires longer, and you can ask more open-ended questions when the answers will be typed.

Of course, even though the respondents are reached through a database you generate, you can't be sure of the demographics/psychographics/geographics of the respondents. They may not fulfill your target requirements. On the other hand, with the right screening questions, you'll reach a broader consumer segment than you could ever hope for from on-site surveys.

If you carefully manage your database, you have the advantage of specific targeting. You can send your questionnaires to members, selected ZIP codes, age groups, business communities, or visitors who spend over $50 a year at the store. Some questions that seem insensitive or irrelevant on a general questionnaire—like age or income—can be taken into consideration in a data-driven e-mail survey.

QUALITATIVE RESEARCH

Although this chapter is devoted to writing a survey, there are other kinds of research you should always keep in mind. A successful survey will generate more questions, and if you have the time, money, and patience, be prepared to enjoy the follow-up studies. Surveys give quantitative answers, numbers. If you want more depth, more nuances, more insights, more clarification, slide over to the qualitative column.

- Online ethnography
- Focus groups
- One-on-one interviews
- Transaction interviews
- Observation
- Projects

Online Ethnography

Listening to the social conversation is currently the hottest form of research. The technology engages citizen and marketer alike, and the many platforms deliver the insights and opportunities no other media can. When you, as a marketer, hear a problem on Twitter or Facebook or Yelp, you can respond immediately and start making longer-term adjustments. You listen to the conversation about your own museum, of course, but also to the many conversations embracing tangential communities of culture, education, and leisure. Online ethnography is as easy as following Twitter, or as sophisticated as the latest big data service, and there are many cost-effective bundlers like socialmention.com and topsy.com that survey several platforms at once. It would be too good to be true, if there weren't a few disadvantages. Although your interns will be proficient in the latest iterations, it's easy to lose sight of your research objectives. The technology seduces one away from options.

Don't think of the social media segment as necessarily younger; it isn't. But the segments are defined by the main intent of social media, which is to communicate with like-minded people, and that can be limiting. You also want to research people whose mind-sets are sometimes on education, or raising a family, or planning a vacation. Fortunately, with the listening capability of the Internet, you can hear them as well.

Focus Groups

Gathering a group of people in a room for ninety minutes and looking at their reactions and interactions is wonderfully insight laden. You can focus on specific questions, dig down for insights, follow up on comments, and branch out into spontaneous ideas. Surveys will leave you with a lot of Why and So What questions unanswered, and those can be clarified in groups after the survey. As said before, you can also pretest your survey questions in groups. The disadvantages are the cost of groups and the small number of responses. The answers and insights you get in groups are directional only; they point to areas of further investigation.

One-on-One Interviews

They're even more insightful than groups. You can ask a lot of follow-up questions. These individual sessions produce responses that people are often too cautious to voice among strangers. They are the only way to conduct transaction research.

Transaction Interviews

These are the phone calls, or e-mails, that follow up on a customer's visit to the auto repair shop, or the vacation hotel. They are frequently used for high-end purchases. Museums would find them useful after a gala or membership event.

Observation

This is the most cost-effective research; it costs nothing but time. The idea is simply to watch visitors as they move in their idiosyncratic ways through your museum. All it takes is fifteen minutes to start observing behaviors that you wouldn't believe if you hadn't seen them with your own eyes. My first example of the phenomenon was hand-holding. Yes, an amazingly high percentage of people walk through museums holding hands! One conclusion to be drawn is that museums are intimate experiences that visitors want to share. Even people who don't hold hands will lean in close to each other. And I observed this behavior in museums all over the world. In my book

Consumer Research for Museum Marketers, I write about many more observations that marketers need to address: the number of minutes spent in the restaurant; the way museumgoers dress; how they examine merchandise in the store; how they take photographs. You need an open mind for this kind of research, a willingness to sit unobtrusively and just look around. Of course, you'll need multiple sessions of watching at different times and with different exhibitions. Then you must discipline your staff to discuss, analyze, and draw implications. It's time consuming but immensely worthwhile in establishing some of the questions to be pursued in surveys and groups.

Projects

Many of the people you want to know can't take a survey or participate in groups. Young children, for instance. And introverts, who don't shine in semicircles of ten. These segments frequently delve into projects with fervor. An easy project is storytelling. Ask respondents to write a one-page story about their experience with museums. This oldest of entertainments seems to come naturally to almost everyone. Leave the setup vague: "Tell me a story about museums." Give your respondents a choice of writing a first-person memoir, a history, poem, or movie plot—the formats are varied and charming, and the insights equally so.

The collage approach was presented by researchers Susie Wilkening and James Chun in a case to get tweens talking . . . to adults, not each other. They gave the young people an assortment of magazines from which to choose any images they wanted, with the goal of assembling "what I like." Some of the unexpected insights were that girls like a variety and quantity of things, sometimes two of a kind, resulting in a mass of stuff in one collage. Boys assembled three to five things, and never duplicated. The takeaway, significant for field trips or family visits, is that girls like to scan broadly, and boys like to dig into particulars.

This exceedingly brief summary of qualitative research is given as counterpoint to the quantitative results provided by surveys. Together, both types of research lead to a better knowledge of the market you need to reach.

IMPLICATIONS AND NEXT STEPS

Museums, know your visitor! They are your other half, and the honeymoon promises to continue for as long as you listen. That means more than taking down answers and tallying up totals; it involves constantly engaging the entire museum staff in asking Why and So What. And also What's Next. The writer brings to this conference table an ear for words, both the words written in the survey questions and the words found in the responses. Writers analyze well; it's in their genes to understand the dropped hints hidden in questionnaire responses and the implications to be deliberated. Rely on writers to start the Whys and So Whats rolling.

Chapter Seventeen

Volunteers

The demand for talented workers now outpaces the supply. If you don't engage them, they will leave. Notice the operative word "engage." It's not higher salaries, flexible hours, or even interesting projects they want from you, but a share in success. And if engagement is important to keep paid employees, it's essential with volunteers. Adequate volunteers are already told that they contribute meaningful support. Good volunteers do more than help out and prop up. It's time to redefine volunteerism and give the good volunteers a stake in the game.

You can't write a job contract for a volunteer, but you can write engaging recruiting and job descriptions, serious feedback forms, and professional memos and conference reports, newsletters, surveys, manuals, and reference letters. Some of the material is covered in other chapters, and can be used for volunteers; all you need to do is add their names to your mailing lists. You'll also find some new ways to communicate with volunteers, and an underlying message to just do it.

JOB DESCRIPTION

The chapter on websites (chapter 18) suggests some ways to enhance your career or job page beyond the facts of the job description. When recruiting paid employees, you want to stress the emotional, cultural, and social benefits of the job. It is the opposite with a volunteer job description; they already know the emotional benefits. Volunteers are already emotionally enticed by your brand; they have chosen it over all the other arts organizations they know and like. Since your goal is attracting the best volunteers, your volunteer descriptions should be filled with specific expectations. Make it more rigorous rather than less. Show that they will hold an accountable niche in the museum. The writing should avoid gushing phrases like "You'll love the friendly environment" or vague phrases like "Help the marketing director." It should give specifics such as: title, physical strength and activity required, schedule, qualifications, and age requirements (for teenage volunteers). You may not get as many respondents, but you'll attract some really good ones. Tight job descriptions, policies, and procedures will also make it easier to phase out a volunteer. Once people know the rules and expectations, you can require that they meet them—just as any workplace would.

Volunteers and Docents

It's important to distinguish between volunteer, intern, and docent. The three types of unpaid jobs are commonly confused and their titles misused. Their respective responsibilities are quite different. The Ogden Museum of Southern Art in New Orleans elucidates the difference this way:
Volunteers in education:

> Ensure our visitors have an enriching experience by assisting with the Ogden's Education activities. Help Museum guests explore the Art of the South by participating in family and adult education programs like Family Fair, lectures, artist tours, and more.

Docent opportunities:

> Docents introduce and expand the knowledge about works of art in the collection through tours and gallery discussions for our visitors of all ages.

The Museum of Contemporary Art Chicago includes time and tenure requirements in its docent descriptions:

> Docents give public tours of the exhibitions to adult visitors and receive ongoing training from educators, curators, and artists. Docents commit to one or two days of touring per month (one or two tours per day), attendance at ongoing training sessions, and a minimum of two years of touring after the initial training.

Internships

The Museum of Contemporary Art zeroes in on its intern expectations with this description:

> The Museum of Contemporary Art internship program welcomes students and recent graduates who wish to broaden their education and professional experience by working and learning in a not-for-profit museum. All MCA departments offer experiential education in a challenging, hands-on environment in

exchange for a substantive contribution from talented and interested individuals.

It also continues with a thorough listing of types of internships available:

- Accounting
- Administration
- Collections and exhibitions
- Curatorial
- Editorial
- Education
- Fund-Raising and Membership
- Graphic Design
- Information Systems
- Library
- Marketing
- Media Relations
- Multimedia: Video
- Multimedia: Web
- Performance Programs
- Photo Archives
- Preparators
- Rental Events
- Retail
- Special Events

It's an encyclopedic view of the workings of a museum, and every one of these internship headings is followed by a sixty- to 140-word description. This remarkably rich list suggests the high-level importance and intensity the MCA places on its internships, which are clearly important opportunities for intern and museum alike. Even if your museum doesn't have all these options, a list of the possible learning opportunities will help attract the specific interns—and qualified volunteers and docents—you value.

Difference between Rigorous and Strict

Your requirements for volunteers, at any level, may not be rigorous, but the adherence must be strict. Whether your volunteers are expected to smile at the entrance or write a daily blog, spell out the job in detail. Don't just describe the job, lay out the component tasks. Give examples of a typical half day of work. This takes good writing because it must be crystal clear and short; nobody voluntarily reads lots of words.

Also learn to delete words. To keep job descriptions short and concise:

- Be sparing with humor
- Avoid insider terminology
- Cut short emotional appeals; if you want people to work, entreat their intelligence and industry

SMALL MUSEUMS: JOB OFFERINGS

Smaller museums face different problems when publicizing jobs in their volunteer workforce. Whereas large museums are inundated with applicants—including job seekers willing to gain experience for no pay—small museums have to be more proactive. It starts on the website home page, so think carefully whether to relegate Volunteer or Support or Opportunities to the navigation bar at the bottom of your home page, where some museums hide it, or announce Volunteer right at the top of the screen. Wherever visitors find your link, reward them with a rousing welcome when they land on your Volunteer or Support or Opportunities page. The website of Hildene, The Lincoln Family Home (of Robert Todd Lincoln, the president's oldest son), in Manchester, Vermont, opens with an irresistible enticement:

> "Research has shown that people who volunteer often live longer." —Allen Klein

Yes, it's a dramatic appeal, but it's tempered with logic and intelligent humor. The volunteer job description continues with facts. The mention of this institution's history is effective, and if your museum has a long backstory, use it. When you recruit for the long term, durability counts. The volunteer appeal continues:

> Were it not for a group of determined group of community volunteers more than thirty years ago, Hildene would not have been saved from development. To this day, volunteers remain an important part of this historic Lincoln site. The Lincoln family's estate is rich in opportunities for volunteer service from the mansion, to the trails, to Hildene Farm.

JOB DESCRIPTION ADDENDUM: LEARNING OUTCOMES

Think about your volunteer opportunities as learning opportunities and consider the format used by educators:

Learning Outcomes for Volunteers

At the end of a volunteer day, the volunteer will:

- Understand the scope of the museum
- Discover new objects in the museum
- Explore new perspectives via the exhibitions
- Discuss ideas with other volunteers
- Get physical exercise
- Explore the business side of the museum
- Survey the history of the era

Some of these will apply to your museum, and you can certainly add your own learning outcomes.

FEEDBACK FORMS AND QUESTIONNAIRES

Start with the assumption that your volunteers will stay with you for a long time, and then stop making assumptions about them. You need to stay in touch with volunteers, discovering how they like their job and whether they might function more satisfyingly—for you and them—elsewhere. You must listen to their comments, complaints, or ideas, because they bring essential perspectives you don't have: the consumer's and the outsider's. They have visited your museum as consumers or they wouldn't be interested in volunteering for you. And they are not insiders; they are not employees who are paid to understand management's agenda. Similar to hired employees, you can't afford the expense of recruiting, training, and acculturating workers only to have them leave after six months. Unlike people on your payroll, the only contract you share is an emotional one.

Employees get a certain amount of employer feedback simply by receiving a paycheck each pay period. There's also a system for telling employees they have good ideas and perform their job diligently; it's called the employee review. For volunteers I recommend the feedback form, available on paper in the volunteer office or online at the Volunteer page of your website. The volunteer starts the process by filling out:

- Name
- Assignment
- Today's date
- Observations
- Conclusions
- Next steps

It asks a lot of the volunteer, but it's the basis for discussion with the director of volunteers. It is to be filled out immediately after the scheduled tour, store duty, or other volunteer/docent/intern job. All volunteers, regardless of how closely they work with a supervisor, complete the form. This is their opportunity to demonstrate their sensitivity to the museum, its visitors, and its operations. It might include visitor insights, merchandise preferences, overheard conversations online or on-site, or the tactical details of an event. Challenge volunteers to add value to their assigned task by spotting issues before they become problems. Plan to respond to these feedback forms in person with the volunteer; also plan to disseminate some of the gathered information to the entire staff, with acknowledgments. It communicates back to the volunteers (a) that you appreciate their contribution and (b) how you'll use their input.

MEMOS AND CONFERENCE REPORTS

Employees communicate regularly with each other just by coming into the office every morning and saying hello to coworkers. Volunteers have neither the regular schedule nor the serendipitous meeting points that allow for esprit de corps. Help keep esprit among your volunteer corps with memoranda. This can be done on a group Facebook page, with a regular e-mail, or a low-tech notice pinned to the wall. The subject of the message is less important than its frequency. Keep it short but interesting. Don't wait for the annual appreciation day, or the monthly assignment sheet, to be in touch. One advantage of an e-mail memo is its familiarity to the retired businesspeople in your volunteer force. These highly efficient producers are habituated to being kept in the loop; they can't shake the ritual of responsibility, and you'd be remiss in ignoring that. You don't have to promote them—much as some would like that—just share with them more often.

The memo format—perfect for writing a timely message:

TO: Volunteers
FR: Director of Education
RE: Temperature control
Perhaps you've notice the change in temperature around the museum. That's because . . .

This kind of hallway chitchat, unless it's strictly confidential, keeps volunteers informed and involved, so release it to your volunteers in a short e-memo blast. It's a part of your daily life, and it can become part of their weekly life. Some information can be used in their dealings with visitors; certainly it will give them a deeper immersion in the organization they have decided to join. And about the hallway reference: Steve Jobs so much liked the idea of workers sparking ideas by informally chatting with each other in the halls, he planned to locate the bathrooms as far as possible from the employee offices; they'd meet serendipitously while heading toward the loo.

The idea was jettisoned, but the concept of casual intersections lives on in management theory.

Sometimes, you'll want to convey more important information, the kind that employees get more formally in meetings. There's an easy way to send a memo to volunteers: use the wording of the media release and send it to your volunteers when you release it to the media.

Awards should always be shared with volunteers, preferably before the media announces the news. You never want some neighbor telling the volunteer first; it diminishes the importance of their contribution in their community. Partnerships with local businesses should always be shared with volunteers. They're important to the life of the museum, and a volunteer should know the alliance long before they're given a coupon for a merchant's product. Many volunteers, who come to you after a lifetime of work experience, understand the importance of business community support. They all need to know about your Main Street friends.

Whenever employees meet in a conference room, they share information. You can replicate that collegiality and crowd wisdom. Within reason, share the results of the meetings in occasional conference reports. The format of a conference report also conveys the scope of the information:

Café Committee Meeting
Date:
Committee Members Attending:
Committee Members Absent:
The Café Committee was convened to discuss nutritional guidelines that are in keeping with local and federal initiatives. The agenda items discussed were . . .

Standard conference reports end with a request to comment and make corrections. You may not want to include volunteers in this aspect of the conference report, but if you do you'll get insights you and your employees can't imagine in the isolation of your offices. Whether they respond or not, engaged volunteers will appreciate learning about the interactions of their full-time colleagues.

The professionalism of e-memos and conference reports, whether or not the volunteer recipients come from a work background, conveys respect. These documents demonstrate your expectation of professionalism from them. In a world where news is casually disseminated by gossip and social media, your authoritative communiqués count more than ever. Museum volunteers hold their employer in high regard and the employer must reciprocate.

QUESTIONNAIRES

Traditionally, nonprofits have tried to convince people to give time and money because it feels good or it's the right thing to do, emphasizing heart-strings rather than logic. Even businesses that promote volunteerism as a feel-good involvement recognize its objective value, the bottom-line improvement, in maintaining their happiness. How to learn what makes volunteers happy? Give them a questionnaire. Word the questions to elicit their thoughts on volunteerism in general and their own role in your museum.

What kind of connections to other people do you want?

_____

How do you see our museum helping you meet those people?

_____

What do you think you'll learn working in our museum?

_____

List some career skills that might be sharpened by working at the museum:

_____

Describe your personal goals outside the museum:

_____

Identify some expertise or experiences you bring to the museum:

_____

You can field this questionnaire among current volunteers and, even better, to prospects. When you understand what they want, you interview them more meaningfully, and offer the satisfying assignments that will retain them.

Here are some questions adapted from the volunteer surveys conducted by the Hammonds House Museum in Atlanta. It was distributed to three database groups: Current Volunteers, Tried to Volunteer, and Lapsed Volunteers. The concept makes superb use of a good database, reaching not only to those already in the fold, but to prospects who once expressed interest and didn't join the volunteer group, and to those who, for reasons to be discovered, chose to quit. Here is the questionnaire, which is based on the online source:

> Orientation Sessions: If you have attended an orientation session for volunteers at the Museum, how would you rate the Orientation on the following points?

- Informative
- Interesting
- Well-organized
- Useful hand-outs
- Convenient day and time

Personal Volunteer Experience: If you have volunteered at the Museum within the last two years, what was your job:

- Helped at an event(s)
- Helped with administrative tasks or gallery sat
- Gave a tour(s)
- Completed volunteer hours for school
- Completed an internship
- Completed community service hours

How did you like it?

- It was what I expected based on description given by Museum staff or in published material.
- I was given the help and supervision I needed to be successful.
- The Museum's staff was prepared for my help.
- I felt that I made an important contribution to the Museum's work.
- I felt that my contribution was appreciated by the Museum's staff.
- I felt that my volunteer time was well-utilized.
- I enjoyed working with the Museum's staff.

If you are a regularly scheduled volunteer, list the two most important reasons why.

_____

Have you volunteered with any other organizations? E.g., Arts/Culture, Educational, Social Services, Religious, Fraternal ___ Yes ___ No

Compare volunteering at our museum to your other volunteer experiences:

_____

If you have not volunteered at the Museum, or have stopped volunteering, what caused you to lose interest?

- Not being informed of volunteer opportunities
- No longer interested in volunteering
- No longer have the time to volunteer
- Family, work, and/or health issues prevent me from volunteering
- Volunteer opportunities don't interest me or relate to my skills
- Didn't enjoy working with the staff
- Was disappointed in or had a bad experience at the Museum
- Have heard things about the Museum that make me reluctant to continue volunteering

- No or slow response to my attempt to volunteer
- Completed my volunteer hours or internship
- Moved
- Event, training, or task that interested me is no longer available

Chapter 16 covers the writing of surveys, and when you decide to send a questionnaire to your volunteers, that information is applicable. Notice my wording "when" rather than "if" you field a volunteer questionnaire. Do it. You need to know what motivates prospective volunteers, and you need to discover what current volunteers overhear, observe, and perceive. Remember that volunteers possess perspectives that you'll never have. Pick their brains.

EXIT INTERVIEW

Volunteers exit, too. And if they form a large chunk of your workforce, you need to hear what they have to say. Like paid employees, who are advised not to speak ill of colleagues they may meet again in another job, volunteers also may be leery of misspeaking. In their case, the standard "why are you leaving" will elicit even blurrier answers; they won't be rational reasons like higher salary or better hours. It's difficult for a departing worker to articulate a precise reason for disaffection.

- When did you first think this was not a good volunteer fit for you?
- What first prompted you to think about doing something else?
- Name one occasion that caused you to reconsider your volunteer work with us.

With this kind of open-ended question respondents can be as vague as they want, but if you listen carefully you'll hear clues to the real reason. Here are other ways to query volunteers who have given notice. These questions are framed around a third person:

- Would you recommend our museum to other people, even if it's not for you? Why or why not?

_____

- How can we be more welcoming to other people?

_____

- How would you describe your job here to a new volunteer?

_____

LETTER OF REFERENCE

And when they leave for other unpaid positions, which good volunteers often do, send them off graciously. Well-written reference letters are part of being a good citizen, and they reap returns for years. A good letter helps keep a good worker in the not-for-profit community. Well-written letters become a forum for you to promote your museum's initiatives, both to the person leaving and to the person reading the letter at other institutions. A collegial letter makes the name on the letterhead look good.

Never shoot off a form letter; they're insulting to the worker, the prospective employer, and you. This template will make an individualized letter easy:

- First paragraph: facts
- Second paragraph: examples
- Third paragraph: relevance to job sought

The first paragraph is short and simply states the volunteer's jobs and skills. Refer to the volunteer by his or her full name.

The second paragraph is the longest, and in it you give specific examples. If Jenny worked every Friday afternoon in the museum store, say so. If Tom guided two tours a month, on Saturday or Sunday, say that. Tell the store size and number of other assistants. If you can supply the average number of people in a typical tour, give that figure. Include talents such as "articulate writer for our *Summer in the County* exhibition," "good math skills," "always fifteen minutes early for the 10 a.m. tours," "tireless researcher on our recent exhibition." Give three examples, speak conversationally, and feel free to refer to the volunteers by their informal names.

The third paragraph demonstrates your broader vision; in it you surmise how the volunteer will fit into the next organization. If you have the name of the organization, employer, or job, it shows collegiality to note the link between volunteer and the new employer. If you're talking to Whom It May Concern, and can't connect the volunteer to his or her new organization, link the volunteer's talents and attitudes to the museum culture as a whole; it highlights your museum's perspective.

The world of good volunteers, even in large communities, is limited, so take every opportunity to understand them. With a thoughtful reference letter you hone your skills as an organization they'll want to stay with.

VOLUNTEERS AND DONATIONS

Several studies over the past few years have shown that individuals who volunteer give more money than those who do not volunteer, making it all the more important to analyze how people give their time, when they want to serve, and what they hope to gain. Volunteerism deserves some of the focused attention currently being directed at fund-raising, and with better communication, you can start the process.

RETENTION

The Gilcrease Museum in Tulsa, Oklahoma, is the rare museum whose volunteers have a club name: the Gillies. Just as book clubs have names, and Retired Old Men Eating Out give themselves an acronym name, business entities embrace names as empowering. Special teams and task forces in corporations are assigned names because they demonstrate that the group has guidelines and an agreed-upon mission. So it is with a volunteer organization; a name implies loyalty to one another, and that's a fine path to retention.

Retention of volunteers is a dynamic challenge. When the economy allows people to go back to work, volunteerism suffers. When retirees start second careers, volunteerism suffers. And, of course, the new reality in the volunteer market, as well as the job market, is social media, which makes it so easy for everyone to scoop up opinions on their employers. They can ask questions and get answers from the gamut of informed and uninformed sources. You can send a constant flow of positive messages and, certainly, you can respond sincerely to negative tweets, posts, and comments. However, it's so much better to avoid negativity in the first place. Recruit for the best volunteers, utilize them to the best of their ability, and rely on them to share and spread the best of what your museum offers.

Chapter Eighteen

Website

Your website is like the lineup of servants, arrayed at the front door of the country house, waiting to be of service to all who come to visit. How do you look?

First impressions matter a lot with websites because for many visitors a website is their first good look at a museum. More than a brochure or an e-mail update, your website invites exploration and a pretty thorough overview of who you are. Visitors who make it to your site spend quite a bit of time checking times and prices, exhibitions and events, ways to support and things to buy. Visitors opt to hang around the virtual institution, and donors, funders, scholars, and the media are obliged to visit. Much as you intend to entice them into the actual building, all visitors rely on the website for a full picture. So take inventory of your assets, and then power up to help the desktop, laptop, tablet, or mobile device user decide where your museum fits in his or her life. Depend on it: however a visitor enters your portal, that visit previews your vast panorama of objects, programs, education, membership, volunteerism, donation, partnership, and ideas.

There are ten major services that the website accomplishes. Don't be daunted by the number; be organized. The job is easier when you write to the task.

Service #1: Definition of your brand
Service #2: Basic information
Service #3: Collection and exhibitions
Service #4: Jobs and careers
Service #5: Donations and donors
Service #6: Museum store
Service #7: Dining
Service #8: Research and scholarship

Service #9: Programs and events
Service #10: SEO/SEM, Search Engine Optimization/Marketing

SERVICE #1: DEFINITION OF YOUR BRAND

Defining your collection, mission, and competitive place in the leisure marketplace is the most strategic task of your website. Strategy plays a bigger role in website development than most people realize. As with any marketing decisions, you have to decide your main market, other feasible target audiences, the strongest departments of your institution, the less competitive aspects of your operation, the visuals, photos, and other graphics that will augment the story, and how you want to handle staff and contact listings. All this, while taking into account the constraints of budget, personnel, and time.

Strategy starts at the front door, with your home page—the first place to establish your brand identity. It sets the tone for every page that follows, and those matter when it comes to landing pages, which are where visitors land after typing in a search word. Every successive page should carry the same DNA, the same look, the same message.

Visuals

The home page should be something special to look at: attractive, different, and worth sticking around with. A designer is essential, and writers usually write better when they partner with a graphic designer; visual people have no compunctions about asking verbal people: "What do you mean?" Visuals, of course, communicate powerfully, and on a home page or landing page, they identify the museum immediately so viewers know they're at the right place. It's all too easy to click away from a weak or generic home page, and good graphics hold attention.

Writers and everyone else select the look of the page. Color, mood, size of type relative to picture, all strengthen the words, and if your staffers are not design professionals, they may struggle a bit articulating why they do or don't like something. Soldier on, and expect to spend some time on this. Your home page look is your opening scene, and it establishes what the players are going to say.

Strive for an uncluttered look. As a caution, consider the words of the *Wall Street Journal* writer in describing the home page of an antiques website: "The site's look is clean and stylish, more like a fashion site than a museum homepage." Know that the favorite word of college students in referring to visuals is "clean." This market segment is not the only one that perceives all things good in the page clear of clutter.

Your home page strategy also includes whom to target as your primary targets, so you'll have to prioritize which communities will be addressed by a tab on the navigation bar. Although these are somewhat standardized, you will prioritize them. It's a strategic decision whether, reading from left to right, you want About Us at the beginning or Visit, whether Education comes next or Membership.

Communities

When you think in terms of communities, you organize the tabs accordingly. Members, for example: Do they get their own tab on the navigation bar, or are they listed with Donors and Volunteers within the Support Us pages? Volunteers and Job Seekers frequently appear on the page headed Careers, but if you have a strong internship program or association with an academic institution, Interns might be categorized with About Us.

The important point is thinking of your audiences as communities, because these are people with similar motivations with whom you will have many conversations across many platforms. Establish contact with them on the website. Of course, many of your communities will be reached via social media, and these are usually indicated at the bottom of the home page with their icons. You can read more about them in chapter 12.

Here is just a fraction of the many different groups that can be addressed on your website:

- Visitors
- Schoolteachers
- School administrators, school boards, homeschoolers
- Scholars—historians, scientists, artists, writers
- Members
- Donors
- Sponsors
- Patrons
- Volunteers
- Interns
- Media on all platforms
- Grant funders
- Business and community partners
- Local officials
- Job seekers

However they are categorized on the home page, your communication with each one will be specific. The broad category of Education, for example: you will write differently to (a) teachers who are interested in field trips, (b) visitors who want tours, (c) members who like your workshops. The writing is easy if you start the appropriate page with:

For grade school teachers interested in a field trip . . .

Our tours are open to all visitors, and they are offered . . .

If you're interested in Civil War letters, our upcoming lecture . . .

As you can see, websites are a complex undertaking, even for the smallest museums. Right from the start, on the home page, this holistic breadth and depth should be hinted at verbally and visually. So plan to gather a team from all your staff to decide what is shown, what explained, what expatiated on, and in what proportion. Get everyone involved early, because, like the weather, it changes daily.

SERVICE #2: BASIC INFORMATION

Your website is tasked with delivering Hours of Operation, Price, Address, Phone, How to Get Here including public transportation, Current Events, and a Map. At the same time it must clearly outline the departments and services. Everything gets organized on the home page, and continues in depth on pages devoted to the details of About Us, History, Your Visit, Education, Programs, Giving, Jobs, Press/Media, and Outreach. You may decide to add Research or Classes instead of Education and Outreach, or to give priority to Facilities and include Research under Education. Language is important here, and you might want to assemble a language committee at the outset to help the writer with a taxonomy of terms.

Put as much of this on one page as can be done legibly; then switch to links. The beauty of the website is that it can dole out information a spoonful at a time; the reader links to whatever additional knowledge he or she needs. For example, on the Your Visit page you can link to pages for driving or public transportation details; some museums provide links to bus and train schedules. A link to an interactive map is desirable if more than 10 percent of your visitors come from outside the area.

Note: even on basic facts, it's wise to know who your consumer is, so you can prioritize your site effectively. Some people will want the nearest airport. Others care if you're open any evening.

SERVICE #3: COLLECTION AND EXHIBITIONS

The purpose of this task is to depict your museum's objects in depth, and you can go as deep as you want. When readers can link from the home page or landing page, or type a word in your internal Search menu, or click on a hyperlink, they indicate that they crave more learning; you then have all the space in the world to expatiate. Art museums broaden readers' knowledge by explaining, for example, the culture of the artist; science museums compare a featured exhibition with the scientific advances of the time; a historic house delves into the preservation of its objects; a botanic garden connects exhibits with home gardens; zoos activate activism by listing animal rights organizations.

This is the time to be creative and goal oriented. And there are so many ways to show not how smart you are but how the visitor can best appreciate your museum.

The website should expand the details of special exhibitions. At a recent exhibition at the Los Angeles County Museum of Art, the James Turrell light displays were arranged in two parts, in two buildings, and each had timed admittance. It was essential to know the breadth of the show before starting out, so as not to miss your entrance time. Even without assigned times, visitors will benefit from knowing how much time to expect to spend. This kind of information belongs on the website.

And what about the growing phenomenon of visible storage? Many museums are opening up their behind-the-scenes collection, and it's a treasure chest for scholars. It requires a lot of time and space, and if you're short of either, you can accomplish this transparency on your website. The writing on the labels in visual storage is starkly factual because the concept is not to interpret but to show the object naked, before it is dressed up for presentation in exhibitions. However, within the spirit of raw data, there is room for synthesis. The Luce Center for American Art at Brooklyn Museum has objects from highboys to silver spoons, stacked in glass cubes up to the very high ceilings. The light is low and the aisles narrow, but the assortment is intriguing and an informative brochure explains how to decipher the accession number accompanying each object. As the brochure says, "You can discover a lot about an object's history at the Museum by just looking at the accession number"—as long as you know how to read it. After reading the number, you can jot it down on the back of the brochure and enter it at a nearby computer station to learn more about the object. And that's the kind of added information that websites were born to deliver.

Limitless possibilities may tempt the unfocused writer to say too much. But an effective website can range wide and deep as long as it hews to a sharp outline that's well edited. Organization is key here, too.

Rules of Thumb

A guideline for writing successive pages is 125 words per screen. That's 125 words for announcing a new exhibition, 125 words about a lecture, 125 words on Family Saturday, or a featured work, or how to contribute. This count does not include the headline or subheads, which are in larger type and provide a verbal snapshot of the topic. You don't have to describe every feature of an event, or the full bio of a lecturer, or the curator's synopsis. If one of the 125 words is a link, readers can choose to read more, or not. One hundred twenty-five words will suffice to describe a subject without unduly boring the reader. This paragraph is 117 words.

If you must write more, without forcing the reader to scroll down, decrease the font size. This is not advisable with museum audiences who skew older. Try to keep the text to three paragraphs and use the "for more information" link to another page if you need more space.

Think of each landing page as a headline and first paragraph of information about whatever the reader has typed in "Search" to find. If they are searching for your hours, the headline reads:

Hours

The first paragraph reads:

Wednesday–Sunday 10–5:30
Thursday 10–7
Cafe 9–2
Store 10–5 (Nov. 29–Dec. 23 10–6)
Garden (May–October) 7–7 (Nov.–April) 9–5
Library 11–3 or by appointment
Tours 12, 1, 2, 3 Weekends
Visible Storage Thursday–Saturday
Restored Outbuildings May–October or by appointment

As you can see, at some point this list will look cumbersome, and that's where you write:

For Other Hours Click Here

The same format applies to every tab on the navigation bar.

SERVICE #4: JOBS AND CAREERS

You have job openings? Congratulations. But even if you're swamped with unsolicited applications for unpaid internships, take advantage of this interest by lavishing the Job/Career/Employment page with all the attention paid the other parts of your website. This objective of this website service is to boast about your museum to a community that is young and enthusiastic. Jobs fascinate two other important communities beside the seekers: the people in your organization who need serious helpers and the proliferating college programs that help educate them. Your requirements for jobs—paid and unpaid, full- and part-time—will be stringent, but lead with charm, not challenge. The Carnegie Art Museums in Pittsburgh treats job hunters with all the verve that they show their donors: full-color photographs, complete information, and more emphasis on the museum than on how hard it is to get a job there. It all starts with a good headline, as Carnegie Museums' web page does:

> Your work might belong in a museum.
> One of Our Museums.

Page Design

Design the Jobs page with the same attention to layout and visual treatment as the rest of the site. Then add the human touch the Human Resources department deserves. Carve out an Our Workplace space in a narrow column at the left side of the screen, and write a few sentences about why your museum is a good place to work. Some suggestions for this left-hand column:

Jobholders' Statements

When it comes to job satisfaction, ask around and see what your curators, registrar, librarian, or conservation team like about their work. No specifics, but rather a few conversational sentences about the research they do, or working with children eager to learn, or collaborating with esteemed colleagues. Cite the employee by initials and job title; this will provide a peek at the kind of work—not jobs—your museum offers. The jobs, of course, will change; the work environment is constant.

Unique Pleasures of the Workplace

Write about why the museum is a great place to work. Write in the first person something like, "Our museum is known for its collection of _____, so we meet interesting scholars and experts from all over the eight-state area." Describe the location, because all potential employees want to envision where they'll spend one-third of their day, and portray your neighborhood. Write:

> We're situated above a small river, and this is just a beautiful place to work.

> Our lovely building is in a residential neighborhood of Victorian houses, and it feels like our work is part of the community.

> Our museum is embraced by the schools, businesses, and organizations in our area, and we can see how our work benefits a much larger community.

Let your building help describe the job. Buildings have personalities, and your architecture, whoever the architect and whatever the vintage, is worth discussing. For example, "Our building has this sweeping staircase curving up three floors. You feel pretty grand going from one office to another." Look for features inside and out to highlight: "Our forecourt is paved with memorial and honorarium bricks of people in our state. Walking in to work you get a sense of what our museum is all about."

These imagined examples are umbrella statements for opportunities. You aren't hiring people to fill slots; you're bringing them on board to add their skills and talents to your mission. And even if the longer column of positions available doesn't immediately offer the right job, the job hunter will still come away feeling that you have good work available. Your website also announces opportunities for volunteers, and that is covered in chapter 17.

SERVICE #5: DONATIONS AND DONORS

This important service is charged with raising money from people who, at this moment, are conversing only with a screen. Do not greet these admirable and highly desired people with a page that looks like a pharmaceutical manual. Giving money to a beloved institution is not a black-and-white transaction. It is a Technicolor, emotional experience, and that's the way your Support page must look. Yes, you need to spell out details, and make sure to dot and cross every deductible "i" and legal "t." You will, of course, send an annual report. But on this web page, first be charming.

As with the Jobs page, leave a narrow column on the left side of the screen for the Pleasure of Giving testimonials. Ask your donors, at every level, for a brief quote on why they are pleased, honored, and fulfilled by giving to your museum. You'll have to be diplomatic about whom to ask, and how to edit. Be sure to inform them that you may have to edit for length. Assure them that you will show them the quotes before you upload them. Also tell them that these will be alternating additions to the page, so they may not see their quote every time they visit. Then start recording their words. With a more complex site, you could show these comments as talking head videos.

And think seriously about the Contact Us page; giving the name and extension of a real person is a smart idea.

SERVICE #6: MUSEUM STORE

The online store is more than a way to make money. It is also tasked with keeping your awareness front and center. The online store is a reason for people to revisit your site, even if they aren't planning a trip to the galleries.

The writer's challenge in fulfilling this task is not to transmit the specifics of an item—the description, price, and net weight are easy—but also to convey the personality and learning that your merchandise represents. Depicting both emotion and details in one page is a good challenge and the writer should remember two rules:

1. Never picture a book cover if it isn't relevant to your museum's learning objectives; if the cover misleads, it's a waste of your valuable web real estate.
2. Select and picture items that relate to your mission.

How can you stay on message visually? Start each description with: "This beautiful scarf relates to our exhibition because of . . ." If you can't relate online items to your collection or a special exhibition, don't feature them. Select representative items from toys, apparel, decor, reproductions, books, stationery, and souvenirs. You needn't go into great detail initially; find one compelling reason why a toy telescope is something an education-minded grandparent should purchase. Even inexpensive toys can have educational value, like the Make Your Own Chocolate kit from the Field Museum in Chicago:

> Aztec legend tells of their god, Quetzalcoatl, bringing the cacao tree from paradise to Earth for people to enjoy. Teach your children why cacao was so special to the ancient Aztecs with our chocolate making kit. Chocolate can be educational as well as delicious!

Then you write about the assorted sizes and adhesive included.

For more expensive items, from a travel telescope to designer chairs for children, a few sentences connecting a gift to learning boosts the museum, as well as the sale. This artist's statement, from designer Verner Panton, quoted as part of a product description in the Dallas Museum of Art online catalog, accompanies his $135 Verner Panton Junior Chair:

> The main purpose of my work is to provoke people into using their imagination and make their surroundings more exciting.

Of course, jewelry, housewares, mugs, and plush toys are big sellers, so show these toward the bottom of the screen, or subsequent pages. They may not relate to an exhibition or your mission, but you can still make them sound like a worthy selection:

> This local jewelry designer uses . . .

> The hand-painted design makes this mug especially . . .

Children will take home a lasting memory of our museum with this . . .

SERVICE #7: DINING

Armies aren't the only voyagers to march on their stomachs; museum visitors need fuel, too. Museums also get mileage out of all aspects of dining: the restaurant, menu, facilities rental, recipes, local food sources, and reservation links. The objective of this website service is to leverage the love of food. It's an important component of museums frequented by tourists or any destination museum. For starters, the dining table is a casual forum for information, where visitors gather to reflect and share what they've seen. It may be the only place for visitors to actually discuss the museum experience with those who accompany them. For larger institutions, it's also a place to regroup, to relax and refresh for the next few hours of visiting. Look at your web information as prescriptive, and head the page:

Take a break for lunch, there's a lot to see in our museum.

And then show off your menu to encourage this dining intermission. To further remind visitors to plan a food break, divide your meal occasions into categories:

Light Snacks: to start your visit, refresh, or end the day

Table-Service Lunch: to relax and talk

Café: for a quick meal with the kids

Your website is a place for learning about food, as Crystal Bridges Museum of American Art expertly shows. The Bentonville, Arkansas, museum states a philosophy about the meals served at its restaurant, Eleven. At each dining opportunity it writes about its partnership with local food purveyors and its intent to "specialize in modern American comfort food with an emphasis on traditions that hail from the 'high South and low Midwest' region . . . the Ozarks." Crystal Bridges talks about its "edible responsibility" to feature local foods and culinary artisans and to tell a story "inspired by the artworks, natural surroundings, and fascinating regional history connected to our Museum." It's a masterful way to connect the restaurant to the museum and its wider universe.

The earned income from restaurants, as well as facilities rentals and the store, is around 27 percent. And while rentals and merchandise represent a large chunk of that percentage, the true value of your restaurant is in building social as well as economic sustainability. Diners who gather as participants in a meeting or guests at an event are only tangentially introduced to your collection and exhibitions. They may not have time to stop after lunch or before the cocktails. But on your website they can see the connection vividly.

Facilities

The Facilities Rental page is such a popular sales space that the details of the transaction risk overrunning the charm of the event itself. Here's where your prospects go to plan romantic weddings, stimulating conferences, and collegial business meetings, not just rent tables and chairs. Make sure the romance, stimulation, and collegiality shines through the mass of information. Remember that two different target audiences visit the Facilities page: the professionals who plan parties and the people who give them. Both want facts, but party givers want delight, as well. Part of this is accomplished by photos of flower arrangements, podiums, and polished-wood meeting rooms. The writer's part is to write the descriptions of the rental facilities and one of the best models is provided by the writer for the New Bedford Whaling Museum in New Bedford, Massachusetts:

> Our open courtyard at the top of Johnny Cake Hill has views of the Seaman's Bethel and Double Bank.

> . . . space features . . . a full size ship model. It is an interesting canvas for cocktails or dinner.

> This room has a panoramic view of New Bedford Harbor. . . . The view as a backdrop is great for wedding photos.

> A spectacular salute to New Bedford's rich history.

Guests come to your venue for parties, conferences, and meetings. Make sure they leave as museum visitors.

SERVICE #8: RESEARCH AND SCHOLARSHIP

Chapter 5 covers how museums educate students, teachers, homeschoolers, and lecture attendees. This part of your website addresses a special constituency that deserves more online attention: scholars. Scholars today come in many different species including academics, authors, investigative journalists, autodidacts, precocious children, family genealogists, and the perennially curious. Museums naturally embrace scholars as part of the family, and now it's time to put that relationship on the website for the extended family everywhere who wants to engage in exploration and critical thinking.

How does a museum accept this challenge? Slowly. Whether you have a librarian, archivist, large education department, or merely a conscientious staffer who is willing to help with questions, put your research/scholarship resources on the home page where everyone can see. It engenders curiosity, and that is a proud service that museums provide to the community—the world community—and the fact of it is as important as the details.

The Dedham Historical Society in Dedham, Massachusetts, lists Research right after Home on its website. That alone signifies its importance. Open the page and you'll see a fascinating list of services, many of which your museum probably offers. And even the casual reader understands that local museums know about town records, street plans, high school yearbooks, and military involvement. Old communities, like Dedham, will preserve knowledge like church and civil records, eighteenth-century newspapers, journals and diaries, social organizations, and Civil War documents. In an era when students are required to explore, think critically, synthesize, and draw conclusions, research is imperative, whether it comes with a small "r" or a larger Research on a website.

For museums without space to display all their objects, be assured that a good writer can find plenty of space on the Research bookshelves of your website. Select any category that's in storage and start a paragraph on your new Research page with:

Did you know that nineteenth-century tall clocks . . .

What our recipe book collection can tell you about Kansas homesteads . . .

Learn more about . . .

The Abbe Museum in Bar Harbor, Maine, includes a concise three paragraphs on the group of Maine Indian tribes known collectively as the Wabanaki and follows it with four links to additional information. It's not encyclopedic knowledge and it needn't be; it's a new awareness, just enough to keep the lifelong learning process alive.

Another excellent website concept is provided by an academic museum, Weatherspoon Art Gallery at the University of North Carolina, Greensboro. The organization of information is simple: images of art on any one of which one can click to open a current exhibition. Keep clicking and you get a good sampling of the whole show, with each image accompanied by one to four paragraphs of text. It's as comprehensive as an art lecture, appropriate for a teaching and learning museum connected to a major university.

Here's how any museum can adapt the concept for its website:

Select five to eight images, sliding or static, depending on what your site and time of staff allow. Don't attempt too many objects; if the page is static, each will be too small, and if the images slide, they'll move faster than the mind can absorb them.

Write a caption for each image, giving title, artist/creator, and one sentence of description or background. Write just enough to inform and intrigue; you don't have to sound like an educator in the caption. If you keep it short, you'll force yourself to be conversational.

Elsewhere on the screen page, write a paragraph summing up the exhibition. This can come straight from the introductory panel on the wall, from the exhibition catalog, or from the curator. If it sounds academic, that's fine. Website viewers have options of what to read, just as they would in a visit to the museum.

Archives of Events

Knowledge pops up where you least expect it. Today's event is tomorrow's history. A timely lecture or fun workshop might be just a diversion for today's audiences; for tomorrow's researchers it is anthropology.

So consider your website a repository of events. Websites endure, and one-off events do not. Unlike exhibitions, which endure forever on a website, events are ephemeral, and ephemera such as event invitations and promotional pieces are useful long afterward for reference. Here are some of the quotidian details in the soon-to-be-tossed-away invitation that should remain retrievable on your website for the reference of scholars and educators:

- Speaker's biography
- Title of the talk or event
- Reasons for holding the event
- Authoritative quotes about the subject of the event
- Food served
- Venue and setting

Certainly, more text-heavy event materials such as programs and other handouts are troves of data and insights and should also be archived on the website. In the world of publishing, these transient pieces might be called ephemera, but in the digital world they last forever. And those are just the printed material to be converted to PDFs. Here is a third category of information that appears on your Exhibition and Event pages at the time, easily saved in archives:

- Complementary programming during the exhibition
- Family days, school, and local library collaborations
- Community and corporate tie-ins

- Names of exhibition lenders and supporters and their affiliation with the museum

Archiving is time consuming and archivists deserve sympathy and praise. Be prepared to verbally document past exhibitions with the title, introduction taken from first wall panel of the exhibition, dates, season, tagline from promotional material, titles of accompanying lectures and workshops, and locations of various activities. That's a lot of writing, but valuable fodder for hungry researchers.

SERVICE #9: PROGRAMS AND EVENTS

This category has gotten out of hand. Thanks to social media, every blip in the routine is treated like an event as it gets headlined on Facebook, tweeted, and commemorated on Instagram. Just because something gets published online doesn't mean it's eventful. So, for example, the photos of installing an exhibition or welcoming a school group might be interesting and newsworthy, but they aren't the main event. These documentations belong on other social media; save your website for the main event. The former are transitory; the latter endures for several weeks beforehand.

There are firm guidelines, if not rules, for writing about an event or program: consistency, interest, relevance, branding. Use the same event title that you use in all your written pieces, from the newsletter to the magazine to the signage inside and outside the museum. Tell why the event or program is relevant to the museum's audiences. If you explain why visitors, educators, and the community will enjoy the program or event, the second rule—interest—will be fulfilled. Finally, remember that the program or event was designed to augment the mission of the museum. It bolsters your brand in the competitive welter of arts and culture organizations, so constantly relate the features of the program or event to your core values. Select visuals for the Events and Programs pages that are used in all other printed pieces. You can add pages on supplementary activities—a series of talks that preview a performance—but make sure they're absolutely relevant and not just amusing. One excellent social media addition to your website is a blog that thoughtfully, and at some length, develops themes from the program. A link to a YouTube video is another apt extension into social media. But again, this will be a carefully scripted and produced piece, informative and worth archiving.

SERVICE #10: SEO/SEM, SEARCH ENGINE OPTIMIZATION/ MARKETING

The underlying task of all website content is to make the virtual visit happen in the first place. It's not just a matter of "build a website and they will come." The pages must be written in such a way that search engines find them. All museum professionals must be alert to the growing power of search engine marketing, and how writers can optimize their words. Search engines identify keywords on every media platform, not just websites, but your web pages are a good place to start.

The simple goal: use the keywords that visitors use when they search for something they want. It's not straightforward, and algorithms won't be mentioned in this chapter. I leave that to your content strategist. There is one writer's rule of thumb that has endured from pre-SEO days: Keep it simple. Edit your thoughts and write succinctly and to the point. Search engines don't do a good job navigating around fulsome adjectives and adverbs. If you can express your thoughts in bullet points of nouns and verbs, do so. Search engines like bullet points.

Some other SEO-motivated writing tips: Use subheads of three words. Assemble no more than five ideas, with five subheads, per page. Don't make the reader scroll down.

Readers read in an "F" pattern—after the first two paragraphs their attention dribbles down to nothing—so put most of your keywords at the top.

Beyond these basic marching orders, plan to confer with your search consultant. That's the expert who can help with the analytics that suggest the best words to use. However, not all content strategists are writers, and they won't know your museum as well as you do. Demand a back-and-forth collaboration as you craft the best words. As always when working with a consultant, ask good questions to get good answers. Here are some of the questions to ask your web content developer:

- Multiple pages: How many multiple pages does our website need for each tab?
- Google: How do we get to page 1?
- Google Analytics: Is it still the gold standard and why?
- URL: Is our URL optimized for search? Is that how people will get to our site?
- Responses to e-mail: How do we analyze the traffic generated by e-mail?
- Referring sites: What websites or other platforms are linking to ours? How do we maximize this flow?
- Top landing page: Where do visitors to our site go first? What keyword have they used?

- I've heard that Google wants fresh information, that search favors what's new. How often should we refresh our website?
- Distracted visitors: So, someone has linked to one of our pages and can't wait to get back to YouTube. How do we keep that itchy person on our website?
- Consistency: Sometimes we refer to our museum as a house museum, sometimes as a historic house. Does this confuse search engines?
- Google AdWords: The keywords it suggests—can't everyone use them?
- Keyword density: Is it true that 5 to 8 percent of any page should contain keywords? And that there should be only five hundred words of content per page?
- Euphemisms: I've heard that we should avoid wit and vivid language and stick with generally accepted terms. Why?
- Pronouns: Ignore them, right? Why?
- Blogs: They're supposed to be good for search, so should we add "blog-ger" to our job descriptions?
- Navigation bars vs. links: Which gets visitors to keep on reading through the site?
- Good writing: True or false? Good writing for an online presence is not the same as good writing for any other media.
- Mindless repetition of keywords: That means not using "science," "scien-tist," and "scientific" on the same page, right? (Well, that's good writing offline, too.)
- Reading level: How do I assess the reading level of our website users and the reading level of our content?

You can probably answer many of these questions right now. But learn to constantly push your content consultant, because SEO changes with every update and post. A major change is the addition of SEM to SEO. Search engine marketing has evolved to a marketing science with a corresponding multitude of experts capable of elucidating it. Keywords are but one manifes-tation of the strategic thinking behind SEM. And if you're not ready to plunge into digital analytics, be confident that plain good writing never goes out of style. Writers have always had five keywords of their own: reader, relevance, brevity, nothing wasted.

OWNED MEDIA

In a world of shared media, where everyone who posts or comments is an author and all content is subject to citizen approval or rebuttal, your website stands distinct. It is owned media, which you create and manage. How it ranks against other media platforms is a question asked endlessly, and there is no answer. Three things are certain: (1) your website represents your museum and its brand as nothing else can, (2) your website maps out more of the information you want to convey than any other platform, and (3) if you organize the major tasks, you can be a beacon of knowledge to more communities than were ever dreamed of.

Chapter Nineteen

YouTube

While Facebook, Twitter, Instagram, and Pinterest provide the platforms to showcase content, YouTube, like blogs, *is* content. With YouTube, you are the primary author, the authority on stage with the microphone. If all platforms are forums, then Facebook is an exhibition hall, Twitter is a town hall, and blogs and YouTube are lecture halls. With Facebook and Twitter, everyone talks back and forth. With YouTube, one voice talks first and Q&A and the comments come later.

YouTube was a sleeping giant that woke up. What started as home videos, and then developed into pretty good amateur comedies and parodies, has now bloomed into a bully pulpit for cultural presentations. People and organizations with something to say are creating channels around a subject, series of talks that appear as regularly as a television talk show, or opinion column. Social media may seem co-opted by the young and spontaneous, but with YouTube there's a wide audience for ongoing learning, research, and scholarship. And museums of every size and type can reach their own slice of that audience with videos geared to their field of expertise. The National Churchill Museum in Fulton, Missouri, has troves of knowledge about England's most famous leader, and from a small space can reach the community of people who follow Winston Churchill.

YouTube is an audiovisual juggernaut that's exquisitely appropriate for museums—and vice versa. With YouTube:

- Museums have a lot of objects and knowledge—the unlimited subject matter that YouTube needs to inform and delight its many followers.
- Museums employ experts—the curators, educators, scholars, librarians, multimedia professionals that YouTube needs to credibly present a four- to six-minute video.

- Museums have a brand—a mission and core values that can attract and retain the niche audiences that YouTube needs as it expands into a network to rival television.
- Museums keep schedules—YouTube videos appear regularly; they are anticipated.
- Museums have a stage set—the backdrop of a video that has become the YouTube requirement for instantly communicating its topic to its targeted audiences.
- Museums demonstrate—and YouTube is made for visual explication.

Target audience, niche markets, networks: YouTube has created thousands of channels that reach very specific communities, and your museum can talk directly to your communities, too.

Museums of any size or resources can utilize YouTube. You can produce a one-off video, or a series. You can create a series for one exhibition, or weekly shows as the Field Museum in Chicago does with its Brain Scoop videos. Developing a YouTube video involves six components:

- Subject
- Expert
- Brand
- Schedule
- Production values
- Demonstration

SUBJECT

Museums own a lot of knowledge on niche subjects, collected for decades as they go about their stated mission. The niche subjects discussed on YouTube appeal to a narrow but densely populated section of the public. Thanks to the Internet, you can reach thousands of people on a subject as arcane as eighteenth-century French mechanical furniture, as the Getty Museum does, or as action oriented as the Frazier Museum, Louisville, Kentucky, does with its how-to videos on samurai weapons.

Do you realize how many four-minute videos you already have stored in your brain, as well as in your galleries? At one local historical society museum, I received a very helpful spur-of-the-moment explanation on the use of white cotton gloves with costume collections. It was fascinating, with a built-in demonstration, and it was spontaneous. It took place in a storage room among racks of archivally protected garments, and if cameras were allowed, I could have produced a video with a mobile phone right then and there. At another small historical society's restored house, a costumed interpreter told me about the history of the pioneers who had moved to a house like the one we were in. We walked up the steep stairs, discussed the meager furnishings, and looked at door handles and window frames. This informative, and informal, conversation was a YouTube video just waiting to be made. At yet another local historical society's museum I learned about itinerant portrait painters. These are the slivers of information that niche audiences crave, and any museum can serve them up.

One roundtable discussion among your colleagues should unearth plenty of YouTube episodes. The short time frame of a four-minute video takes the intimidation out of the job. Some by the way are even shorter, like the ones produced by the Frazier Museum. All a YouTube video takes is someone who can talk engagingly to the camera and the unseen viewer beyond. Here's the framework:

> This is . . . [describe object]
>
> The [name of museum] added it to its collection because . . .
>
> Look at this [show a detail] . . .
>
> It demonstrates [tell what it demonstrates, proves] . . .
>
> The artist [cabinetmaker, merchant, king, seaman] who made [designed, used, enjoyed, commissioned, found] this object probably lived a life of [describe the history or context] . . .
>
> Today [relate or contrast the object to current experience] . . .
>
> Here at the [name of museum] we think this is important because . . .

YouTube videos are informative, direct, clear, focused. Take a trial run with your smart phone and see how you might design one for your museum.

Archived Material

You may have hidden YouTube treasure in your archives. There are dozens of stories in those photographs and ancient footage, and you don't need to be a Ken Burns to deploy them well. Here are some ways to write a script around a photograph:

> This is the kitchen of [name of historic house]. Ever wonder how they made dinner . . .
>
> Look at the people in the background. You can tell by . . .

These are the [objects] the newcomers brought with them. Do you know why they were so precious?

The setting of this [subject of photo] is significant because . . .

The [name of museum] is lucky to have this footage because it shows . . .

Or borrow this unintended suggestion from a posted comment to the British Golf Museum's YouTube video:

I cannot express how elated I am to view this swing of James Braid. All my golfing life I have tried to emulate his swing through his writings.

The footage and the comment become a YouTube video with the addition of Mr. Braid's commentary, edited from his writings. Read excerpts from the written documents in your archives; a good letter or diary is about as informative and poignant as you can get, and that's what YouTube is all about.

Finding Subjects

Select your four- to six-minute topic by using the book club selection process. Start with a room of eight people; ask each to think of three topics from their recent experience. Then ask everyone to write a one-sentence rationale for any topic they like. It's the writing of the rationale that winnows out the least interesting, and points to the most promising and doable videos. You'll soon have a short list of topics that your table of experts find promising, and the beginning line of narrative to prove that they can actually be taken to completion.

EXPERT

YouTube videos are characterized by a respected and well-liked person who talks informally straight to the camera, right to the viewer. The format of YouTube started as a single person, frequently at home, who knew a lot about a topic he or she wanted to share with people who also cared. The subject could as mundane as makeup and beauty (from the No. 2 most popular YouTube channel in 2013) or as esoteric as how to ship antique statues (from the Getty Museum's encyclopedic library of YouTube videos), but it is always of passionate interest to the viewer who then stands to become one of your followers. In museums, there is no shortage of experts who are passionate and knowledgeable about their specialty. Emily Graslie is one expert who created her own channel, called the Brain Scoop; she is now employed by the Field Museum and delivers highly engaging talks every week on subjects ranging from romantic ants and meteorites to the antler room and skinning wolves (parental guidance advised).

At the Frazier Museum of History in Louisville, historic interpreter Gerry Rose dons a tricorn hat to tell you his stories about history. YouTube videos are very personal, and that one-to-one approach helps museums connect with their constituencies in ways they never could before.

Here's the same framework as above, but from the point of view of the personality of the speaker:

This is [object] and I find it fascinating because . . .

People are always asking me . . .

When I show visitors this [object] they always . . .

Look at this [detail]: I'll take my finger out of the way so you can see it better. Notice how . . .

Part of my job is to [relate job to object or gallery] . . .

I'm in my office today, so I'll be doing some work visitors don't usually see. . . .

I love [name of museum] because of [object] like this. . . .

Note that last line: it relates to the museum itself, the institution that collects, preserves, and, via YouTube, interprets. YouTube flourishes as media because of its clearly defined topics. These are the areas of knowledge that comprise your mission, your brand, and YouTube will attract an audience of loyal followers much as blogs do.

BRAND

A good YouTube video has an intriguing title, like "Brain Scoop" from the Field Museum, or "Churchill Chats" from the National Churchill Museum. This title brands your museum because it describes content that is distinctive to you. Remember that YouTube is the platform that allows you to author a message; your on-camera authority is associated with you; the location is your own building and galleries; your message holds the stage for four to six minutes; your audience is now worldwide and reachable any time of day. Just don't forget to tell all those people your name.

Some people will follow you on YouTube because there's an icon at the bottom of your website. Thousands more follow their curiosity by typing a keyword in a search box and landing on your YouTube video. When their inquiries take them to your site, introduce yourself immediately.

The National Churchill Museum starts its video with a title card that reads:

The National Churchill Museum presents Churchill Chats

At the end, remind captivated viewers who made it possible:

The Brain Scoop is brought to you by The Field Museum, Chicago

Another rule of branding reminds on-camera personalities to mention the marketer's name. In the Brain Scoop series, presenter Emily Graslie references the museum in a way that seems perfectly natural and conversational. Here are some ways your on-camera presenter can refer to the museum in the course of the video:

My colleagues here at [your museum] tell me that . . .

See this [object, detail of object]? The [your museum] curators told me that . . .

This woman sits at a [desk] similar to several in [your museum] and . . .

Here's a part of [your museum] visitors don't see. We're taking a behind-the-scenes . . .

The more videos you create for YouTube, the stronger your brand. The Getty has many series including "Animals in Art" and "Making Art." But you don't need vast resources. It requires some quality time to confer on stories and it's worth the effort. Highlighting a theme unique to your museum and then following up with regular episodes reinforces your mission and core competencies. Continuity attests to your vision. It shows that your values will endure, and that you have the strength to follow through.

As your viewers see additional videos, they become more familiar with your institution and its distinctive knowledge. If they then become followers, congratulations! That "repurchase" is everything a brand hopes for. By the way, you need a strong brand not just to collect clicks and followers, but donors and partners.

SCHEDULE

Continuity leads to the thorny question: How often is continuous? Regular YouTube videos are essential, according to Dixie Lee Clough, a museum professional with an unerring eye for good YouTube videos. They don't have to be daily, or even weekly, but they do have to recur. They must be awaited. YouTube's strength as a branding tool is familiarity, consistency, and trust. Your followers have to know that you will be there.

A regular schedule is demanding, and it helps you establish the length of video you can deliver on time. One of the values of YouTube is anticipation; your viewers expect the next installment. Experts suggest no more than four minutes; produce a longer video and the comments can hurt: boring, pointless, and poor quality are just some of the reactions you'll read. Of course, you are none of the above, but you have to edit yourself. Write as much as you have to say, because it's easier to whittle down than to add on. Then whittle.

PRODUCTION VALUES

When YouTubers started out, theirs was a cottage industry, but even then it never looked tacky. It was certainly personal, idiosyncratic, and off the cuff, but never low value. As YouTube expert Dixie Clough would say, the recipe might be delicious, but nobody wants to eat a sagging cake. And no one wants to view a shabby video. So it matters that you have production values such as a believable speaker, nice voice, appropriate wardrobe, pleasing setting, easy-to-understand graphics, and clear audio. Most YouTube videos today have good lighting, without blurry shadows or hot glares. Getting a lighting expert to set you up might be a good investment. In other YouTube videos, there may be no fancy sets in evidence. In truth, of course, there are some rather sophisticated production values at work, but they are made to appear informal.

The Set

The Churchill Museum's YouTube series features an excellent YouTube set: uncluttered yet representative of the subject and tone of the videos. It consists of two comfy chairs for the interviewer and his guest, with a library bookshelf behind and a small bust of Winston Churchill on the table between them.

The Frazier Museum of History varies its set depending on the topic, and adds costuming to set the stage. For a series of videos on a Napoleonic exhibition, the interpreter wore a tricorn hat. For a series on samurai martial arts, the speaker wore a kimono.

The series of videos on early twentieth-century golf from the archives of the British Golf Museum, St. Andrews, Scotland, is delightful though raw. Some of the videos are titled "Lessons from History," others are "Swings of Champions," and though the footage is old and blurred, dedicated golfers will love the close-up view of legends and the hole-by-hole journey through iconic golf courses and links. The outdoor settings capture the sweep and lore of golf, the brand of the British Golf Museum. One charming scene focused on the quandary of James Braid, whose ball got stuck in a crevice of a stone wall. Typical English country landscaping, typical golf situation.

Sometimes a YouTube video will take your museum outside a set, especially if you're a garden or zoo or conducting field research. But pick your shots carefully. Some sites look so interesting they detract from the speaker, and unless that person has built a strong brand as a spokesman the set will trump your museum. A well-known science YouTuber, Derek Muller, has transcended the simple set for explorations far and wide. His visit to a buffered sound studio is fascinating; however, Muller's well-earned celebrity over the years gives him permission to stretch the YouTube rules. His channel, Veritasium, is worth watching as a model of how YouTube can promote knowledge beyond the walls of the museum.

Casting is important. YouTubers used to act singly, talking directly to the camera, with no supporting actors. Their personality carried the show. The genre has evolved to allow an occasional sidekick or interviewees, but the star system remains in place. Whether it's the museum blogger performing his or her comments on camera, or an interpreter from the museum, or a professional with expertise and believability, certain rules apply: pleasant voice, appropriate wardrobe, neatness, easy smiles, and sincerity. YouTube is built on likeable experts their followers want to return to, time after time.

Competent production matters more all the time as YouTube breaches the space previously held tight by television. The contrast between a YouTube video and television remains sharp:

- Four-plus minutes, rather than thirty minutes
- One personality vs. cast of characters
- Real person vs. an actor in a role
- Low budget vs. big budget
- One-person show vs. team
- Narrow, niche audiences vs. broad-market segments
- Thoughtful content vs. easy-listening content

However different YouTube may be from television, just remember that now it competes with the big kids, and will have to stay sharp; not costly, but knowledgeable. Museums are lucky; they have the thoughtful content.

DEMONSTRATION

Video is all about demonstration and usage. You get to show how a sword is held, how a musical instrument is played, how an animal is fed. You can indicate how people interact with your objects, even if preservation requires that you don't touch. As for the increasingly interesting world of preservation, it's a natural for YouTube videos. Video lets you demonstrate more than things; it shows how to navigate your galleries and gives a sense of the space that eliminates the fear that many people have of museums. YouTube takes viewers behind the scenes and makes back rooms and labs interesting. There are many ways to bring the stuff of museums to life, and YouTube invigorates your stories in ways you'll never get tired of telling.

THE ARCHIVING ADVANTAGE

Museums do a wonderful job of collecting, preserving, interpreting, and educating, and it has a skilled ally in YouTube. YouTube tells the world about the entirety of a collection. It preserves knowledge with the fervor of a medieval monk. And it interprets and educates with the agility of video and sound. A most mesmerizing YouTube video is the stop-action unlocking of an eighteenth-century French mechanical table, presented on the Getty Museum channels. You see a hand inserting a key, and then drawer after hidden drawer opens. There is no other way this fragile possession could be demonstrated to so many people. Other videos showed calligraphy being drawn and mosaic tiles being positioned. If you have exhibition videos, consider archiving them on YouTube. One such was situated in a wall monitor at the Field Museum's 2013 *Scenes from the Stone Age: The Cave Paintings of Lascaux*. It demonstrated blade making and stone bowl carving and was accompanied by the quiet, rasping sound effect of scraping and grating, carving and etching. The visual was doubly instructive because of the slow, methodical sound, testifying to the patient craftsmanship of early man and firmly rebutting the stereotype of "caveman." This is interpretation at its finest. YouTube helps you preserve sounds and actions for posterity.

With technology so new, and the strategies so different, it's helpful to look at other people's work. Any content creator and Internet consultant will tell you the same thing: look at other examples and find the ones you'd like to borrow. The list of references for this chapter at the end of the book should give you a good tutorial.

YouTube is exciting because it permeates a layer of audience that is hard to touch: museum lovers who want more. They can't visit every day, they can't stay for twenty-four hours, and they can't carry you away with them. Still, they love to learn about everything, and short, rigorous videos quench that thirst. Each social media has its strategy, and YouTube is maturing into a very strategic tool. It's a writer's dream assignment: a strong visual and strong reason for writing about it.

Chapter Twenty

Writing Tips

In conclusion and in brief, these words of wisdom have guided writers across the ages and disciplines.

1. Keep it short. Plan to spend a lot of time making your copy short. Heed the words of Blaise Pascal, seventeenth-century man of letters: "I have made this longer than usual because I have not had time to make it shorter."
2. Write in longhand. Pretend you're in a meeting, where it's considered impolite to be seen working on your laptop or tablet, and write your thoughts on a piece of paper. Write it out by hand, understanding that you'll have to transcribe it later, as well. Believe me, you'll think first and write succinctly.
3. Read it out loud. You'll hear the clinkers that your eye missed.
4. Pretend your college professor has limited to you to one page, after which she'll stop reading and grade you on whatever is on the first page.
5. In selecting adjectives, use only one comma and one "and"—three adjectives—it forces you to pick the most descriptive ones, rather than those that flaunt your vocabulary.
6. Rethink the rule of three. Writers love threesomes too much. I was one of them, but I now realize that the chanting quality of a list of three makes people yawn. Three is too many if two examples suffice.
7. Avoid adverbs . . . assiduously.
8. Replace cliché phrases like "tough as nails" with one adjective like "adamantine."
9. Don't be too proud to use clichés if they make they point. Don't use too many.

10. Write your paragraph as bullet points. With your thoughts in list form, it's easy to spot the repetitive or inessential ones. Then put them back into sentences.

11. "Try to leave out the part that readers tend to skip." Elmore Leonard, the hard-boiled detective writer, said this. How to know what readers find skippable? Save your day's writing for twenty-four hours and then reread it. You'll be more objective.

12. Use quotations. They've made it to the quote websites for a reason. Also, it adds authority to your own writing if you're smart enough to borrow wisely. It's easy to research quotes in numerous online sources. Next time you need to use the Shift+F7 key to find a synonym, look for help from quotations.

13. Write captions for every visual. Captions are the candy of publications, little nuggets of sweet information, small enough to pop into your brain at an instant, nonsating, and always leaving you wanting more. I think they're easy to write because you have a photograph to feed you the idea.

14. Use foreign words where appropriate. Museum, *musée, museo,* 博物馆, *bówùguǎn.* Visitors from all over the globe are visiting your museum. Although most museum exhibits are visual enough to carry the weight of communication, foreign words add depth and meaning, without which no communication is complete. Don't rush out and hire translators. Do, however, select a few areas to enrich with other languages.

15. Run from buzzwords. Buzzwords are worse than clichés because they're just trendy and embarrassingly overused. Because they sneak onto the page without warning, you have to know what they look like. Of the one hundred terms listed on Adam Sherk's website, I have selected the twenty-five I personally hang my head in shame for writing.

- Leading
- Innovative
- Dynamic
- Smart
- Savvy
- World class
- Sustainable
- Next generation
- Best practices
- Groundbreaking
- Empower
- Scalable

- Stakeholders
- Repurpose
- Synergy
- Disruption
- Customer-centric
- Sticky
- Silo
- Organic growth
- Unique
- Strategic partnership
- Iconic
- Robust
- Outside the box

Be alert, and if you suddenly feel proud about using a word, it's probably a trendy one. It happens all the time. Find some synonyms.

References

REFERENCES FOR CHAPTER 1: AUDIO TOURS

Byrne, D. *How Music Works*. San Francisco: McSweeney's, 2013.

Conn, S. *Do Museums Still Need Objects?* Philadelphia: University of Pennsylvania Press, 2010.

Gill, N. S. "Is 'First Do No Harm' from the Hippocratic Oath? Myth vs. Fact." About.com, Ancient/Classical History. Accessed February 2, 2014. http://ancienthistory.about.com/od/greekmedicine/f/HippocraticOath.htm.

"Jeff Koons." Museum of Contemporary Art, Chicago, guide program. 2008.

"LEGO Advert: Let's Build." LEGO YouTube video, 0:59. Posted November 1, 2013. http://www.youtube.com/watch?v=rwQqkX3qZak.

Sangster, C. "RP and BBC English." BBC online. http://www.bbc.co.uk/voices/yourvoice/rpandbbc.shtml.

Solway, D. "Directors' Guild." Culture, *W*, November 2008. Accessed February 9, 2014. http://www.wmagazine.com/culture/art-and-design/2008/11/grynsztejn_viso.

Underhill, P. *Call of the Mall*. New York: Simon & Schuster, 2005.

———. *Why We Buy: The Science of Shopping*. New York: Simon & Schuster, 1999.

Vanderbilt, T. "When Pedestrians Get Mixed Signals." Sunday Review, *New York Times*, February 1, 2014. Accessed February 2, 2014. http://www.nytimes.com/2014/02/02/opinion/sunday/when-pedestrians-get-mixed-signals.html?_r=0.

REFERENCES FOR CHAPTER 2: BLOGS

"About the Museum." National Museum of the American Indian online. http://nmai.si.edu/about/.

Brochure, Luce Center for American Art at Brooklyn Museum, New York.

Brooks, D., and G. Collins. "Happy New Year, Politicians. Seriously." *New York Times*, January 4, 2014. Accessed January 6, 2014. http://opinionator.blogs.nytimes.com/2014/01/04/happy-new-year-politicians-seriously/?r=0.

Brown, J., J. Culbertson, J. Grimes, K. Harringer, M. Johnson, S. Samuels, and S. Van de Berg. *Museum of Life and Science Animal Department Blogs*. Accessed December 30, 2013. http://blogs.lifeandscience.org/keepers.

"Career Opportunities." Cleveland Museum of Natural History online. http://www.cmnh.org/site/AboutUs/CareerOpportunities/SecGuard.aspx.

"Early Illinois Folk Art, 1825–1925: Exhibit Extended to October 27, 2014." *DuPage County Historical Museum Newsletter* 4, no. 2 (Fall 2013). Accessed March 3, 2014. http://www.dupagemuseum.org/PDFs/2013Fall_Newsletter.pdf.

Eisner, J., and Y. Ten. *Stories Yun Told Me* (blog). Accessed December 30, 2013.

Furlong, A. "Flowers and Honey, BEEcause of Bees." *Indianapolis Museum of Art Blog*, July 12, 2013. http://www.imamuseum.org/blog/2013/07/12/flowers-and-honey-beecause-of-bees/#more-20911.

Gopnik, A. *Paris to the Moon.* New York: Random House, 2000.

"The Life Before You." BurkeMuseum.org. http://www.burkemuseum.org/brand/.

"Map: Luce Center for American Art." BrooklynMuseum.org. http://www.brooklynmuseum.org/opencollection/research/luce/lucemap.php.

McMaken, B. "In Vogue and Out." *DuPage County Historical Museum Newsletter* 5, no. 1 (Winter 2014). Accessed March 3, 2014. http://www.dupagemuseum.org/PDFs/2014Winter_Newsletter.pdf.

National Museum of the American Indian. *All Things Green* (blog). http://blog.nmai.si.edu/main/all-things-green/.

———. *A Song for the Horse Nation* (blog). http://blog.nmai.si.edu/main/a-song-for-the-horse-nation/.

"The New Colossus." *Wikipedia.* Accessed December 30, 2013. http://en.wikipedia.org/wiki/The_New_Colossus.

Nordquist, R. "Listicle." About.com, Grammar & Composition. Accessed March 15, 2014. http://grammar.about.com/od/il/g/Listicle.htm.

Okrent, A. "The Listicle as Literary Form." *University of Chicago Magazine,* January–February 2014, 52–53.

Pulitzer Foundation for the Arts, and Contemporary Art Museum, St. Louis. *Contemporary-Pulitzer Blog.* http://www.pulitzerarts.org/resources/blog/.

Saetta, E. "That's a Wrap: Protecting the 'Burghers' from Construction." *Cross-Sections* (blog), September 17, 2013. http://cantorscience.wordpress.com/2013/09/17/thats-a-wrap-protecting-the-burghers-from-construction/.

Simon, N. "Museum 2.0 Rerun: Answers to the Ten Questions I Am Most Commonly Asked." *Museum 2.0* (blog), September 18, 2013. Accessed March 2, 2014. http://museumtwo.blogspot.com/2011/04/answers-to-top-ten-questions-i-am-asked.html.

Tate Museums. *Tate Debate* (blog). http://www.tate.org.uk/context-comment/search?f[]=im_vid_46:1849&f[]=im_vid_31:1212&solrsort=is_end_date%20asc,%20is_start_date%20asc,%20is_published_date%20desc.

———. *TateShots* (blog). http://www.tate.org.uk/context-comment/audio-video/search?f[0]=im_vid_31%3A2327&solrsort=is_end_date%20asc%2C%20is_start_date%20asc%2C%20is_published_date%20desc .

Tenement Museum. "Something to Smile About." *Notes from the Tenement* (blog), September 30, 2013. http://www.tenement.org/blog/something-to-smile-about/.

———. "A Standing Ovation for the Jewish Rialto." *Notes from the Tenement* (blog), February 25, 2014. http://www.tenement.org/blog/a-standing-ovation-for-the-jewish-rialto/.

Van de Berg, S. "Who Weighs More? Round 2." *Museum of Life and Science Animal Department Blogs,* December 15, 2013. http://blogs.lifeandscience.org/keepers/2013/12/15/who-weighs-more-round-2/ .

Wright, R. "Mask That Likely Inspired the Seahawks Logo Discovered in Maine Museum." *Burke Museum Blog,* February 20, 2014. http://burkemuseum.blogspot.com.

REFERENCES FOR CHAPTER 3: BROCHURES

Booklet, John and Mable Ringling Museum of Art, Sarasota, Fla.

Booklet, Kunstmuseum Basel, Basel, Switzerland.

Brochure, Crystal Bridges Museum of American Art, Bentonville, Ark.

Brochure, Deere-Wiman House, Moline, Ill.

Brochure, DuPage County Historical Museum, Wheaton, Ill.

Brochure, Georgia O'Keeffe Museum, Santa Fe, N.M.
Brochure, Marine Museum, Biarritz, France.
Brochure, McFaddin-Ward House, Beaumont, Tex.
Brochure, New Museum, New York, N.Y.

REFERENCES FOR CHAPTER 4: E-MAIL

Miller, C., and S. Clifford. "Retailers Fight Exile from Gmail In-Boxes." *New York Times*, September 15, 2013. http://www.nytimes.com/2013/09/16/technology/for-retailers-new-gmail-has-one-tab-too-many.html?pagewanted=1&adxnnl=1&adxnnlx=1382288509-rSJCB75Ndf8pQvc8zBf4pg.
Stevens, G., and W. Luke. *A Life in Museums: Managing Your Museum Career*. Washington, D.C.: AAM Press, 2012.
Tenement Museum. "Waking Up at 97 Orchard Street." *Notes from the Tenement* (blog), March 7, 2013. http://www.tenement.org/blog/waking-up-at-97-orchard-street/.

REFERENCES FOR CHAPTER 5: EDUCATION: LEARNING OUTCOMES

"Bloom's Taxonomy Action Verbs." Clemson University online. http://www.clemson.edu/assessment/assessmentpractices/referencematerials/documents/Blooms%20Taxonomy%20Action%20Verbs.pdf.
"Buffalo State Students Study Museums as Part of the Year of the Teacher." *Burchfield Penney Art Center Blog*, November 14, 2013. http://www.burchfieldpenney.org/general/blog/article:11-14-2013-12-00am-buffalo-state-students-study-museums-as-part-of-the-year-of-the-teacher/.
"Churchill Museum School and Museum Programs." NationalChurchillMuseum.org. Accessed January 7, 2014. http://www.nationalchurchillmuseum.org/churchill-museum-programs.html.
"FAQ." Tenement Museum online. http://tenement.org/group_faq.html.
"Homeschool Happenings." FortWorthMuseum.org. http://fortworthmuseum.org/homeschool.
Kraybill, A. "What's the Value of an Art Museum Field Trip?" ArtMuseumTeaching.com, September 16, 2013. http://artmuseumteaching.com/2013/09/16/whats-the-value-of-an-art-museum-field-trip/.
"Mark Twain Quotes." BrainyQuote.com. http://www.brainyquote.com/quotes/authors/m/mark_twain.html#qI1IOO07mPLWVJYU.99.
Mettille, C. "Buffalo State Students Study Museums as Part of the Year of the Teacher." *Burchfield Penney Art Center Blog*, November 14, 2013. Accessed February 1, 2014. http://www.burchfieldpenney.org/general/blog/article:11-14-2013-12-00am-buffalo-state-students-study-museums-as-part-of-the-year-of-the-teacher/.
"Museum School." Brochure, ForthWorthMuseum.org. http://fortworthmuseum.org/sites/default/files/PDFs/Museum_School/2014/Museum_School_Spring_2014_Class_Brochure1.pdf.
National Science Museum, London. *Talk Science* (blog). Accessed December 21, 2013. http://blog.sciencemuseum.org.uk/talkscience/.
"Professional Development Opportunities." Tenement Museum online. http://tenement.org/education_workshops.php?utm_source=The+Tenement+Museum+Newsletter+List&utm_campaign=305eba8e07-April_2013_Newsletter&utm_medium=email.
"School Groups." Tenement Museum online. http://www.tenement.org/groups-school.php.
"Template: Average Height around the World." *Wikipedia*. http://en.wikipedia.org/wiki/Template:Average_height_around_the_world.
"Winter Classes 2014." John Michael Kohler Arts Center online. http://issuu.com/jmkac/docs/classes_web.

"Workshop." WingLuke.org. http://wingluke.org/teachers.htm#undermyskin.

REFERENCES FOR CHAPTER 6: ENVIRONMENTAL GRAPHICS

Collins, G. "Serving Museum Patrons Something More." Fine Arts & Exhibits, *New York Times*, October 27, 2013, 4.

Din, H., and W. B. Crow. "Museums Unfixed in Place and Time." *American Alliance of Museums* newsletter, January 2014. Excerpt from "Unbound by Place or Time," Museum, American Alliance of Museums, July/August 2009.

Dinardojan, K. "Telling the Olympic Story, Far from Sochi." *New York Times*, January 15, 2014. Accessed January 21, 2014. http://www.nytimes.com/2014/01/19/travel/telling-the-olympic-story-far-from-sochi.html?Hpw&rref=travel&_r=0.

Dobrzynski, J. H. "High Culture Goes Hands-On." Opinion, *New York Times*, August 10, 2013. http://www.nytimes.com/2013/08/11/opinion/sunday/high-culture-goes-hands-on.html?_r=1&.

Harris, N. "Capital Culture: J. Carter Brown, the National Gallery of Art, and the Reinvention of the Museum Experience." University of Chicago Women's Board program, November 6, 2013.

Lyall, S. "Seeking Clarity on Fees at the Metropolitan Museum." Art & Design, *New York Times*, October 7, 2013. Accessed April 27, 2014. http://www.nytimes.com/2013/10/08/arts/design/seeking-clarity-on-fees-at-the-metropolitan-museum.html?_r=0.

Marie, Laura. Quoted in visitor comments section. In-gallery laptop at Brooklyn Museum. September 21, 2013, at 3:44 p.m.

Pace, E. "Gaillard F. Ravenel, 55, Curator of Design at National Gallery." Arts, *New York Times*, September 16, 1996. Accessed January 7, 2014. http://www.nytimes.com/1996/09/16/arts/gaillard-f-ravenel-55-curator-of-design-at-national-gallery.html.

Vitra Design Museum (Basel). Exhibition brochure for Louis Kahn—The Power of Architecture, February 23, 2013–August 11, 2013.

REFERENCE FOR CHAPTER 8: GUIDED TOURS

Gopnik, A. *Paris to the Moon.* New York: Random House, 2000. Book Summary, BookBrowse.com. Accessed August 11, 2013. http://www.bookbrowse.com/reviews/index.cfm/book_number/671/paris-to-the-moon.

REFERENCE FOR CHAPTER 9: LECTURES

Conn, Steven. *Do Museums Still Need Objects*. Philadelphia: University of Pennsylvania Press, 2010.

Kaplan, M. Informal discussion about presentation skills with faculty members at Columbia College Chicago, 2005.

Mead, R. "Renaissance Man: The Met's New Director." *New Yorker*, July 27, 2009, 52–59.

REFERENCES FOR CHAPTER 10: MAGAZINES

Andrews, B. "Newly Analyzed Star Is One of Ten Largest Ever Discovered." *Discover*, March 12, 2014. http://blogs.discovermagazine.com/d-brief/2014/03/12/newly-analyzed-star-is-one-of-ten-largest-ever-discovered/#.U1QiplfJH2o.

Eiland, W. "Value of Collections." *Museum* 92, no. 1 (January/February 2013): 2.

Macdonald, S., ed. *A Companion to Museum Studies*. Chichester, UK: Wiley-Blackwell, 2011 (as previewed in Google Books). Accessed March 15, 2014. http://books.google.com/books?id=oQ8c6kRgH1IC&pg=PA220&source=gbs_toc_r&cad=4#v=snippet&q=text&f=false.

REFERENCES FOR CHAPTER 11: NEWSLETTERS

Circa. E-newsletter of Drayton Hall, Charleston. http://e2.ma/message/jpm3d/vqnu8b.
"Help Bring Ravinia Music into Public Schools." Ravinia Festival, e-mail received October 10, 2013.
Interiors. Newsletter of Drayton Hall, Charleston. http://draytonhall.org/news/newsletter/.
"Mission Statement." International Museum of the Horse online. www.imh.org.
"Nålbinding—A Practical Fiber Art." Vesterheim.org. http://vesterheim.us4.list-manage.com/track/click?u=6ad9c0cef0af2e3a0fda81f4c&id=0da2d9318f&e=fe54520d43.
Quinn, D. Technology Workshop, Oak Park, Ill., April 2010.
"Shop Online: Equation Watch." Science Museum, London, online. http://www.sciencemuseumshop.co.uk/valentines?uid=UA-542777-25&utm_campaign=SM+Online+Shop+-+Valentine%27s+Day+2014+-+Last+Chance+-+Non-Clickers&utm_medium=email&utm_source=Science+Museum+Shop.

REFERENCES FOR CHAPTER 12: PINTEREST, TWITTER, AND SOCIAL MEDIA STRATEGIES

Brooks, D., and G. Collins. "Happy New Year, Politicians. Seriously." *New York Times*, January 4, 2014. Accessed January 6, 2014. http://opinionator.blogs.nytimes.com/2014/01/04/happy-new-year-politicians-seriously/?r=0. {%222%22%3A%22RI%3A13%22} [accessed 7-25-14]
Dixon, M. "What Would You Ask a Museum Curator? Twitter Can Help." *Guardian*, September 5, 2013. Accessed January 5, 2014. http://www.theguardian.com/culture-professionals-network/culture-professionals-blog/2013/sep/05/ask-a-curator-twitter-museums.
https://twitter.com/TJMonticello/status/48506518456293376 [accessed 7-25-14]
"Jean-Paul Brunier." Twitter.com. https://twitter.com/jeanpaul19.
Lee, S. "Who Is Jean-Paul? A New Way to Market Impressionism." A&E, *Chicago Tribune*, July 28, 2013. Accessed January 25, 2014. http://articles.chicagotribune.com/2013-07-28/entertainment/ct-ent-0729-jean-paul-20130728_1_fashion-art-institute-impressionism.
"OPAL Explore Nature." Twitter.com. Accessed August 17, 2013. https://twitter.com/OPALnature.
"Other Public Surveys." Natural History Museum online. http://www.nhm.ac.uk/nature-online/british-natural-history/uk-biodiversity-portal/get-involved/citizen-science-projects/.
Phalen, A. "How to Use Hashtags Correctly across Social Networks for Marketing." *Command Partners* (blog). Accessed January 25, 2014. http://commandpartners.com/blog/how-to-use-hashtags-correctly-across-social-networks-for-marketing.
Rudden, J. "Five Social Media Myths We Need to Dispel." *MediaPost*, December 6, 2013. Accessed March 15, 2014. http://www.mediapost.com/publications/article/214995/five-social-media-myths-we-need-to-dispel.html.

REFERENCES FOR CHAPTER 13: PUBLIC RELATIONS

"All Politics Is Local." *Wikipedia*. http://en.wikipedia.org/wiki/All_politics_is_local.
"Early American Music Historian David Hildebrand to Speak at Old Sturbridge Village Oct. 3." Old Sturbridge Museum online, October 3, 2013. Accessed December 21, 2013. http://

www.osv.org/news/early-american-music-historian-david-hildebrand-to-speak-at-old-sturbridge-village-oct-3.

Itzkoff, D. "Arts, Briefly." *New York Times*, October 19, 2013, C2.

Kapos, S. "Exec Who Managed Modern Wing Capital Campaign Departs." *Shia Kapos Takes Names* (blog), *Crain's Chicago Business*, August 28, 2013. http://www.chicagobusiness.com/article/20130828/BLOGS03/130829793/exec-who-managed-modern-wing-capital-campaign-departs.

Merritt, E. "Museum Jobs That Didn't Exist in 2003." *American Alliance of Museums* newsletter, December 17, 2013.

"N.Y. Maritime Museum Afloat in Troubles." *The Chronicle of Philanthropy* (blog), June 27, 2013. Accessed December 31, 2013. http://philanthropy.com/blogs/philanthropytoday/n-y-maritime-museum-afloat-in-administrative-troubles/70741.

Pogrebin, R. "Cut Adrift by Its Would-Be Rescuer, Seaport Museum Seeks a Lifeline." *New York Times*, June 25, 2013. Accessed April 27, 2014. http://www.nytimes.com/2013/06/26/arts/design/cut-adrift-by-its-would-be-rescuer-seaport-museum-seeks-a-lifeline.html.

Seitel, F. *The Practice of Public Relations*. Upper Saddle River, N.J.: Pearson, 2014. See especially chapter 12.

"SFMOMA Appoints Two New Deputy Directors during Its Transformational Expansion." SFMOMA.org, November 26, 2013. Accessed December 21, 2013. http://www.sfmoma.org/about/press/press_news/releases/979 .

"SFMOMA Museum Store Offers Creative Gifts for the Holidays." SFMOMA.org, November 21, 2103. Accessed December 21, 2013. http://www.sfmoma.org/about/press/press_news/releases/978.

"SFMOMA Unveils New Grand Stair Design." SFMOMA.org, November 14, 2013. Accessed December 21, 2013. http://www.sfmoma.org/about/press/press_news/releases/976.

Sheets, H. "Ian Berry: Teaching Students How to See." *ArtNews*, January 20, 2014. http://www.artnews.com/2014/01/20/ian-berry-teaches-students-how-to-see/.

Testimony by Dr. Ford W. Bell, President of the American Association of Museums, to the House Appropriations Subcommittee on Commerce, Justice, Science, and Related Agencies. March 22, 2012. http://aam-us.org/docs/advocacy/fy13-ford-bell-cjs-comments-testimony-3-22-12.pdf?sfvrsn=0.

"Old Man House Collections Come Home." BurkeMuseum.org, October 24, 2013. Accessed December 21, 2013. http://www.burkemuseum.org/info/news_browse/old_man_house_collectionspr.

"2014 Calendar." Garfield Farm and Inn Museum online. http://www.garfieldfarm.org/calendar.html.

REFERENCES FOR CHAPTER 14: SOLICITATION LETTERS

Arndt, N. "The Pullman Porter, On and Off the Rails." *OnStage* 30, no. 1 (September–December 2013): 5.

Buffett, W. E., Chairman of the Board. *Letter to the Shareholders of Berkshire Hathaway Inc.* March 1, 1993. http://www.berkshirehathaway.com/letters/1992.html.

———. *Letter to the Shareholders of Berkshire Hathaway Inc.* March 1, 2013. http://www.berkshirehathaway.com/letters/2012ltr.pdf.

Field Museum. Membership mailing for exhibition *Opening the Vaults: Wonders of the 1893 World's Fair*. January 2013.

"Fundraising with GiveForward." Giveforward.com. Accessed December 8, 2013. http://www.giveforward.com/s/learn.

McCullough, D. *John Adams*. New York: Simon & Schuster, 2001.

The Millennial Impact Project. *The 2013 Millennial Impact Report*. TheMillennialImpact.com. http://cdn.trustedpartner.com/docs/library/AchieveMCON2013/Research%20Report/Millennial%20Impact%20Research.pdf.

National Museum of Women in the Arts, Washington, D.C., mailing, December 2013.

"Season's Greetings from AMA." E-mail, December 9, 2013.

"2014 Atlanta Film Festival—Bring Artists to Atlanta." Kickstarter.com. Accessed December 15, 2013. http://www.kickstarter.com/projects/1550800358/2014-atlanta-film-festival-bring-artists-to-atlant?ref=home_location.

REFERENCES FOR CHAPTER 15: STORE

Bryson, B. *At Home*. New York: Knopf Doubleday, 2011.
"Collectible Toys and Figurines: Elizabeth I." Frazier History Museum online store. Accessed February 22, 2014. http://store.fraziermuseum.org/ProductDetails.asp?ProductCode=501607.
"Elephant." Out to Africa. Accessed February 22, 2014. http://www.outtoafrica.nl/animals/engelephant.html.
Grossman, L. "Jonathan Franzen: The Wide Shot." *Time*, August 23, 2010, 42–46, 48.
"Massachusetts Butterfly Species List." North American Butterfly Association. Accessed February 22, 2014. http://www.naba.org/chapters/nabambc/construct-group-page.asp?gr=All.
McCullough, D. *Truman*. New York: Simon & Schuster, 1993.
McLaughlin, K. "Recipe: Put Feather in Cap, Call It Macaroni, Add Cheese." *Wall Street Journal*, @KatyMcL December 27, 2013. http://online.wsj.com/news/articles/SB10001424052702303345104579284283130907604 .
Meacham, J. *Thomas Jefferson: The Art of Power*. New York: Random House, 2012.
Montebello, P. Quoted in P. Daniel, "From the Editor." *Sarasota Magazine*. Accessed August 23, 2013. http://sarasotamagazine.com/blog/2010/08/01/from-the-editor-6/.
"MSA Integrated Marketing Program." Museum Store Association. Accessed February 22, 2014. http://www.museumstoreassociation.org/App_Themes/Public/Documents/Promote/2014MediaKit.pdf.
"SFMOMA Products." SFMOMA Museum Store, SFMOMA.org. Accessed February 22, 2014. http://museumstore.sfmoma.org/sfmomaproducts.html.
Shapley, H., and B. Starzee. "Exhibit A: The Museum Store," *Gift Shop*, Winter 2011. Accessed February 21, 2014. http://www.giftshopmag.com/issue/2011/03/gift-shop-stories/category-profile/exhibit_a_the_museum_store/.
"Sir Henry Raeburn." National Galleries of Scotland online collection. Accessed February 22, 2014. http://www.nationalgalleries.org/collection/artists-a-z/R/4399/artist_name/Sir%20Henry%20Raeburn/record_id/2469.

REFERENCES FOR CHAPTER 16: SURVEY QUESTIONNAIRES

Brown, T., and T. Suter. *MR*. Instructor Edition, 116–23, Mason, Ohio: South-Western, Cengage Learning, 2014.
DeVault, G. "Social Media Market Research versus Surveys Research: Choose Market Research Tools Based on Best Fit, Not on Popularity." About.com, Marketing. Accessed February 24, 2014. http://marketresearch.about.com/od/market.research.surveys/a/Social-Media-Market-Research-Versus-Surveys-Research.htm.
DiStaso, M. W., and D. S. Bortree, eds. *Ethical Practice of Social Media in Public Relations*. London: Routledge, 2014. Accessed February 24, 2014. http://www.routledge.com/books/details/9780415727532/?utm_source=adestra&utm_medium=email&utm_campaign=sbu5_jcd_3rf_1em_5com_47699_febrr.
"Questionnaire Design." Pew Research Center for the People & the Press. http://www.people-press.org/methodology/questionnaire-design/.
"Strategic Planning Survey." Delaware Art Museum online. http://www.surveymonkey.com/s/QTXSRGP.
Wallace, M. *Consumer Research for Museum Marketers*. Lanham, Md.: AltaMira, 2010.
Wilkening, S., and J. Chung. "The Mall over the Museum." *Museum*, September–October 2009, 42–51.

REFERENCES FOR CHAPTER 17: VOLUNTEERS

Allen, E., and B. Doladee. "Talent Optimization—Culture: If You Build It (Right) the Talent Will Come (and Stay)." Vaya Group White Paper, 2011. Accessed February 16, 2014. http://www.brandchannel.com/images/papers/534_vaya_group_wp_talent_optimization_culture_12-11.pdf.

Davis, R. "You Asked for It: How Can We Create an Excellent Volunteer Program?" *Museum*, March–April 2013, 15–16, 57.

"Internships: Overview." Museum of Contemporary Art Chicago online. http://www2.mcachicago.org/employment/internships.

Isaacson, W. *Steve Jobs.* New York: Simon & Schuster, 2011.

Knoepke, D. "Volunteers Need to Benefit from Their Charitable Work." *The Chronicle of Philanthropy* (blog), August 26, 2013. Accessed January 31, 2014. http://philanthropy.com/blogs/measuring-up/volunteers-need-to-benefit-from-their-charitable-work/213.

"Volunteer @ the O!" OgdenMuseum.org. http://www.ogdenmuseum.org/getinvolved/index.html.

"Volunteer Opportunities: Frequently Asked Questions." Gilcrease Museum online. http://gilcrease.utulsa.edu/Support/Volunteer-Opportunities/Volunteering-FAQ.

"Volunteer: Overview." Museum of Contemporary Art Chicago online. http://www2.mcachicago.org/employment/volunteer.

"Volunteers." Hildene.org. http://www.hildene.org/volunteers.html.

"Volunteer Survey." HammondsHouse.org. http://www.hammondshouse.org/volunteer-survey.html.

Weber, L. "The One Question to Ask in an Exit Interview." *At Work* (blog), *Wall Street Journal*, February 21, 2013. http://blogs.wsj.com/atwork/2013/02/21/the-one-question-to-ask-in-an-exit-interview/.

REFERENCES FOR CHAPTER 18: WEBSITE

"Are Your CPG Brands Maximizing the Return on Your Digital Investment?" Accenture, dunnhumbyUSA, and comScore Research. http://www.brandchannel.com/images/papers/534;CPG%20White%20Paper.pdf.

"Art History: Redux." Weatherspoon Art Museum online. http://weatherspoon.uncg.edu/exhibitions/show/?title=art-history-redux.

Bell, F. W. *You Asked: How Are Museums Supported Financially in the United States?* Embassy of the United States of America, March 14, 2012. http://iipdigital.usembassy.gov/st/english/pamphlet/2012/05/201205155699.html#axzz2tJmDmroR.

Breitkopf, S. "Check, Please! Museums and Destination Dining." Originally published in *Museum News*, September/October 2007. http://www.manask.com/images/articles/aam_museums_destination_dining.pdf.

Brochure, Luce Center for American Art at Brooklyn Museum, New York.

Cohen, A., and D. Quinn. Workshop for Online Marketers, Oak Park, Ill., January 30, 2010.

"Eleven Restaurant." Crystal Bridges Museum of American Art online. http://crystalbridges.org/eleven/.

"Employment." CarnegieMuseums.org. http://www.carnegiemuseums.org/interior.php?pageID=11.

Graham, R. "Antiques for the Twitterati: The HighBoy.com, a New Antiques Website, Is Taking On 1stdibs in an Effort to Make Vintage Furniture Accessible to the Smartphone Set." Design, *Wall Street Journal*, February 27, 2014. Accessed March 2, 2014. http://online.wsj.com/news/articles/SB10001424052702304610404579403260830122126?mg=reno64-wsj&url=http%3A%2F%2Fonline.wsj.com%2Farticle%2FSB10001424052702304610404579403260830122126.html&fpid=2,7,121,122,201,401,641,1009.

Maschner, H. "Making Natural History Accessible to All." *Museum*, March–April 2013, 27–31.

"Research." Dedham Historical Society online. http://dedhamhistorical.org/research/.

"The Spencer Museum Brings Work by Art World Luminary James Turrell to Kansas." Spencer Museum of Art online, August 13, 2013. http://www.spencerart.ku.edu/about/mediareleases/20130813.shtml.

http://store.fieldmuseum.org/field-favorites/for-kids/kits-and-puzzles/make-your-own-chocolate-kit.html [accessed 7-25-14]

"Verner Panton Junior Chair." Dallas Museum of Art online catalog. http://store.shopdma.org/vepajuch.html.

"Wabanaki: Culture, Continuity, Courage & Change." AbbeMuseum.org. http://www.abbemuseum.org/research/wabanaki/index.html.

"Weddings & Receptions." New Bedford Whaling Museum online. http://www.whalingmuseum.org/visit/rentals/weddings-receptions.

REFERENCES FOR CHAPTER 19: YOUTUBE

British Golf Museum YouTube channel. https://www.youtube.com/user/britishgolfmuseum/videos .

Brooklyn Museum YouTube channel. http://m.youtube.com/user/brooklynmuseum.

"Can Silence Actually Drive You Crazy?" Veritasium YouTube video, 10:33. Posted February 18, 2014. http://www.youtube.com/watch?v=mXVGIb3bzHI&list=TLi0f8swHDnDruNSE9dIimCEngY3xedUws .

Carter, C. "10 Most Popular YouTube Channels by Subscribers." IgniteSocialMedia.com, May 9, 2013. http://www.ignitesocialmedia.com/social-media-trends/top-10-most-popular-youtube-channels-by-subscribers/.

"Churchill Chat: Paul Reid." National Churchill Museum YouTube video, 6:52. Posted March 4, 2014. http://m.youtube.com/watch?v=6ToJloaUUNg.

Clough, D. L. "Fundamentals of YouTube Videos." Session at American Alliance of Museums Annual Meeting, Baltimore, Md., May 21, 2013.

Frazier Museum YouTube channel. https://www.youtube.com/user/fraziermuseum.

Getty Museum YouTube channel. http://m.youtube.com/user/gettymuseum.

Graslie, E. "The Brain Scoop." Field Museum YouTube video series. http://fieldmuseum.org/explore/brain-scoop.

"Inside the Exhibit—Oil Painting of Napoleon." Frazier Museum YouTube video, 0:55. Posted December 25, 2013. http://www.youtube.com/watch?v=H2IlLK8AaY4&list=UUI-EPRixxRCYQhTfCit4v1w.

Kapos, S. "Field Museum Hires Famed YouTube Science Geek." *Shia Kapos Takes Names* (blog), *Crain's Chicago Business*, June 3, 2013. http://www.chicagobusiness.com/article/20130603/blogs03/130609979/field-museum-hires-famed-youtube-science-geek#.

Kaufman, L. "Chasing Their Star, on YouTube's Terms." Business, *New York Times*, February 2, 2014, 1, 5.

"Nathaniel Russell House." Bob Vila YouTube video, 5:16. Posted October 26, 2011. http://www.youtube.com/watch?v=VDhpwTUPbLw.

"1904 Harry Vardon v James Braid, Murrayfield GC.avi." British Golf Museum YouTube video, 2:49. Posted March 29, 2012. http://m.youtube.com/watch?v=kIsVJUiD4II.

O'Leary, A. "The Woman with 1 Billion Clicks, Jenna Marbles." *New York Times*, April 12, 2013. http://www.nytimes.com/2013/04/14/fashion/jenna-marbles.html?_r=1&.

Rosman, K. "Tips on Finding YouTube Stardom: A Conversation with Online Video Stars and Internet Marketers." Technology, *Wall Street Journal*, July 8, 2013. Accessed March 8, 2014. http://online.wsj.com/news/articles/SB1000142412788732336870457859384085675884.

"Snake-Haired Monster." Getty Museum YouTube video, 1:33. Posted April 25, 2012. http://m.youtube.com/watch?v=Rm6LkuZfEis.

"Statistics." YouTube.com. http://www.youtube.com/yt/press/statistics.html.

"Unlocking an 18th-Century French Mechanical Table." Getty Museum YouTube video, 2:39. Posted April 14, 2011. https://www.youtube.com/watch?v=EblnaLMjdNg.

Veritasium YouTube channel. Accessed March 9, 2014. http://www.youtube.com/1veritasium.

REFERENCES FOR CHAPTER 20: WRITING TIPS

Bade, D. "Johannes Brahms." *Performances Magazine* (Los Angeles Philharmonic), January 2014, 40. www.showgoer.com.
Fields, J. "The Power of Brevity and Deletion." JonathanFields.com. Accessed November 24, 2013. http://www.jonathanfields.com/brevity-deletion/.
Jenkins, D. "Newly Released Books: 'Communion Town' by Sam Thompson, and More." Books, *New York Times*, December 25, 2013. Accessed January 4, 2014. http://www.nytimes.com/2013/12/26/books/communion-town-by-sam-thompson-and-more.html?_r=0.
Johnson, K. "Sophisticates' Sketchbooks." *New York Times*, May 27, 2011, C19.
Leonard, E., "Writers on Writing: Easy on the adverbs, Exclamation Points and Especially Hooptedoodle," *New York Times*, July 16, 2001 http://www.nytimes.com/2001/07/16/arts/writers-writing-easy-adverbs-exclamation-points-especially-hooptedoodle.html [accessed 7-12-14]
Pascal, B. Quoted in F. R. Shapiro, F. R., *The Yale Book of Quotations*. New Haven, Conn.: Yale University Press. Section: Blaise Pascal, p. 583. Accessed May 8, 2014. http://quoteinvestigator.com/2012/04/28/shorter-letter/#return-note-3700-1.
Sherk, A. "The Most Overused Buzzwords and Marketing Speak in Press Releases." *Adam Sherk* (blog), June 29, 2010. Accessed January 1, 2014. http://www.adamsherk.com/public-relations/most-overused-press-release-buzzwords/.

ADDITIONAL REFERENCES

Bennett, B. B. "Urban Schooling: Policy, Practice, and Hope in Chicago and Our Nation." Panel presented by University of Chicago Women's Board and Urban Education Institute at the University of Chicago, February 26, 2014.
Buxton, B. *Sketching User Experiences*. San Francisco: Elsevier, 2007.
Cuno, J. *Whose Muse?* Princeton, N.J.: Princeton University Press, 2004.
"E. B. White: Quotes." GoodReads.com. https://www.goodreads.com/author/quotes/988142. E_B_White.
Gayford, M. "Reading Van Gogh." *ArtNews* 109, no. 1 (January 2010): 70.
Jackson, C. "How Art Affects the Brain: A New Exhibit Explores Science and Aesthetics." Arts & Entertainment, *Wall Street Journal*, January 22, 2010. http://online.wsj.com/news/articles/SB10001424052748703699204575017050699693576.
Koolhaus, R. *Project on the City*. Cambridge, Mass.: Harvard University Press, 2002.
Macdonald, S., ed. *A Companion to Museum Studies*. Chichester, UK: Wiley-Blackwell, 2011.
Miranda, C. "Painting the Sun and Sculpting Fog." *ARTnews*, March 2013, 60–62.
White, E. B. "Charlotte's Web." New York: HarperCollins, 1952. Text copyright renewed 1980.

ADDITIONAL WEBSITES

http://artisnaples.org/museum
http://www.ecommcode.com/Hoover/hats/HooverHats.html
http://gamification.org/education
www.GoFundMe.com
http://www.michenermuseum.org/about/press/\

Index

Abbe Museum (Bar Harbor, ME), 210
Abraham Lincoln Presidential Library and
 Museum (Springfield, IL), 73
academic museum, 11
accountability, 16
accreditation, 49
actor, 4
advertising, 140, 149
advocacy, 35
Albright Knox Art Gallery, 59
Alfred Lunt and Lynn Fontanne. *See* Ten
 Chimneys
Allen Memorial Art Museum, Oberlin
 College, 135
American Alliance for Museums, 148, 150
American Museum of Natural History
 (New York), 75, 89
animals, 17; horse, 19–20
announcer, 80
architect, 68, 72
architecture, 69, 206
archival footage, 82
archive(s), 11, 23, 211–212, 219
archiving, 225
Art Institute of Chicago, 67, 69, 71, 77,
 85–86, 88, 99, 131, 146–147
Art Museum of Delaware, 41
Art Museum of the Americas, 156
the arts, 70
ask letter, 151
audience, 97, 100, 103

aural learning, 65
authenticates, 119
authority, 15, 77, 88, 128, 217
author(s), 15, 128, 137, 217
authorship, 75, 77, 107, 128, 137

Baker Museum of Art, 69
Bessemer Steelworks Museum, 122
Black History Month, 16
blog, 43
board members, 13
booklet, 35
bookstore, 43, 163–165
botanic garden(s), 22, 33, 63, 68, 86
brand(ing), 18, 20, 41, 55, 61–62, 68, 78,
 93–94, 101, 115, 122–124, 200–201,
 212, 218, 221–222; building of, 112;
 identity, 71; message, 19; personality,
 80; reinforcement, 71–72. *See also*
 mission; rebranding; story(ies)
British Golf Museum, 220, 223
Brooklyn Museum, 63, 70
Bryson, Bill, 164
budget Manager, 2
Buffalo State College, 59
Buffett, Warren, 158
buildings, 72, 73
bullet points, 228
Burchfield Penney Art Center, 59
Burke Museum at University of
 Washington, Seattle, 18, 41–42, 50, 143

buyer, 161

café, 62, 67–68
calendar (of events), 120, 123
call to action, 108
campuses, 68
Cantor Arts Center at Stanford University, 16, 18–20
capital campaign, 34–35
caption(s), 18–19, 107, 111, 134, 156, 228
careers. *See* museum careers
Carnegie Art Museum, 205
Cedar Rapids Museum of Art, 166
Chicago Botanic Garden, 23, 61, 72, 117, 157, 163
child. *See* children
children, 2, 6, 31, 67, 141
Churchill, Winston. *See* National Churchill Museum at Westminster College
Cleveland Museum of Natural History, 23
clichés, 227
close ended, 178
collecting policy, 18
collection, 202–203
college syllabus, 51
color palette, 80
community(ies), 15, 19–20, 93, 121, 127, 129–130, 139–140, 149, 152–153, 200–201
conferences, 49
conference report, 193
constituents, 49, 60
Contemporary Art Museum (St. Louis), 27
content, 11, 20, 43
content strategist, 213–214
core message, 80
core values, 122
counter card, 66, 70, 161–162, 166, 169. *See also* table tents
Courtauld Gallery (London), 168
creation myth, 157
cross-cultural references, 88
cross merchandising, 70–71
crowd, 39
crowdsourcer, 129
Crystal Bridges Museum of American Art, 33, 52, 61, 145, 208
culture, 8
curator, 2, 4–5, 22, 77

Dallas Museum of Art, 207
database, 26, 46, 118, 120–121, 183, 194
Dedham Historical Society, 210
Deere-Wiman House, 31
Delaware Art Museum, 180
Denver Art Museum, 58
designer, 5
destination, 10
dining, 208
director, 105–108
Disney Hall (Los Angeles), 73
display, 5, 13
docent, 4, 6, 85–91, 119, 164, 187–188, 191
donor(s), 4–6, 9, 11, 49, 107, 118, 151, 206
Du Page County (IL) Historical Museum, 24, 27, 34, 36

earned media, 140
Edelman, Daniel J., 150
educator, 2, 5, 29, 33
employees, 107, 120
engage (engagement), 139, 150
ephemera, 211–212
ethics, 150
exhibition(s), 8, 29, 75, 202–203
exhibition design, 2
exit interview, 196
experience, 2
external links, 44
event(s), 16, 41, 65, 101–104, 108–109, 115, 123, 133, 140, 142, 153, 156, 169, 199–200, 202, 209, 211–212

Facebook, 17, 127–128, 192, 217
facility(ies) rental, 29, 34, 68, 70, 208–209
family(ies), 58, 141
Field Museum, 57, 68, 153, 207, 218, 220, 225
field trip, 13, 27, 31, 51–52, 185, 201
field trippers, 53
focus group. *See* research
food, 22
Fort Worth Museum of Science and History, 56, 58
Franklin Institute, 40–41, 64, 67
Frazier Museum of History, 169, 219, 221, 223

garage, 63
Garfield Farm Museum, 145
Gehry, Frank, 72
Georgia O'Keeffe Museum, 34
Getty Museum. *See* J. Paul Getty Museum
Gilcrease Museum (Tulsa), 198
Goodman Theatre, 158
Gopnik, Adam, 27, 89
government relations, 147
grant proposal, 131
graphic designer, 111
guards, 58
Guggenheim Museum, 72
Guggenheim Museum (Bilbao), 72
guide. *See* docent

Hammer, Frances and Armand Building, 76
Hammonds House Museum, 194
headlines, 144
heritage museum, 22
High Museum of Art, 134
Hildene, The Lincoln Family Home, 190
historic house, 32, 86, 131
historical society, 22
Holocaust Museum (Berlin), 72
homeschooler(s), 11, 165, 201, 209
Hoving, Thomas, Jr., 71
Huntington Library, 62

immigrants, 53
Indianapolis Museum of Art, 17
insights, 178–179
Instagram, 17, 19, 217
installation, 5
intellectual property, 123–124
International Horse Museum, 122
interns, 16, 23, 60
internships, 145
interview, 80, 180
interviewer bias, 180

Jefferson, Thomas, 133, 164
jobs, 56, 57, 204; and careers, 204–206; description of, 187–191; or occupations, 53
John A. and Mable Ringling Museum of Art. *See* Ringling Museum

John Michael Kohler Art Center. *See* Kohler Art Center
journalism, 16
journalist(s), 16–17, 140
J. Paul Getty Museum, 135, 218, 220, 222

Kahn, Louis, 73
keyword(s), 2, 7, 17, 134, 136, 213, 214
Kickstarter.com, 153–154
Kohler Art Center, 60, 103
Koons, Jeff, 10
Kunstmuseum (Basel), 35

label, 78
lapsed member, 120
layout, 111
learning (vs. teaching), 2, 9, 50
legislators, 34–35
letter from the mayor, 113
letter of reference, 197
Libeskind, Daniel, 72
library, 63
lighting, 80
Lincoln, Abraham, 164
listicle, 24
lobby(ies), 63, 65, 73
local artists, 166–167
logo, 44, 116
Los Angeles County Museum of Art, 76, 203
Lower East Side Tenement Museum. *See* Tenement Museum.
loyalty, 88, 101
loyalists, 117, 129

Manet (Edouard), 2, 131
Marine Museum, 30
Marmottan Museum (Paris), 83
Matisse, Henri, 10
McFadden-Ward House, 33
meeting planner, 29
member(s), 46, 105, 107, 118
membership, 29, 34, 151, 159
merchandise, 46, 118, 161–172
Merchant's House, 156
Metropolitan Museum of Art (New York), 71, 135, 166
Millennials, 155
Mills College, 167

mission, 18–19, 31, 55, 76, 93–94, 101, 105, 122, 221
mobile, 10
mobile devices, 5
de Montebello, Philippe, 166
Monticello, 133
multicultural, 6
Musée Branly, Paris, 62, 78
Musée des Arts Decoratifs (Paris), 66, 169
Museum of Arts and Design (New York), 65
Museum of Contemporary Art, Chicago, 58, 64, 107, 163
Museum of Life and Science, 17, 19, 23, 25
Museum Store Association, 165

narration, 7
narrative, 76
narrator, 2, 4, 6, 80
National Churchill Museum at Westminster College, 55, 116, 123, 222–223
National Galleries of Scotland (Edinburgh), 168
National Gallery of Art, Washington, DC, 63, 69
The National Museum of the American Indian, 19–20, 25, 103, 107, 110
National Museum of Women in the Arts, 152
National Postal Museum, 116, 122
National Science Museum, London, 58
Native American, 19
Natural History Museum (London), 129
natural history museum(s), 89
neighborhood, 17
Neue Galerie, 152
New Bedford Whaling Museum, 209
New Museum (New York), 31
New York Historical Society, 66
newsletter, 39, 43
news release, 142
niche audiences. *See* niche markets
niche markets, 34, 135, 149, 218
niche populations. *See* niche markets

Oakland Museum of California, 150
Oberlin College, 135

Ogden Museum of Southern Art, 136, 188
Okrent, Arika, 25
Old Colorado City Historical Society, 122
Old Sturbridge Village, 143, 145
older people, 6
Olympic Museum (Lausanne), 73
on camera, 77, 81
online ethnography, 183
online store, 171, 206
online surveys, 182
on-site questionnaire, 182
open ended, 178
orientation, 195
owned media, 140, 214

paid media, 140
parental, 52
parents, 52, 67
parking lot, 73
partners, 11, 146–147
partnerships, 29, 33
Pei, I. M., 63
performance(s), 11, 34, 120
Phillips Collection, 169
photographer, 141
photographs, 156
Pinterest, 19
pr (public relations), 139–150
pre-qualified respondents, 182
preservation, 225
primary source(s), 53
principal(s), 49, 60
programming, 29
publics, 139–140, 149
Pulitzer Foundation for the Arts, 27

Q & A, 97, 100, 104, 111

Ravinia Music Festival, 117
rebranding, 56
recreated village, 32
registrar, 22
Renoir (Auguste), 131
research, 29, 52, 155, 167; focus groups, 173, 179, 180, 184; observation, 184; one-on-one interviews, 184; online ethnography, 183; projects, 185; qualitative, 183; quantitative, 183; storytelling, 185; transaction

interviews, 184; website, 209–212
researchers, 15
restaurant, 63, 67
restored villages, 68
retail, 70
Ringling Museum, 6, 23, 36, 61, 144
Roosevelt, Theodore, 164
Ruskin, John, 42

San Francisco Museum of Modern Art, 142, 167
scholarship, 21, 78, 209–212
school tours, 27
science museum(s), 89, 133
Science Museum (London), 118
script, 5, 6, 77, 85–86
sculpture gardens, 68
search engine, 17
search engine marketing, 125, 213–214
seasonality, 156–157
Seattle Art Museum, 12
Seattle Seahawks, 18
self-guided tour, 89
Seurat (Georges), 131
shelf talker, 161, 163
shopping bags, 168
signage, 68, 70
Skidmore College, 144
slide presentation, 53
Smart Museum, University of Chicago, 120
social conversation. *See* social media
social media, xi, 15–16, 27, 124, 127, 128, 130, 133, 136–137, 141, 150, 156, 158, 183–184, 193, 198, 201, 212, 217, 225
social sharing, 39
Solomon R. Guggenheim Museum of Art. *See* Guggenheim Museum
Sonoma State University, 167
sound, 2, 75, 225
South Street Seaport, 142
souvenir(s), 53, 65, 170–172
speaker, 93–101
speaker introduction, 98
Speed Art Museum, 130
Spencer Museum of Art at the University of Kansas, 103, 105, 108
staff, 120
standing features, 111

standing titles, 26
Stanford University, 16. *See also* Cantor Arts Center at Stanford University
star architects. *See* architects
store, 39, 43, 46, 62–63, 118
story(ies), 21, 31, 32, 43–44, 76, 78, 157–158
story conference, 33
story line, 5
storyteller, 6, 155
strategic, 46, 76, 126
strategy(ies), 32, 34–35, 76, 79, 105, 127, 151–152, 154, 156–157, 159, 199, 225
student(s), 49; college, 7, 54, 60
Sydney (Australia), 63

table tents, 163
tagline, 44
talking points, 147
Tamástslikt Museum, 123
Tang, Frances Young Teaching Museum, Skidmore College, 144
target, 46, 200
target audiences, 104
targeting, 134
Tate Museums: Britain, 18; Liverpool, 18; Modern, 18, 67; St. Ives, 18
teacher(s), 49, 60, 165
team, 2, 5
Ten Chimneys, 40, 46
Tenement Museum, 16–17, 19, 22, 40, 43–44, 46, 53, 89, 117, 168
testimonials, 158, 206
theater, 63
Tissor, Jacques, 2
title card, 83
Toledo Museum of Art, 58, 65
tone of voice, 4, 91, 103
tour guide. *See* docent
toys, 165–166
traveling exhibition, 75
TripAdvisor, 175–176
Truman, Harry S., 164
Truth, Sojourner, 16
Twain, Mark, 49

Ullens Center for Contemporary Art (Beijing), 168
Underhill, Paco, 6

University of Arkansas, 52
University of Chicago, 120
University of Florida, 61
University of Kansas, 103, 107
University of North Carolina, Greensboro, 210
University of Washington, Seattle, 23, 42, 50
U.S. Postal Museum. *See* National Postal Museum

Van Gogh Museum (Amsterdam), 71
vendors, 169
Vesterheim Norwegian-American Museum, 60, 124
video, 42, 53, 75–84
visible storage, 203
vision, 12, 107
visitor studies, 2, 5
visual(s), 41–65, 75–84, 85–86, 91, 100
visual culture, 69
visualize, 76
voice(s), 6, 11, 16, 20, 75–76
voice over, 77, 81
volunteers, 107, 120
volunteer questionnaire, 194–196

wall text, 8
wayfinding, 67
Weatherspoon Art Gallery at the University of North Carolina, 210
website, 11, 39, 43, 137, 140
Westminster College, 55
Whistler, James McNeill, 42
Whitney. *See* Whitney Museum of American Art
Whitney Museum of American Art, 62–63
William Morris style, 66
Wing Luke Museum of the Asian Pacific American Experience, 22, 53
Worcester Art Museum, 150
work experience, 56
workshop(s), 51, 118, 166; craft, 60
Wright, Frank Lloyd, 72
The Writers' Museum, 1

Yelp, 175, 183
Yiddish Theatre, 19
youngsters. *See* children
YouTube, 6

ZIP codes, 46
zoos, 68